Charles H. Jones

A Biography

has been donated
by the family to
libraries throughout
Georgia

Mercer University Press
July 2003

Charles H. Jones

Charles H. Jones

A Biography

Richard Hyatt

Mercer University Press
Macon

ISBN 0-86554-759-9
MUP/H571

6316 Peake Road
Macon, Georgia 31210-3960

First Edition.

∞The paper used in this publication meets the minimum requirements of American National Standard for Information Sciences—Permanence of Paper for Printed Library Materials, ANSI Z39.48-1992.

Library of Congress Cataloging-in-Publication Data

Hyatt, Richard, 1944-
Charles H. Jones : a biography / Richard Hyatt.— 1st ed.
p. cm.
Includes index.
ISBN 0-86554-759-9 (hardcover : alk. paper)
1. Jones, Charles H. (Charles Hubert), 1927-
2. Businessmen--Georgia--Biography. 3. Real estate developers--Georgia--Biography. 4. Ocmulgee Fields, Inc.
I. Title.
HC102.5.J66 2003
333.33'092--dc21

2003004185

Contents

Acknowledgments

Though many people have aided in the research and writing of this book, I am most indebted to Charles and Ves Jones for their time and cooperation. Their willingness to be interviewed numerous times and their patience throughout has been nothing short of amazing.

My sources for this book were virtually all oral. I cannot begin to name all the people who were so generous with their time by allowing me to ask question after question. I want to thank R. Kirby Godsey for his support. And I want to thank Mercer University Press for patience beyond understanding.

Photographs

Left to right: Jackie, Charles, Ben.

The family. (l-r, standing): Betty, Dad, Jackie; (seated): Charles, Mom, Ben.

Back row, second from left is Ben.
Front row, third from left is Betty;
Charles is second from right.

Charles (l) and Ben (r).

Charles and Ben.

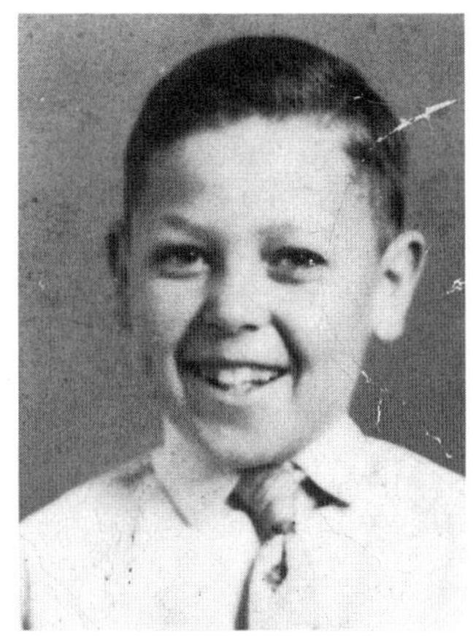

Charles always had the winning smile.

Charles (r) with the late Robert Trice of Thomaston in Central Park.

Charles in Navy attire.

Ben and Charles (r).

Charles dressed well.

(L-r): James Ferguson, Charles, and Ben.

Daddy at the Ambassador Hotel, 1958.

Bud Moss (left), chair of Industrial Authority. Gov. Jimmy Carter (middle), Charles (far right).

(L-r): Rev. Julius Hope State NAACP; Mayor Ronnie Thompson (seated); Charles (standing); and John "Blue Moon" Odom.

Buckner Melton (left), Carl Vinson (third from left), Charles (far right).

Johnny Mitchell gives Charles a hand.

Mercer University President Rufus Harris with Charles.

(L-r): Gov. Zell Miller, Charles, Terry Coleman, and David Lucas.

(L-r): Doug Skelton, Charles, Damon King.

(L-r): Mercer University President Dr. R. Kirby Godsey, Charles, Gov. Joe Frank Harris, Johnny Mitchell.

Charles with R. Kirby Godsey.

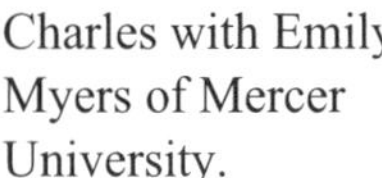

Charles with Emily Myers of Mercer University.

(L-r): R. Kirby Godsey, Charles, and Doug Skelton.

R. Kirby Godsey and Charles.

The Board of Governors of the Mercer University School of Medicine meets with President R. Kirby Godsey and Dr. Richard E. Barry, former dean. Seated left to right around the table are Dr. Barry, Chairman Charles H. Jones, President Godsey, Buckner F. Melton, Mrs. Connie Plunkett, and William P. Randall. Standing are Hugh M. Gillis, G. H. Achenbach, Dr. Otis Williams, Charles A. Harris, Albert Billingslea, Bert Struby, C. O. Smith, Dr. Milford B. Hatcher, Mrs. Jane B. Turton, and Joe Frank Harris.

(L-r): Jackie, Charles, Betty.

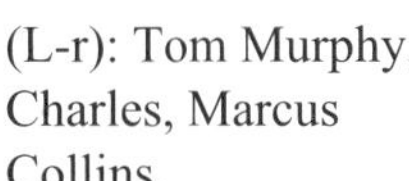

(L-r): Tom Murphy, Charles, Marcus Collins.

Charles with Doris Lawrence at the Woodruff House.

Charles and Don Leeburn.

Charles with son Dwight.

Dwight, Charles, and Tracy.

Charles with daughter Judy.

Charles with son Jeff.

Charles and Ves Jones.

(L-r):Nora Bell, Charles, Ves, and David Bell.

Charles and Ves at a Habitat project in Peru.

Ves, Charles, and Millard Fuller.

Charles and Ves in Peru (Machu Pichu).

“The King,” Charles, and Ves in Las Vegas.

(L-r): Jan, Ves, Charles, Tracy holding Connor, and Dwight holding Barron.

Charles at the farm in Bollingbroke with grandchildren Connor and Benjamin Blake.

Charles with Connor.

Charles with Benjamin Blake.

Charles with the grandchildren, Connor and Barron.

Charles, the boys, and harvested carrots.

Charles and his home-grown tomatoes. Senator Hugh Gillis will be taking some home.

Charles in Bryce Canyon.

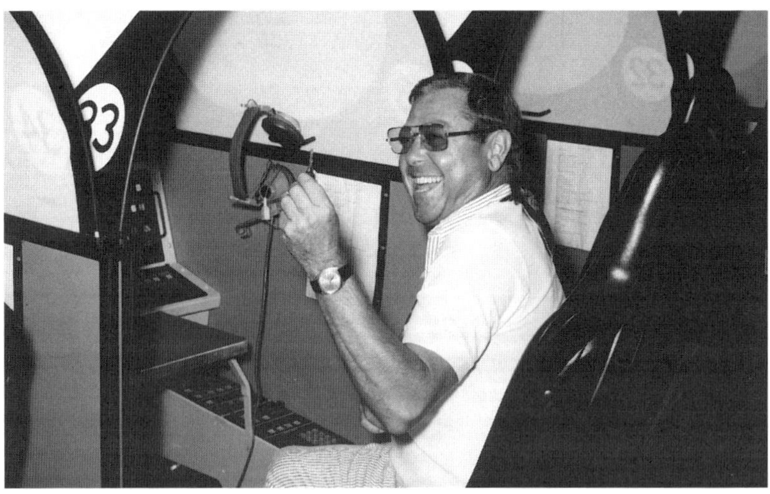

Charles and the USS Lexington in Pensacola.

Chief Charlie. Ronnie Thompson seated on Charlie's right.

Charles's smile.

Charles as a wave-rider on a lake in North Georgia.

Charles roller-blading in Florida.

Charles aboard the USS Carl Vinson in the Pacific as a guest of Georgia College and State University.

Charles with Chief Cox.

Charles and the author at Uncle Robert's grocery store.

Charles always shoots straight.

1

Lucky Lindy

Lindy, his friends called him. As in Lucky Lindy. The Lone Eagle. In 33 1/2 hours flying solo over the Atlantic, Charles Lindbergh had advanced from barnstorming daredevil to hero, just a brief stop on his way to legend. This spunky young man with the magical nickname who was buzzing around the town square had come into the world on the twenty-first day of May 1927, the day that Lindbergh and the Spirit of St. Louis set down in Paris. So Charles Lindbergh Jones he was.

Or so he thought.

Bounding up the steps of the stately Upson County Courthouse, Charles Jones went right inside. He was 16 years old and in need of a Social Security card. This was his business to take care of so nobody went along to hold his hand. But his mother had carefully described which office to go to and there he went, confident in himself and his world.

From behind the counter, the clerk smiled and looked down on the polite, neatly-dressed high school student. She asked if she could help him. He said he went to school at Robert E. Lee and that every day after school he was working for Mr. Ed Beach at the Silver Town Theater. He said he needed a Social Security card.

"What's your name?" she asked.

"Charles Lindbergh Jones," he said, as proud as he could be.

Getting all the vital statistics she needed from the young man, she excused herself and went back to the dusty, dimly lit records room. She was gone less than fifteen minutes. All he could do was wait. When she came back to the counter, she wore a puzzled look on her face. She told him she couldn't find a Charles Lindbergh Jones in her files.

Now he was puzzled.

"I'm Charles Lindbergh Jones," he said, repeating the story he had told so often. "I was born right here in Upson County, on the day Lindbergh landed in Paris. My mama and daddy named me after him."

Again the clerk went to look, and again she came back with nothing. Except one thing. "We do have a Charles Hubert Jones that was born on that day," she explained.

Hubert?

He didn't know anybody named Hubert. Neither did his friends. Something was wrong, very wrong. But right there in front of him on those papers was that name. And this Charles Hubert Jones fellow on the list was born on the same day in 1927 that he was. And according to those official records, the two of them shared the same mother and same father.

"I felt all empty inside," he says, remembering that day in living color.

His face told the story even if he couldn't. He was devastated. One minute the boy knew who he was, the next minute he didn't. His identity had evaporated, just like that. He had always been Lindy. Everybody knew that. It set him apart from his friends. For even then, years after his famous flight, Lindbergh's name was magical and to the wilted teenager, that name made him special.

Charles Augustus Lindbergh accomplished his first solo flight at Souther Field in Americus, Georgia—just down the road from Thomaston. Four years later, barely twenty-five, he took off from New York City with four sandwiches, two canteens of water and 451 gallons of gas. When he landed in France, he had to stall his engines to keep from injuring the thousands of excited onlookers who clustered around him on the runway. Back home in America, he was a hero. People in New York threw ticker-tape parades in his honor and the President of the United States, Calvin Coolidge, presented him with the Congressional Medal of Honor and the Distinguished Flying Cross. Songs were written about him, and before he was thirty years old publishers insisted he write his life story. Thanks to him, the world got smaller.

People looked at May 21, 1927—the date Charles Lindbergh became the first person to fly solo across the ocean—as a landmark day in their lives. Other generations would have Pearl Harbor, the day JFK was shot, the day man first walked on the moon and the day terrorists flew planes into the World Trade Center. That generation had Lindy.

Charles Hubert Jones had nothing. Not even a name.

"Who in the hell is Hubert?" he thought.

The certificate they gave him when he graduated from elementary school in Molena, Georgia said Charles Lindbergh Jones as plain as day. Folks all over Upson County knew the story about him being named for Lindy. He had told anybody who would listen. But right there in front of him, the paper work said otherwise. He was somebody else, somebody he didn't know. A nobody. He was a Hubert. It was like getting to heaven and being told he wasn't on the roll. He didn't know what to do or what to say. All he could do was stare at those official papers.

Who the hell was Hubert? More importantly, who was he? He thanked the woman at the counter for her help then ambled back down the courthouse stairs. Shoulders slumped, he walked back home. There had to be an answer. Only there wasn't. Even now, several decades later, Charles Jones doesn't fully understand what happened. He accepts, but he doesn't understand. When he got home that day, his mother tried to console him. But to him, it was as if his mama and daddy knew something he didn't.

His mother, Jewel Becham Jones, thought back to the days right after he was born. She remembered her husband Ben telling her he would take care of the boy's birth certificate. He had gone to town to get a sack of flour and some lard and said he would go to the courthouse.

Years later, Charles Jones believes he knows what happened that day. His uncles must have been in town when his father got there and before going to the courthouse they probably got together at one of the pool halls on the Thomaston square. After enjoying a couple of beers, Ben Jones finally went across the street to the courthouse. When they asked him his new son's name, he didn't have a clue. He didn't know the baby's name, much less Charles Lindbergh's. Some how, the baby became Charles Hubert Jones.

At sixteen, it was a blow. In his seventies, it still is.

"Maybe I didn't belong. Maybe I was an orphan. I didn't know what to think. It was bewildering. God, I've had most of my life to accept it. And I guess I have. But it was like I lost my personhood that day," he says.

By now, he has been Charles H. Jones many more years than he was Lindy. That doesn't mean he is as proud of Hubert as he was Lindbergh. Hubert is a name he doesn't wear very often, using only his middle initial to set him aside from the rest of the Joneses. He's accepted, he says. Yet today, when he parks his car on the street outside the courthouse in Thomaston, he can point to the door he entered that day in May 1943.

Losing his name was a blow for that shy boy from out in the country who marveled at the paved streets around the square when he first came to town. He wanted to be somebody, and until that day he thought he was. Stripped of his name, he had to start over, to find himself, to fly solo instead of flying with Lindy.

And it is a saga that hasn't ended.

2

Family and Childhood

Ben Jones could see only as far as his World Books would let him. His cousin used to sell encyclopedias and for Ben and his boys those volumes on the shelf painted pictures of mysterious worlds. People, places, and things his son Charles never thought he would be able to see.

His father had a self-imposed passion for geography and if the books didn't quench his thirst he kept stacks of colorful maps handy. Pouring over the maps by the light of an oil lamp they would meticulously chart the building of the government dams in the Tennessee Valley or track the killer storms that always seemed to be threatening Florida.

For young Charles Jones, those unusual places they read about in the reference books or located on the maps might as well have been in another universe. As a little boy, his world extended only to the far boundary of the family farm—one his father's family had stubbornly planted for several generations.

From his earliest memory, they had lived in Thunder, an obscure community in northwest Upson County, Georgia. The town got its name from Thunder Springs, which until litter and trash filled it up would boil over with enough force to make a sound like thunder. Old-timers told stories about grown men being carried into the air when those geysers would erupt, creating a ride that would rival Six Flags Over Georgia or Disney World.

The county adjoining on the north was Pike, which was formed in 1822, with landowners getting their acreage from a spirited lottery. It was named for United States Army General Zebulon Pike. He was an explorer who in 1805 led an ambitious expedition that traced the Mississippi River all the way to its source. Pike, who was killed in the War of 1812, first climbed the Colorado mountain that came to be known as Pike's Peak. Before the white men arrived, this section of Georgia had been Indian territory, part of the Creek Nation—a tribe Charles Jones would get to know decades later.

Ben Jones' five brothers had moved away to Atlanta and to Alabama, going to work for the railroad and for cotton warehouses. Giving in to the boll weevil whose presence turned hordes of Georgia cotton farmers into city dwellers, his brothers vacated the farm like so many other Southerners did in the 1930s. Not Ben. He stayed at home, determined to work the land that his father had farmed not far from the foot of the Pine Mountain range in the northwest corner of the county. Ben Jones was a farmer. Before he died, he had several other professions in his life, but he always considered himself just a farmer.

The Jones family was poor, but then so were their neighbors. That was just part of living in rural Georgia. They raised corn and cotton, wheat and oats and crops that put three meals a day on the table. Near a creek, two or three miles from the house, Ben had a blacksmith's shop where he could care for his tools and make shoes for the mules. He also had a grist mill where they could grind their own cornmeal and flour. Charles and his big brother Ben, as soon as they could walk, would trail behind their father picking up the wheat. When the cotton would come in, the two boys, hardly old enough for school, would hitch a mule and haul the bales to the gin two or three miles away in Molena.

In those days, you measured a farmer's success by whether or not he survived, and sometimes survival was measured by that squirrel you shot early that morning. Ben Jones managed, raising enough to feed his growing family and to keep alive the fleeting hope that somehow life would be better next year. It was just that—hope.

Ben Jones also ran a tiny store that was stuck on the other side of the farm from their home. His store was small and simple, offering mainly staples. He sold flour, salt, and sugar—things people couldn't grow themselves and things they didn't want to go all the way to Molena to buy. Jones took cash, but he would also accept produce, eggs, or chickens. He could take these items to town and get cash or barter them for things his family needed. When he wasn't around, the rest of the family would man the store.

Life was quiet and dusty. There was only one paved road in the whole county—US 19, from the Spalding County line to Zebulon, the county seat. That big event did not come until 1931. Like most roads in the state of Georgia, the road that passed by the Jones' place was nothing more than packed Georgia clay. Traffic had not yet been invented. Passing cars were still something to be celebrated.

Sometimes, when they were working out in the cotton patch, someone would stand straight up and cup a dirty hand around his ear. Work would stop.

"Shhhhhhh. Be quiet," somebody would say.

And everybody was.

Out there, somewhere in the distance, there was a very faint noise. An engine. At first, you could just barely hear it. Then it would get closer. Until finally, they could spot a swirl of dust rising on the horizon. A car was coming.

"Over yonder, way over the hill, it was the mailman," Jones says. "He came about three times a week and him coming was a real big deal to us. Other than that, we didn't see no more than one or two cars or trucks a week."

Life was slow but hardly sad. Boys had time to be boys and girls had time to be girls. The kids had simple fun, playing marbles, hide-and-go-seek, dodge ball, and Red Rover. In the summertime, somebody usually dammed up an icy creek, turning it into what passed for a swimming hole. Dangling from the trees were vines that would swing the kids out over the water like Tarzan. If you fell in, everybody laughed. So did you.

There was always Sunday school and church and August revivals where sanctified folks congregated for all-day singings and dinner on the grounds. There was enough New Testament gospel and okra there to feed everybody who showed up. Folks were washed in the blood of the lamb in the same creek where the kids did their swimming and the Baptist preacher did his baptizing. Most of the time, the Jones family traveled to church in a two-mule wagon. A quilt was spread out on the back of the wagon for the kids to sit on. They would cross the creek without the benefit of a bridge.

Riding in the back of that bouncing wagon was a test of faith.

"With wooden spoked metal wheels on a country road and with nothing to absorb the bumps, it could be a long, long journey," Jones says. "And I'm sure the Lord appreciated it, too."

Sometimes a large tent would be set up in nearby Molena and folks would flock in there to watch a moving picture, usually a shoot 'em up cowboy movie that the kids would enjoy. And on some Saturday afternoons, folks from a three-mile circle would gather at the creek for a fish fry. There would be plenty of fishing, singing and visiting.

If nobody was looking, the youngsters could get together and sneak a seasonal feast of their own. There were apples in the orchards and in the summer there were peaches hanging so heavy they made the limbs on the trees bow like weeping willows. Up in the nearby mountains, there were blackberries to pick, though you had to fight off the chiggers to get at them.

Long before he started to school, a pecan tree that his granny had planted particularly challenged him. It was a menace, standing next to the well in back of the house, seeming to invite him to climb. One day he answered the call while the rest of the family was down in the field tending to the crops.

Pulling himself up limb by limb, he started up the tree. Very slowly. Very carefully. Looking around, he was twelve feet off the ground. He wasn't careful enough though and he fell. And when he slammed against the ground, he hit his head on one of the decorative rocks his mother had circled around the bottom of the tree.

"It knocked me wacky," he says. "I thought: 'This is it!' My folks were down in the field working and I started running. I was hurting and I was yelling. 'I'm dead! I'm dead!' Everybody could hear me. My head was hurting so bad that I thought I had to be dead."

Before there was time to play there was always work. It wasn't something kids were encouraged to do. Work was something they were expected to do. Not childish chores, but real work. Farming was a family thing. Everybody had to pitch in if they were going to make it. Jones understood. Nobody had to teach him or any kid in that part of the world that lesson. He just knew. Work came natural to him and he soon learned that with it came rewards.

He was barely five years old when his father invited him to take the plow, and Ben Jones might as well have asked his youngest son to become a doctor. Charles Jones thought he was coming up in the world. And to him, it was about time. It wouldn't be long before there would be other promotions. Then he might be trustworthy enough to take the mule to the barn all by himself, to feed it, to take the bridle off, and to put away the plow. He wasn't old enough to spell responsibility yet, but he relished the word.

His older brother Ben, a year and a half older than he, always got to do things before he did and like most little brothers, Jones was impatient and jealous. He wanted to be as big as his brother, not just the *little* brother. So when he was barely tall enough to reach the handles on the plow, Charles accepted his father's call and joined the others in the field, trying to plow a straight row behind that big old mule.

Jones wasn't old enough to know about Wall Street, crashing stock markets, Great Depressions or Mr. Roosevelt's New Deal and wouldn't have cared if he was. But in a boyish manner, he knew his family was poor—and he resented that. He also knew that Uncle Lewis, his father's older cousin across the road, owned a tractor and they didn't. And while his family harvested their crop of wheat by hand, Uncle Lewis, over on the other side of the road, scooted effortlessly down the rows astride that impressive tractor. For young Charles, there was a lesson there.

One day, he promised himself, he would be the one with a tractor.

"With all the clarity I could muster, that was a sign to me, a class in Business Administration 101. If Uncle Lewis could have a tractor, I could have a tractor. You can do great things, but first you have to have a tractor. Even at that age, I understood that," Jones says.

And while his father taught him to dream of faraway places, his mother instilled in him the practical side of life. How the world worked. How folks got their tractors. Ben Jones was the one with the dreams. Jewel Jones knew how to make those dreams come true.

"My initiative toward commerce came from her and her alone," says Jones. "It was an influence and an action. If a door is closed, then keep knocking on other doors until one is open. She was that way, my family right or wrong, my family first. My wanting to see the world came from my Daddy and him alone. I put it all together for myself. I learned that you usually have to have the commerce before you can make the dreams happen. It was that way with that tractor. You had to work for it."

A friend of his brother's had come to visit Ben. The boy was the same age as Charles and lived more than five miles away. He rode over to the Jones' place on his very own bicycle. Charles was jealous and resentful, feelings that were new to a boy of just seven or eight. All he knew was that the other boy had a bike and he didn't. He shared his feelings with Granny.

"I felt bad about having those feelings. I went to church like I was supposed to and I knew I wasn't supposed to feel that way. She told me to be grateful that he has that bicycle. Then ask the Lord to give you the knowledge and strength and one day, you'll have a bicycle of your own. That's the way it was, too. Later on, after I had earned the money for one, I did get me a bicycle," he says, proud of the lesson she taught him.

His grandparents, Sally Bennett Jones and William Jefferson Jones, lived two or three miles away in Molena. Charles always looked forward to those weekends when he would get to go and stay at his grandparent's house. Sitting on their porch, Granny would read her Bible and tell him stories. He was a good listener and a good learner and her life was a story to tell.

Granny was a tiny woman, weighing less than 100 pounds. She was a Baptist preacher, a missionary really. As a young person and a new bride, she got the call to go west sometime after the Civil War, in the early part of the 1880s. Leaving her parents and her family behind, she and her young family loaded all they had on a covered wagon and bravely took off. They made their way through Tennessee and St. Louis, down into West Texas and ended up near Odessa, where Granny preached the gospel and buried three of her children. Her little ones were victims of epidemics that raged among the frontier people. When life there got unbearable, she had to write home and ask for enough money to get them back to Georgia.

Back in Georgia, she still was a devout churchwoman, starting two Baptist churches, including a small congregation in an area people around Pike County called "Over the Top." It really was over the mountain, an isolated part of the county that was infested with bootleggers and scalawags. Anybody could tell you that folks over there were more interested in moonshine then they were Mathew, Mark, Luke, or John.

Into the middle of these folks and their sin went Granny and her little God-fearing church. She was fearless, faithful and single-minded. While wearing this godly demeanor, she was also tough. She thought they needed to hear about the Lord. Her grandson never forgot those stories she told him, remembering them when his own life would run into roadblocks.

"I ask myself what Granny would do," Jones says.

There was plenty for Charles Jones to learn right there at home but his parents wanted a much more formal education for their sons and the two daughters who would follow. His father had gone only through the tenth grade and his mother had graduated from high school. They didn't need a wall full of diplomas to know that their children were going to need an education if they were to be something in the world.

His Uncle Robert also harped on the growing need for an education. Charles often went to visit his uncle who farmed and operated a one-room store with two gas pumps.

Charles could earn 50 cents a day helping his uncle in the store and on the farm. The building still stands, sitting up off the ground on piled up rocks and still decorated with fading signs that advertise Royal Crown Cola and Honey-Bee snuff. "It felt like a big old store when I was a little boy. Uncle Robert sold flour and meal, canned goods and all kinds of drinks. He always had that whole place filled up."

As a boy, he was intrigued with Uncle Robert. He enjoyed being there at the store with him, just the two of them. When they weren't busy, the older man and the little boy could talk for hours. Regular customers would drop by to match him for a Coca-Cola, an event that always fascinated his nephew. They would flip a coin into the air and the one that called it right got a free drink.

"Match you for a dope," the customer would say, producing a coin.

"Not today," Uncle Robert might say.

"That's not fair. You beat me twice last week," they'd tell him.

After they left, his uncle would tell Charles that he had a feeling he would lose. Then, a couple of days later, that same fellow would come back into the store. This time Uncle Robert would match him.

Heads you win. Tails you lose.

"All right, you ready?" he'd say, tossing a coin up into the air.

"And you know what?" Charles recalls. "Uncle Robert would win. He won more often than not and when he did lose, he would always try and figure out why."

Between customers, he planned his crops.

"He had this formula," Jones explains, remembering the hours they spent together in that tiny store. "One year, he would plant corn, fertilizing it with soda. He'd do that a second year then plant nothing the third year. He did the same thing with cotton. Folks around there laughed at him, but he made money because he let his land rest and he saved money on fertilizer. People would come in the store and ask questions about what he was doing then sort of laugh at him behind his back. He knew what he was doing. He would tell me, 'Son, you have to get an education. Knowledge is important. You can't get it here. You have to go to school to get it. You have to get your mind beyond those clouds up there in the sky. You have to soar, and the more you soar, the more there is.

There is more to life so keep going and keep thinking.' I can hear him telling me that today, plain as day."

Long before Charles was born, there was Uncle Luther.

His success would also underscore the boy's determination to do whatever it took to get an education. When Uncle Luther was 18, he was helping his father feed into the cotton gin. Some how, the sleeve on his shirt got caught in the machine and his injured right arm was lost at the shoulder.

Arm or not, William Luther Jones went on and raised a family, making his living as a farmer. Then, in his forties, with two children and a farm to keep up, he saved his money and enrolled at Gordon Institute, a two-year college down the road in Barnesville. He wanted to be a teacher. Folks around there were shocked. They couldn't understand why he would want to do this, why he thought he needed this book learning. This was 1922 and 1923, long before the term non-traditional student had been coined.

During the school year, he would stay in Barnesville, near the campus. Weekends, he might manage to get a ride home. Sometimes, Ben Jones would drive the 15 miles to Gordon and pick up his brother. In the summer, he was back home in the fields, making a living. Sometimes, Charles would go out to Uncle Luther's farm and spend a week helping him. Out in the fields, he would tell his nephew about learning and school. Even as a boy, Charles could see how very much Uncle Luther valued an education. He made sacrifices and he didn't quit—just like Granny.

After getting his teaching degree, Luther Jones became a schoolteacher in both Upson and Pike counties. After that, he was elected as the ordinary in Pike County where he served more than twenty years. To his nephew, he was always an example of a man who knew what he wanted and what he needed to do to get it. He was also living proof of the importance of an education.

Charles Jones also wanted to learn. His brother, Ben, was already in school and he couldn't wait for his first day of school. Finally it came. That morning, he cut across the field on his two-mile walk to Thunder and its one-room wooden schoolhouse. He was timid, nervous, and afraid. He didn't know what to expect or what would be expected of him. Then he met Doris Lawrence, and some how he knew things were going to be all right.

It was her first year as a teacher. Two years later, when the school at Thunder was consolidated into the larger one in Molena, Lawrence left the profession. After rearing her family, she began a lifelong career as a postmistress. But those years in that country schoolhouse was one that she would never forget—and neither would Charles.

"She was so gentle to me. I thought I was slow. The other kids were learning and I just couldn't learn as fast as they did. I had to repeat, repeat and repeat, just to keep up. Mrs. Lawrence would come by my desk and put her hand on my arm, telling me it was going to be all right. If I made an error, she didn't chastise me. She would put me at ease," Jones says.

His brother sat next to him, which added to his pressures. Ben was a year ahead of Charles but that didn't mean the little brother didn't intend to keep pace with him. He had the desire to be a good student, but there were times he had his doubts. Cursive writing was something that really came hard to him. His right hand just didn't want to cooperate. Mrs. Lawrence would put her hand on top of his and patiently guide his unruly hand across the page as one by one he shaped the letters.

"Now you do it," she would say. "I'll be back in half a hour."

He wanted to do well. For himself and for Mrs. Lawrence.

"Through her, I found out that I liked to learn. It is still a passion for me. That was an important lesson for me," Jones recalls. "I guess I just liked the way she did business."

Teaching school was a simple business then. There was no state or county bureaucracy to control the way Mrs. Lawrence taught and there were few funds for the schools to use. Luxury was an unknown commodity. This was several years before Governor Ed Rivers first paved the way for free text books for Georgia school children so students often had to share their text books. Playground equipment was usually scarce. The equipment consisted of one basketball, one softball, and one bat. If the softball rolled into the kudzu, play was stopped until the ball was found.

There was no such thing as a school lunchroom. Lunch came from home and from the land. Some children enjoyed lunches of fried rabbit and squirrel, baked sweet potatoes and homemade biscuits their mothers had prepared that morning. After school, there were plays, carnivals, and other activities and when these were held, all the families showed up, often coming miles to show their support.

Under Doris Lawrence, school was fun. She talked about the joy of reading and words. She introduced her students to books, encouraging them to learn lengthy passages by-heart—passages that some of them still remember today. She was kind and considerate of their feelings and expected the same from each one of them in return.

She also showed the young people that there were things to be learned in the world outside their drafty little schoolhouse with its pot-bellied stove in the center of the room. Bending the rules, she decided one day that all of them were going to take a little trip.

"I have a big surprise for you," she announced to the class. "Pack a lunch, we're going to play hooky."

When the day came, not one student was late and nobody was absent. That morning, sitting in their chairs, they were excited as only school kids can be. They all wanted to see what Mrs. Lawrence's surprise was. Finally, it was time to go. Leaving the school house single file, she guided them down the road toward

Thunder Springs, an area that today is the site of a 4,000 acre Boy Scout camp on Elkins Creek near the Flint River.

"It was a wonderful day for us. We went swimming in our overalls. We climbed on the rocks. We walked through the woods. Mrs. Lawrence would stop on the trail and point out the different kinds of plants and trees that were all around us. The first thing she showed us—and I remember it to this day—was how to identify poison ivy. She said that was what we wanted to avoid, and that if any of us were to see any poison ivy to warn the rest of the class. Learning was fun, and it sure did beat picking cotton," Jones says.

Before that year was over, the county was short on funds and the school board decided to close the one-room school in Thunder effective the following fall. That meant that all of the children in that community would be sent to school halfway across the county to Molena in Pike County.

That didn't set well with Ben Jones. He didn't want his kids having to walk that six or eight miles to school every day. They should be riding to school on a bus. The area around Thunder wasn't densely populated and easily ignored, but he believed the children who lived there deserved a bus. Uncle Luther, who was by then the county ordinary, helped Ben draw up a petition making that demand. Ben went around to everybody in the community rallying their support and collecting their signatures on his petition.

"That was my first lesson in politics," Charles Jones says. "I don't know how many people my Daddy got to sign his petition, but it was sure effective. By the next year, a school bus came out and took us into Molena every single morning."

There wasn't money in the budget to go out and buy one so the county school board commissioned Otis Tillery, a local mechanic, to build them a school bus. He used the chassis of an old truck and he turned it into passable transportation. The bus he created would be used to haul students from Crest, McCrary,

Smack-ma-nard, Dripping Rock, and Thunder to Molena every morning.

To the kids, it was the Concorde, taking them non-stop across an ocean.

"Oh, my God," Jones remembers. "You got a school bus coming there, dark in the morning with its lights on. You've got your lunch in a sack just waiting on it. It stops, you climb on it and there's kids sitting on there you've never seen before and they only live three or four miles from you. The doors shut and you take off. Man, that was exciting."

School in Molena was vastly different than school with Doris Lawrence. Instead of all the grade levels being together in a single room, Mrs. Alida Bartlett taught only the second and third grades in one classroom. To Charles Jones, this was uptown.

Molena was a town of more than 60 residents. It was dissected by the Midland and Gulf Railroad that connected Columbus and Atlanta. The town had flourished during World War I and was still a thriving little village. Sometimes, riding on a train that had picked him up in nearby Warm Springs, President Franklin Delano Roosevelt would stop there. It wasn't an official presidential visit, but nevertheless it was an event that always drew a crowd.

"We would know when he was coming and people in that territory would get in their Model T Fords and be there an hour before his train was supposed to stop. Kids would get anxious and we would be playing in the streets next to the tracks," Jones says.

FDR had become a part-time Georgian, spending large parts of the year at the Little White House, a home he built on land that until then had been a weekend getaway for wealthy investors from Columbus. Even before he was elected president, Warm Springs had become his personal retreat from the pressures of Washington and the world.

In the waters of Warm Springs, Roosevelt had found temporary relief from his polio—a crippling disease that sentenced him to a life walking with cumbersome braces or sitting in a wheelchair. He wanted to share this relief with others and polio victims from around the world began to come there for treatment. Roosevelt was a beloved figure to weary Georgia farmers. He might have been the President of the United States, but he was also a neighbor, living hardly thirty miles away.

Ben Jones, like so many other Americans, was devoted to FDR. Listening to a battery-operated radio he hooked up to a car that he usually used to listen to the music of the Fruit Jar Pickers and the Grand Ole Opry on Saturday nights, the Jones family would listen to Roosevelt's speeches. They would be joined by neighbors who were equally enthralled by Roosevelt's folksy talks that soon became known as Fireside Chats.

Sometimes, Ben and Jewel would take the family to Warm Springs where they would wait outside the gate of the Little White House for a glimpse of the president riding in his open-topped Ford Roadster. Using hand controls and escaping the watchful eyes of the Secret Service agents who were assigned to guard him, he would drive all over that part of Georgia, even making visits to his favorite backwoods moonshiners. This drove his bodyguards crazy but must have helped Roosevelt keep his sanity.

Waiting on the side of the road outside his unpretentious compound or waiting for that train to arrive in Molena, it was difficult for young Charles to connect this smiling man who always waved to them with the fellow they heard making speeches on the radio.

And finally, his train would be arriving in Molena.

"You would hear the train coming way down the track. I don't know if they needed to stop there for water or whether they scheduled it so people could see him. But I remember him sitting in his private car, smiling and waving to us," Jones says.

Years later, in the spring of 1945, Charles was home on leave from the US Navy, when word came on the radio that Franklin D.

Roosevelt was dead. He died in his sleep down the road in Warm Springs. Once more a train carrying FDR would pass through little towns like Molena and once more people would line the tracks. For people Charles' age, he was the only president they could remember.

By the time Charles started to school there, Molena was a flourishing Georgia town. It had twelve stores, a bank, a post office, two cotton gins, two cotton warehouses, and a blacksmith. There were enough people around there for them to need both a Baptist and Methodist church. Down the road in Concord there was an accredited high school. They were proud to say that there was even a doctor in the area. Dr. John Henry Grubbs delivered all four of the Jones children and practically every other baby in the county. He practiced medicine there for more than forty years.

School in Molena may have been uptown to her third grade son, but Jewel Jones wanted much more for him and her three other children. She studied what was happening in the world and she accurately decided that in the future farming would not be a vital part of this evolving world. If her children were going to make it, they had to move to town. She shared her views and opinions with her husband but Ben Jones wouldn't budge. He was born a farmer and he intended to die a farmer.

Jewel kept pushing her husband, reminding him how much better the schools in Thomaston were—especially Robert E. Lee Institute, a high school that was far better equipped than the one close by in Concord. She reminded Ben that he could always get a job in one of the cotton mills or one of the other factories. She was determined that their children were going to enjoy all of these opportunities and she wasn't to stop until they got there.

Thomaston wasn't that far away in miles. But until then, it had only been a place the Jones family would visit on special occasions—for a July 4th parade or to see the colorful lights at

Christmas. Life there seemed so different than the one they lived out in the country.

In Thomaston, there was no mud and no dust. On the four sides of the courthouse square, they even had paved streets. Robert E. Lee Institute was a local school with a statewide reputation. Just a few years before, the old building had burned and in its place was built a sprawling new layout. To a little country boy who had always worn his big brother's hand-me-downs, the place seemed huge. Robert E. Lee was a military school, and all the students wore spiffy Army uniforms and freshly polished shoes that you could see your face in.

This was a world vastly different from Thunder or Molena where every day the country children rode to school on what had once been the bed of an old truck. Instead of scheduling their life around the seasons and the planting of the crops, people in town ran their lives by the shrill sound of the whistle at the cotton mill, a daily whistle that signaled when one shift ended and another began.

Giving in to his wife's thoughtful and continual prodding, Ben Jones finally relented. The family would move. This natural born farmer finally took a regular job in Thomaston at Martha's Mills, a division of B.F. Goodrich, the tire manufacturers. Like just about everybody else in town, he would be setting his watch and the tempo of his life by the sound of that mill whistle.

At the age of nine, Charles Jones was leaving behind for good the farm and a fading way of life. "Going to Thomaston had always been like going to the World's Fair," he says.

Now it was going to be his home.

3

War

He was thirteen and he needed a vacation. Since he and his family had moved into Thomaston, Charles Jones had kept busy. He cut leaves and made brooms he sold for 10 or 15 cents each so folks could sweep off their front yard. He delivered movie flyers door to door, earning a quarter a week and two free tickets to the theater. He gathered liter out of the woods and tied it together for tinder. He delivered the Atlanta Constitution seven mornings a week, until he found out that some customers didn't pay their newspaper bills on time. He cut grass for 15 cents a yard, saving enough money to invest in an $8 push mower. He delivered milk, until he decided he didn't like getting up that early.

And though he decided very early that money is life's common denominator, dollars and cents were not his primary motive. "Money has always been just a by-product of working," he says. "It's our claim on the goods and services of this world."

From the very beginning, Jones discovered a natural knack for making and saving money. Like his friends, he enjoyed spending and buying, but there was always something to save for, always a reason to keep some cash stashed away. He didn't use a bank. He didn't think he could afford one. He hid his growing savings in his room at home. And the summer he turned thirteen, he decided it was time for him to spend some of that money on a vacation.

He had studied those maps his father always kept around the house and he had seen some eye-catching places in the newsreels they showed at the local theater so there were plenty of interesting destinations from which he could choose.

He chose Memphis, Tennessee. Not because Memphis was an exotic city and not because he knew anyone there. His choice finally came down to the fact that when he checked the schedules at the bus station they had a bus leaving for Memphis at the very time he wanted to leave.

Even in 1940 protective parents did not ordinarily allow their teenaged sons to buy round-trip bus tickets and take off on a 500-mile journeys halfway across the country. But for some reason Ben Jones did not stand in the way of his impulsive son. Somewhere in the back of his mind were his own private dreams. He had always wanted to go places and to see things but for him the chances had never come. And if they had come his way, he didn't have the gumption to take them.

Fears or not, his father didn't say no.

"Young boys didn't just take off alone like that back then so that had to be pretty strong medicine for Daddy to swallow. But looking back on it I think that he understood how much I really wanted to go," Jones says.

Memphis wasn't the attraction. Going was.

His family had never traveled very much. There were getaways to the creek on Saturday afternoons and there were regular trips up to Atlanta to visit his Uncle Walter and his Uncle Mac. That was about all. Traveling wasn't an option to many people at that time. It wasn't just money. There were no interstate highways and no well-marked four-lanes. Unpaved roads and worn out tires made trips in an automobile a dusty, sometimes dangerous adventure. Even family funerals were avoided if the roads were going to be wet and slippery.

So when Charles Jones boarded that Greyhound in Thomaston, it was a throwback to his granny's decision to hitch up the horses and get on that covered wagon and start her journey west. Ahead of her was an unmarked, untamed frontier. In Memphis, her vacationing grandson would face more modern concerns, though to the naïve 13-year-old from Thunder they proved to be just as wild.

His eyes were wide as the big bus pulled away from the square. He was on his way and on his own. The bus headed through Atlanta, then across the Chattahoochee River and into Alabama. It meandered through scores of little towns, up Highway 78 to Birmingham. As soon as he would get a little comfortable in his seat, there was another crossroads at which to stop.

Out of Birmingham, the bus pushed into the hills of Alabama, through Jasper, and dozens of other little towns he had never heard of. Finally, it made its way into north Mississippi, through Hamilton, Ponotoc, and Tupelo.

Cotton patches lined both sides of the road, making him think of home and the hours he had spent on his knees picking cotton back in Molena. It seemed to him that the bus driver didn't pass a single service station without stopping to pick up a new passenger or to let somebody off. He was enjoying the sights, but by that point, Charles Jones was a weary traveler. "Was this ever going to end," he wondered to himself. It had been only hours since he left Georgia but to his increasingly numb backside it felt like days.

"It beat me to death," he says.

Finally they arrived in Memphis. This was supposed to be his vacation spot but nothing would have prepared him for the seamy sights he saw around that rundown bus station. He walked around town a little while. He saw the mighty Mississippi and looked into the store windows at Goldsmith's, the city's premier department store. But after that endless ride on Greyhound, he was too tired to do very much. Pretty soon, he began searching for a hotel.

"Needless to say, I didn't have enough money to see the ducks at the Peabody," he laughs, though it certainly wasn't funny as walked the streets and looked for a hotel that was within his meager budget. At last, he counted out his money and checked into a hotel he could afford. "I don't know how to describe it other than to say it was less than acceptable."

One night was all he could afford and one night was all he would need. Even with his door bolted, there were times the frightened teen began to think he might not even survive that single night in Tennessee. The streets outside the hotel were littered with wine drinkers and wine bottles and so was the seedy hotel.

"And those folks weren't ready for bed at 10 o'clock either," he says.

Colorful lights from the flickering neon signs outside his window kept waking him up and so did the occasional screams from somewhere down the hall. If there had been a bus leaving for Georgia during the night, Charles Jones would have climbed aboard right then. None of this made him swear off traveling, however. There were plenty of places left to see. But it did teach him the value of knowing where you're going and what you'll be doing when you get there.

"Needless to say, I never went back to Memphis," he says, laughing.

Back in Georgia, he had a little time and a little money left and he decided he would spend the rest of his so-called vacation at a summer camp one of his friends was attending outside of Atlanta. Finally, he came home to Thomaston.

"And I got the biggest hug I ever got from my Daddy," he says.

His little trip did not turn out to be the vacation he had dreamed about, but even the wine bottles and late-night neon could not dim his enthusiasm for that experience.

"I got to see those mountains," he says. "I had never seen mountains before."

His brother was working at the mill with his father but Ben Jones wouldn't let his youngest son work there. There were jobs available at the plant and he could have made more money working a shift there after school but his father said no several times. Charles didn't understand. Looking back, he concludes that his father must have figured that Charles would be better working around people. So instead of the mill, he went to work for Ed Beach at the Silver Town, a job he would have through most of high school.

Beach was a veteran theater operator who came to Thomaston from Fernandina Beach, Florida. He knew the movie business and he enjoyed it. In this ambitious teenager, Beach found a willing pupil. He offered responsibility and Charles grabbed it.

He would come early and stay late, usually not going home until it was close to 10 P.M. Beach had a daughter younger than Charles but no boys so his new employee became like a son to him. He didn't tell his boss that he wasn't much of a hunter or fisherman, so Beach took him rabbit hunting and fishing. Years later, Beach arranged for Charles to get a full scholarship to Duke University to study theater management—an offer he appreciated but did not accept.

With the encouragement of his boss, the youngster soon began noticing the movies and actors of the 1940s, ones that he had never really watched very closely before—from Clark Gable to Gary Cooper to Betty Grable and her million dollar legs.

Working at that theater a few miles from the town square broadened his horizons and his finances. There were the pretty girls he would help to a seat— ones who smelled good, he says. There was also Lowell Thomas and his newsreels putting on that screen as big as life beautiful places he had never seen before: The Alps, London, Montego Bay, Paris, Rome, and Hawaii. These were faraway destinations that you couldn't get to on a Greyhound. At the theater, Charles could dress up with Spencer Tracy or ride a horse with Henry Fonda. For a couple of hours, in a darkened theater, he could lose himself in situations that were foreign to Thomaston, Upson County, and Charles Jones.

> Being there, I was learning so much and I didn't even realize it," he says. "It expanded my world. In those old movies, I saw people dressed differently than we did. I saw big cities and big buildings. I saw people getting on planes, on trains and on ocean liners. I saw tall mountains. I saw the seashores. By the grace of God, I wanted to go to every one of the places I saw on that screen, never dreaming I really would one day. All of that elevated me. It gave me an appreciation of the width and the depth of our world. Our world, I learned, is a big, pretty place. I finally figured out for myself that you might have to leave home to go where the action was.

Being accepted by his peers in town was never a major issue for this boy reared on a farm in Thunder. He was too busy to let it be. But while most of the boys his age in Thomaston were interested in catching touchdown passes and hitting cleanup, Charles Jones had other things on his mind. Not that he didn't enjoy winning. He may not have played much football or baseball, but on the tennis court, others soon found out how innately competitive he was. He didn't know when to quit if a match was on the line.

> I played some football when I was a kid and I soon decided that there had to be a better way to live on this earth than to go out in 102 degree temperatures and have somebody knock you down on the ground all day. I decided having money in my pocket was far more important than running a football. Economics was important to me. I was

> willing to work and I was willing to be disciplined to work. It was my decision. It wasn't a sacrifice or something I dreaded. I looked forward to working every day. I saw it as a way to enhance my education and my life.

Working hard also was a way to put himself on an economic level with his friends and classmates, the ones whose fathers were the bosses at the cotton mill. Using terms he learned on the farm, it was a way to get a tractor. Such things were important to him. It wasn't envy. It went deeper than that. He didn't covet. He just went out and bought things he thought he and his family needed or deserved.

Others might have bought themselves a new bicycle or a new shotgun. Not Charles Jones. Carefully saving his money and cultivating something new they called credit, on his own he bought his mother and father a new dining room suite with room for six. He also bought new silverware and China. The whole family was there when the truck delivered his purchases. This made the teenager experience the satisfaction of giving for the first time in his life. His parents would use those furnishings until they died.

> I guess I saw a need," he explains. "More than anything, that old table and those old chairs bothered me. I didn't do that for everyone else. I did it for me. I didn't know at the time that I was doing it for, but I know that now. Only after I got up off the mat a few times did I come to that conclusion. I did it for my own peace of mind, and joy, and acceptance of the fact that we needed that table. I thought I was doing it for Mama and Daddy but looking back on it, I was doing it for Charles.

Located only a few blocks from the town square in Thomaston, Robert E. Lee Institute was one of the state's premier schools. Founded in 1875, it became a military school in 1929. Boys in Confederate gray uniforms counted cadence and marched in step, hoping to live up to the military bearing of their school's legendary namesake. The school had earned a well-deserved reputation around Georgia for its academics and its discipline. It was a point of pride for the community and for the parents of the students who went there.

Around the school campus, there was also a strict social strata. For Charles Jones, this proved to be intimidating at times. He didn't talk about this openly and maybe he didn't even realize it, but he wanted to fit in with the fraternities and the clubs that were so much a part of the social life of the more affluent students who attended R. E. Lee. And he decided he would start with the clothes he wore.

Parents shopped for the clothes his classmates wore and they bought them right there in Thomaston, like everybody else did. He decided that his wardrobe was going to be imported from Atlanta and that he was going to pick it out himself. His family may have been poor in the pocketbook, but he wasn't poor in spirit.

Catching a bus again, he took off for the big city. After checking out the price range on their clothing, it didn't take him long to determine that neither Rich's nor Davison's nor any of the other major department stores would become his personal clothiers. In an era before discount stores or outlet malls, Charles found his way to Pryor Street where his dollars would go much further. It wasn't the stores that appealed to him. It was their bargains. Those clothes fit him and his budget.

> I would go up there to Atlanta with maybe $15 to buy clothes for the fall season. This was long before discount stores or anything like that. I would walk up and down the street going in the different stores looking at clothes and looking at their price tags. I would find a shirt or a pair of

> pants with a faulty seam. I'd know they had a fault, but nobody else would. Say a tie would be 95 cents, a pair of trousers would be $2.95 and a gabardine sport coat might be $5 or $6. They were seconds, but nobody back home would know that. As far as they knew, the clothes came from Rich's or Davison's. Nobody ever came up to me and said a thing. All they knew was that I would come back home with a completely new wardrobe—from Atlanta.

Charles Jones didn't consider this a sacrifice. Nor did it make him feel superior. More than anything, it gave him an air of independence, a feeling that was much more important to his attitude than those snappy clothes he wore. It set him apart, and he liked that.

None of this stopped Charles from having an active social life. His sister remembers a favorite high school girl friend of his who often made him special gifts—mainly candy and chocolate fudge. Around the Christmas season, their house always was filled with sweets, from divinity to old-fashioned pull candy. When his girl friend would give him her gift of homemade candy, Charles would politely pass it around to his brother and two sisters.

"You could have one piece and one piece only," she says. "Then he would hide it. He had shared it and now it was his and his alone. The three of us would spend untold hours looking all over the house for that candy. But if Charles ever found even a piece of it missing—look out!"

Like Charles Jones, Jimmy and Preston Bentley had moved to Thomaston from out in the country. With common rural backgrounds, the three of them began lifelong friendships and so did their families. Jimmy and Preston's father was elected to the Georgia General Assembly—first the House and later the Senate. The elder Bentley also befriended Charles, often inviting him to join their family for Sunday dinner. He later asked the 14-year-old high school freshman to join Jimmy and Preston and become a page in the Georgia House of Representatives.

Young people came to Atlanta from all over the state to serve as pages during the General Assembly. Legislators usually gathered in early January, meeting for 40 days of work. It was a two-week commitment for the three youngsters from Upson County, who stayed in Mr. Bentley's room at the now legendary Henry Grady Hotel.

The hotel was named for the renowned editor of the Atlanta Constitution who first coined the phrase "New South." It was located on Peachtree Street on what is now the site of the cloud-tickling Peachtree Plaza Hotel. The Henry Grady became to several generations of state lawmakers the home-away-from-home headquarters of Georgia government.

For the small town boys, those were heady times, times that would influence each one of their lives. Jimmy Bentley became a close ally of future governor and United States Senator Herman Talmadge and went on to enjoy a prominent career in state government and Georgia politics. Decades later, on the heels of an unexpected change from the Democratic to the Republican Party, Jimmy Bentley became an unsuccessful candidate for governor himself. Preston Bentley became a teacher, first in Europe and then in Atlanta.

Charles Jones paged several years for Mr. Bentley in both the House and the Senate. Those experiences in Atlanta and in government spawned his lifelong fascination and interest in local and statewide politics. Many years later, he would make two unsuccessful runs for the Georgia Legislature himself.

> For me, this was a great experience. My Lord, here was Ellis Arnall, who had just been elected governor of Georgia. Gene Talmadge, who I had heard about all my life, was around. They were making laws and having debates. It was all very

> exciting for me. When the House wasn't in session, we would go over and watch the Senate. And when Mr. Bentley was busy in committee meetings or something, Jimmy and I would walk up and down Peachtree Street on our own. We could walk around Davison's. We could eat supper at the S&W Cafeteria and we could have an ice cream cone at Lane's Drugstore, which to me was like heaven.

Mr. Bentley even took the boys to meet the governor. "I remember going into the governor's office to shake his hand. Ellis Arnall was sitting at this big desk eating a package of peanuts and drinking chocolate milk from one of those glass half-pint bottles like they used to deliver to you on your front porch. He was eating peanuts and drinking milk, and I remember thinking, 'He's in no better shape than me.'"

During the day, pages lined the walls of the House chambers, which usually was a loud and lively room. Everybody, it seemed, was smoking, many of them cigars as long as the barrel on a shotgun. There was no air conditioning so the long narrow windows on either side of the speaker's podium might be open for fresh air, letting in the clatter of the traffic outside on Washington Street. There were no microphones or sound systems so there was no volume control on the rowdy debates.

Pages were at the beck and call of the elected officials who would raise their hands if they needed them. Pages made sure the demanding House members—all of them men and all of them white—had the proper bills on their desks. They delivered messages. They tapped members on the shoulder and let them know that constituents from back home were waiting for them outside in the crowded hallways. They went into the side rooms and got cold Coca-Colas for the representatives who, at the risk of missing an important vote, couldn't leave their desks. To the amazement of the naïve youngsters, some of the members used those soft drinks as mixers, openly pulling bottles of their favorite booze right out of their desk drawers.

Every evening, the wide-eyed teens hung around the halls of the Henry Grady, where sometimes more state business was conducted than the capital. There was wheeling and there was dealing. Some of it above the table. Some of it below. All of them were Democrats for no God-fearing Georgian would admit to being a Republican. Around the halls of the old Henry Grady, you were either a Talmadge Man or an Anti-Talmadge man.

Arnall stayed around the hotel out of self-defense. So did the Talmadge forces, longtime adversaries of the current governor. Roy Harris of Augusta, an influential figure who had been the Speaker of the House, held court upstairs in the Paradise Room every night. Power brokers and headline-makers from all over the state came and went. Formal votes were not taken at the Henry Grady, but arms were twisted and minds were changed—often with an open bottle of bourbon sitting on the table.

For the small town youngsters this was an up-close view of political science coupled with doses of harsh reality that R. E. Lee's well-meaning teachers could not offer in high school government class.

"I was sitting there seeing how government really works," Jones says. "It was exciting, it was enlightening and it was rewarding. Seeing how things unfolded, I could go back home and when my civics teacher would be explaining something about government I could say, 'That's not how they do it up there.' It was a remarkable part of my life."

As he got older, people began to comment about Jones' unruly shock of hair in the front. They noticed how much it made him look like one of the Talmadges when it drooped on his forehead. Folks started calling him "Little Gene." Jones was still in high school when Herman Talmadge came through Thomaston for one of his rafter-rattling speeches on behalf of his father, Gene. Charles Jones had the honor of introducing him there at home.

These were also remarkable times for him and for the world. Jones remembers being part of a Sunday afternoon touch football game on the elementary school playground near his house. It was December 1941 when he got home his father shared some startling news with him and his older brother.

"Son, you know we're at war," he said, matter of factly.

In the early morning hours of December 7'1941, Japanese planes had surprised the ships and sailors at Pearl Harbor, a United States Navy base in Hawaii. Bombs had destroyed most of the American fleet. Until then, few people in America or in his hometown had ever heard of that secluded installation. In a single moment, it became a spot the world would never forget. In the coming years, they would learn of many other obscure places in the world.

"My daddy kept up with the war every day. He would read the newspaper and look at his maps. He would listen to radio reports and listen to President Roosevelt when he spoke. He told my brother and me that to him it looked like we both would be going into the military when we got out of high school," Jones says.

Their father was right. His boys did serve. And so did most of their classmates and neighbors. Even while they were in school in Thomaston, they were affected by the war effort. Some folks were taking defense jobs in Mobile, Jacksonville or Savannah, building ships in the Navy yards. Men a few years older than Ben and Charles were enlisting in the Army, the Navy, or the Marine Corps. You would see them around town wearing their uniforms. Soon they would leave. It wasn't long before there were reports that some of those young guys they knew at R. E. Lee had been killed somewhere on a faraway battlefield with a name you couldn't pronounce.

Like the rest of the world, his life was forever changed.

> Good God, it was a geography lesson for us every single day. We had an electric radio by then and at night we would sit there listening to Kaltenborn and Edward R. Murrow reporting from England. We wouldn't miss them. If I did miss a report, Daddy would mark a map and show me where the battle was taking place. He would say, they are moving this way or that. At the theater, I would watch the Movie Tone news. I would hear about the war in Russia and see news reels about how our soldiers were doing," he remembers.

Being in a military school, they were studying battlefield maneuvers and tactics in their classes. Jones also signed up for a local Civil Defense unit, reporting for nighttime duty at the sheriff's office. There were reports of enemy soldiers coming ashore in Florida and rumors that submarines had been seen near America's southern ports. In support of the war effort, the government began rationing certain food items along with gasoline and tires.

"Actually," Jones says, "rationing didn't really mean so much to us because we didn't have much money to buy gas or tires anyway."

His generation, like it or not, was growing up. He was little more than fourteen years old when Pearl Harbor was bombed so World War II followed his class all the way through high school. It consumed them. It was in the news and it was all around them—even in an isolated mill town.

For them, it was a wakeup call to reality.

> On the front page of the newspaper every day, they run the list of the casualties. You start identifying with them. You're a junior in high school and next year you'll be

> graduating. News was serious. Allies were being captured. People you know are being killed. Fellows a year or two older than you are going into the military. They're going somewhere for basic training. They come home on leave. You see them at home, wearing their uniforms. They're sent to the Pacific. Six weeks later, they're dead. We learned that this old world was a serious place to live and that the world was getting closer to us every day.

Once they shared dreams and goals and plans. Most of the young people wanted to rear families of their own and now they came to wonder what kind of world their children would encounter. Some of them talked about going to college and getting an education. Some of them thought about moving far away and finding new homes and new lives. Some of them were just going to work third shift right there at Thomaston Mills—just like their mother, father, and the rest of their family had done for as long as they remembered. Fear and uncertainty brought on by war and rumor of war had long ago forced young people to put those simple dreams and goals on hold.

Whether he understood it or not, Charles Jones' plans changed the afternoon he left that game of touch football on the school yard. His father's news that day never went away. It stayed with him. America was at war and so were the young people in Thomaston.

Life would just have to wait.

4

The Navy

All he had was a dime and a pay phone, so he had to call collect. His father's car was in a parking place outside the federal courthouse in Macon, Georgia. His father was at home in Thomaston, and Charles Jones was alone in a phone booth at Union Station in Atlanta, about to board an evening train for Washington DC, about to become a full-fledged member of the United States Navy.

When the operator said who was calling and where he was, Ben Jones was surprised and curious. He accepted the call and the charges. He didn't know what was going on. He thought his youngest son was in Macon. What was he doing in Atlanta and why would he be calling home?

It was almost time for him to board his train so Charles had only a few minutes to bring his father up to date. That morning he had borrowed the family car for a leisurely seventy-mile drive down to Macon. He promised his folks he would be home by dark.

The preceding spring, before he graduated from high school, he had signed up for a special Navy training program. That was months ago. Now, in early 1945, he had received an official letter in the mail telling him to be at the Navy headquarters in the federal courthouse in Macon that particular day. He had assumed they would just give him his college assignment while he was there and let him go back home.

Uncle Sam had other ideas.

The Navy had a ticket with his name on it and they expected Charles Jones to be on a train leaving Macon that very afternoon. No hometown good-byes. No parties. No negotiations. No kiss from mama. No luggage. He was in the Navy now.

"We were already at the station in Atlanta by the time I could call home," he says. "We were changing trains on our way to Washington. I only had time to tell my daddy where the car was parked."

The preceding spring, he had worn a cap and gown as a member of the Robert E. Lee Institute's Class of 1944. War had been part of their education and as they walked across the stage at graduation, each of them knew it would be part of their future. Charles Jones had been resigned to that for a long time and even before he graduated, he began to make plans. This was something a young man did on his own. He didn't talk it over with his parents. He talked it over with himself.

Factoring all of those things into his plans, he had looked at his options. Four years of ROTC training at Robert E. Lee had given him a taste of the Army and the way it operated. Tracing infantry and artillery units across Europe on his father's maps gave him other hints. So did the patriotic newsreels he watched at the Silver Town. Like most young men at that time, he had very few options. Their options were the Army, the Navy or the Marines. Or, they could just sit home and wait to be drafted, an option few red-blooded American males wanted to take. Charles Jones realized if he did that he surely would be ordered to hit the dusty trail into the United States Army.

> I wasn't too enthralled at crawling on my stomach in the grass outside of some little town in Europe, so the Navy had quickly become my choice. I figured out that it was the Navy that took those guys to the frontlines. Then they would leave and go back for more. More than anything,

there was the travel. I had heard of guys on ships to Hawaii and other exotic ports. There was Pensacola and all that white sand. A lot of people went to San Diego, and Southern California had a definite appeal. I could imagine myself on some beautiful island somewhere in the Pacific. So even before we graduated, I signed up for one of the Navy's special programs.

Earlier in the war, the Navy VR7 Program had created those special training programs on selected college campuses throughout the United States. Under those plans, eligible young men could sign up while they were still in high school. They were committed to the Navy, but their enlistment was deferred. When they received their high school diplomas, they would be assigned to a college or university where they would get their basic education in math and science. They were considered to be on active duty while they were attending those college classes. This assured the Navy of a pipeline that would send them a steady stream of well-prepared young men. Such programs had been active throughout the war years at Mercer University in Macon, the University of Georgia in Athens, and several other colleges and universities in the Southeastern part of the United States.

So when Charles Jones got that letter telling him to be at the Navy recruiting headquarters in Macon that day, he drove down there in his father's car to get his college assignment—not to report for basic training in the US Navy.

I figured we would discuss how all of that would work and which college I would be attending. I thought I would have a few weeks to go home and pack and make final plans. There were 12 or 15 other guys in that room with me in Macon. We all were in the same boat. They told us we were all going to be on a train leaving Macon that very day at 4:30 or 5 o'clock. I said, 'You don't understand, I'm supposed to be in the VR7 program.' They knew that already. The problem was, those programs had been eliminated.

By early 1945, the war in Europe was beginning to wind down. The Navy no longer needed that steady pipeline of potential leaders. Their personnel needs were changing dramatically and they had shut down the VR7 program all together. The young men who were already signed up for it were being assigned into the regular Navy. Charles Jones was one of them. He was going to school all right—only in the Navy they called it basic training.

So there he was, standing in a phone booth in the train station in Atlanta, telling his father that he wouldn't be home that night and neither would the family car.

Instead of home, Jones, along with the other surprised recruits, was headed for Washington, on his way to basic training at a Navy base near Bainbridge, Maryland. With the extensive training in military decorum he already had under his belt in high school, Jones was put in charge of his unit. He would stay there in that role for three other training companies. When he signed up, he harbored those dreams of travel. Maryland was not included in those dreams. But getting off the train in the nation's capital did inspire him.

"Seeing that capital dome and all those other historic buildings I had only read about, I imagined it was like the feeling when you first get to heaven. It was overwhelming," he says.

Staying there for those other training sessions, he had plenty of time to find his way around wartime Washington. He went to the Washington Monument, the Lincoln Memorial—all the things a tourist might do. It wasn't as exotic as Hawaii or as balmy as San Diego, but it was Washington, a place he had read about all of his life. The experience was particularly thrilling and inspiring for a young man barely out of high school who had yet to celebrate his eighteenth birthday and who had never really been away from home—except for that one sleepless night he spent in Memphis.

Finally, one of the officers asked Jones what type of permanent assignment he might be interested in. He thought about it and said he was interested in flying. He was told that there were openings for twelve men in the US Naval Air Transport Service. And they were based in Miami, Florida. "What a sacrifice," he said. Soon Jones was boarding another train, this one going back south.

Arriving at the Navy base on the outskirts of Miami, there was a single hangar on the airstrip. The Air Transport unit did not have a permanent home. They were attached to whatever base they were needed. It was a small group, no more than a dozen men. They kept on the move, and most of their destinations were just as sunny and scenic as he had dreamed about watching those features on the theater screen back home. From Miami—which a travel agent would hardly consider as hardship duty—they might go to Key West, to Trinidad, to Cuba, to Puerto Rico, to Panama, or to Jamaica.

Within a couple of weeks, Jones was trained as a flight engineer. His primary job was to see to it that the airplanes were properly loaded. They were flying large four-engine transport planes throughout the hemisphere. They would deliver mail. They would deliver military equipment and whatever else might be needed. They would haul personnel to their new assignments. Often time, their cargo included airplane engines and other heavy items.

"My job was mainly to balance the weight in the plane. The planes were unfinished inside and after the cargo was loaded we would sit on benches that were on the side of the plane. So you might have one of those huge airplane engines and there we were belted in right next to it," he says.

By this time, the war was almost over. Peace was on the horizon in Europe and in the Pacific. Their assignment was quickly changing and Jones' outfit began to drift throughout the United States fulfilling a variety of duties. They delivered planes to bases in California, Texas, and Florida. Staying in first class hotels and eating in fine restaurants, they spent time in Hollywood, New Orleans, Phoenix, and Dallas. Coming into Texas, he called his brother Ben who was stationed there. Ben met him on the airstrip in an Army jeep.

"It was like working for Delta," Jones says. He was the small town kid in a unit of experienced men, guys who had been around. Most of them were more than ten years his senior. They knew the system. They knew all the angles. They knew how to extend their trips, turning a trip from California back to Miami into a two-week journey with nice stops in between. They looked after Jones as if he was their little brother. His buddies were nearing discharge and when he told them he had always wanted to see the Pentagon, they arranged a trip to Washington—just to look over their military records. The next day, they returned to Miami.

It was like Delta, and at times it was a frolic. But there also were frequent flights to Panama, trips that always reminded them why they were wearing their uniforms. A large military hospital was located in the Canal Zone and many of the severely wounded soldiers from the Pacific were brought there for treatment and recuperation.

Jones and the Air Transport Service often flew there to pick up bed-ridden patients who were being sent to Miami, Atlanta and other veteran's hospitals for more extensive treatment or therapy. Covered with canvas walls, the inside of the plane would be turned into a flying hospital ward. The plane soon would be filled with young men just like Jones—wounded men whose bodies would never again be the same.

"My God, I thought. What has been done to them? I'd look at those fellows and think, 'Why me? Why am I so fortunate.' That brought the war home to me in ways I can't describe," he remembers.

He was barely nineteen years old and he had been in the Navy for two years. Now the war was over. The Navy offered him a chance to extend his stay in the Air Transport Service. An assignment to Paris was dangled in front of him as an inducement. He would be sent to France to be part of the massive effort that would move the war machine back home. For a young man with long-standing visions of travel, Paris was definitely tempting. But somehow he sensed that it was time for him to get on with his life—whatever that life would be.

The Navy had equipped him with new confidence, new ideas and new dreams, things he didn't have in large doses before he left home. He had worked with and around young men from all the country, some of them with degrees from some of the nation's best colleges and universities. He had compared himself to them and he felt satisfied with how he stacked up beside them.

When he graduated from high school at Robert E. Lee, he didn't really know what he was capable of, much less what he wanted to do with his life. Now, he had decided that he was capable of just about anything. Long ago, he had proven that he could work and work hard. And maybe he could also learn.

It was time to find out and there was so much to consider.

He remembered Granny, and how she bravely took off for the frontier in that rickety covered wagon, not knowing what to expect when she got where she was going.

He remembered spending those lazy afternoons in Uncle Robert's little store, looking out at the clouds and talking about how large the world was. He remembered Uncle Robert telling him over and over about the need for an education.

He remembered Doris Lawrence and that one-roomed schoolhouse in Northwest Upson County, how encouraging she was how she showed him he could learn as well as the others and how learning could actually be fun.

He remembered his Uncle Luther—in his forties, one arm and all—full of life and promise, making all the sacrifices he did just so he could get a college education.

Now it was his turn.

5

College Graduate and Business Man

Milling around on the grass outside the classroom, the grizzled veterans were ready for another war. Seven of them were in Miss Marion Bush's English class and seven of them had just failed a pop quiz. "She's not fair," one of them grumbled. "She's treating us like trash."

One day they had been young soldiers fighting for Truth, Justice and the American Way, and the next they were older students trying to learn enough to pass an English test. The eighteen– or nineteen-year-old freshmen in Miss Marion's class were passing. The grownups weren't. And to those fellows who had just come home from the war that seemed just plain un-American.

"This isn't any way to treat people who had gone off to save the world. She's got pets. Those young guys are just her pets. That's what it is," one older student complained.

Charles Jones was among the seven. Following in the footsteps of his Uncle Luther, he had enrolled at Gordon Military College as soon as he was discharged from the Navy. He had found courage and confidence he didn't know he had while he was in the Navy, but not enough of either to apply for the University of Georgia or Georgia Tech. He preferred to stay in Barnesville, closer to home and on a small campus with less than 600 students instead of one with thousands.

Founded as Gordon Institute in 1872, it became a military school in 1927, serving students in both high school and prep school. In 1972, it finally would give up its military program and become Gordon College—a two-year school and a flourishing part of the University System of Georgia.

Jones started to class there late in the fall of 1946. He was going to school in the daytime and running a drive-in restaurant at night. There were thousands of young men like him across the country, trying to make the tough transition from soldier to citizen.

Jones was one of about a dozen World War II veterans who overnight found themselves at Gordon. They had the GI Bill to pay their way and the only concession the college administration gave them was to waive the ROTC requirement figuring these young men were well versed in military discipline. The former soldiers, some of them in their thirties, were suddenly in classrooms, sitting next to young people who had never fired a shot in anger or seen a Nazi up close.

As for Jones, he had never seen action on the frontlines either. He had nothing to say when he joined the others after class that day. But he was still a Navy veteran, and like the other older guys in that class he had failed Miss Marion's unannounced test. "We were big shots," he says. "We were veterans."

Every Friday, Miss Marion gave the students in her class a list of fifty or sixty vocabulary words that they were supposed to know and be able to use in a normal conversation by the following Monday. That wasn't part of their textbook. It was just something that she said would help them if they were going to be able to communicate out in the world. She made it clear to the students that this was a major assignment. She would accept nothing less than 95 percent on those tests. That Monday, she had given them a surprise test on Friday's words. "Repulsive," Jones still remembers. "That was one of the words."

Repulsive was not a word Jones had used before or heard before and when it showed up on her test that Monday morning, he was lost. Repulsive was not the only word he didn't understand. He found himself part of the whining group of veterans who after getting their tests back on Tuesday were standing around outside the building complaining that the younger students were Miss Marion's favorites.

The veterans never did figure out how she knew or how she heard, but Wednesday Miss Marion began class with a stern lecture that was directed squarely at them.

"Gentlemen, I understand that some of you in my class say that the reason the four freshmen here passed this test is because they are the teacher's pets." She paused, letting her words sink in. "And if I were you…in the class of Marion Bush…and I felt that way…I would want to be one of Marion Bush's pets."

As she lectured to them, Jones felt increasingly uncomfortable. He sheepishly thought over what she had just said. He was embarrassed. At that moment, he hardly knew Miss Marion, and knew even less about her growing reputation there at Gordon Military College. But he heard what she said that morning, and he listened. And what she said began to make sense to him.

Charles Jones didn't realize it then, but sitting in that classroom he was slowly coming under the spell of another strong influence on his life—one he would never escape.

A native of Barnesville, Marion Bush had graduated from Gordon Institute in 1913—a classmate of the late United States Senator Richard Russell. After receiving a bachelor's degree from Shorter College, she earned a Master's Degree from the University of Georgia. She came back to Gordon as a member of the faculty in 1928—beginning a career in the classroom that would stretch for forty-four years. She never married and devoted her life to education. She became a fixture on the campus and in the community teaching both English and music as well as serving as

Dean of Women. She was also the organist and choir director at the First Baptist Church of Barnesville.

As soon as class was over, Jones couldn't wait. He hopped out of his chair and hurried straight to the front of the room, stopping at the edge of her desk. Tears were welling in his eyes. "Miss Bush," he said, "I want to be one of your pets."

More than that, he went to work. Recovering from that failing test score, Jones made an A-plus in her class. He later would make the Dean's List in two of the three quarters he was a student at Gordon. It was Miss Marion who showed him that he could not only learn, he could make good grades. He could excel, she told him.

And he did.

"I honestly had never considered myself that good, that smart. But Miss Marion showed me the joy of learning. She made us memorize verse after verse and even today I can recite the words of those poems. Just ask me. I could never repay her for what she did for me at Gordon. It changed me and it changed my life," he says.

What she was telling them was that a person should do what they need to do to succeed. Don't let your feelings for someone else be an obstacle to your success. Jones says people today ought to hear what she was saying. "Be a teacher's pet in your own life. If you have a boss who is hard on you, become his pet."

After three quarters in Barnesville, he applied to the University of Georgia. Armed with good grades from Gordon, the GI Bill and his savings from the Navy, he thought he was ready for Athens. He rode up there in a crowded automobile with three other students—plus their luggage and their belongings. The car belonged to Smith Haywood, business school student from nearby Thomaston, Georgia. Jones was the only one in the car who was going to the university for the first time.

With the GI Bill paying the veterans' tuition fees, post-war campuses were overrun with college students, many of them married veterans returning to class after serving in the military. The University of Georgia was no exception. They were breaking enrollment records every time they held registration. So when Jones arrived for class that fall, there was no room at the inn. They had registered far more students than they had dormitory space. He ended up staying his first few weeks in a city park in Athens.

"It had a clubhouse or something and they put cots in there for us. It was really something. After a couple of weeks, I was able to move into Clark Howell Dormitory, where Smith Haywood and some of his friends lived. I was really fortunate. The school and the town were flooded with students. People were living everywhere, in trailers, in spare rooms, anywhere there was room. Folks were piling into all kinds of temporary housings all over town. Me? I ended up in one of the choice dormitories on the whole campus. Like so many times in my life, I was just plain lucky," he says.

For the first time since he was in elementary school back in Thomaston, Jones was a full-time student. He thrived, soon becoming an active member and a natural leader in a variety of campus organizations. His newfound confidence extended from the classroom to his extra-curricular activities and Jones—as he later would exhibit in the real world—discovered that he enjoyed leading much more than following.

In the years that followed at Georgia, he was a member of the Gridiron Secret Society, ODK, Blue Key Honor Society and was president of the Demosthenian Literary and Debate Society. Most of the time, he was a Dean's List student in the university's School of Business Administration, majoring in marketing. In 1950, during his senior year, he was inducted into Who's Who in American Colleges and Universities.

He continued to live in Clark Howell, a dormitory that was located near Sanford Stadium. In the late 1940s, it was a choice campus address and he promptly found that even dorms needed leadership. Soon after he moved in, he became acquainted with the proctor—a student who was part of the dormitory's management team. The proctor worked closely with the dorm mother, a very strict woman named Mrs. Westbrook. Jones and the proctor were walking toward town one day and Jones asked him how he got that job. He described the process and the responsibilities to Jones. Then he really got Jones' attention. "You get your room free and you get $90 a quarter," the proctor said.

By the next day, Jones had introduced himself to the proper authorities and let them know that if that job ever came open, he wanted it. He became the proctor at Clark Howell during both his junior and senior years. With those perks, came responsibilities and also trouble—trouble that a proctor had to avoid.

Mrs. Westbrook treated the students who lived in that dormitory as if they were her children. That style didn't set well with many of the residents who were World War II veterans used to dealing with crusty sergeants rather than doting dorm mothers.

As the proctor, Jones found himself placed squarely in the middle with ninety-six students to defend. They asked Jones to intercede on their behalf and he tried to explain to Mrs. Westbrook that these were men, not boys, and that they ought to be treated with respect.

"Unlike me, those guys were real soldiers. I told Mrs. Westbrook how they had been through some trying times, life and death kind of things. I know you also have some very young freshmen living here. But if you will just leave those older guys alone, things will be all right, I told her. Eventually, she listened to me. She became a very beloved figure to us. I remember one Christmas how we all gave her gifts," he says.

But before things settled down, Jones became involved in an incident that threatened to push Mrs. Westbrook over the edge and cost him his job as proctor. Clark Howell had a spacey entranceway and lobby. Down the hall were rows of dorm rooms and going up from the lobby were the stairs to the other floors. The dorm mother's apartment was right there on that first floor, near the opening to the stairway.

The plan seemed simple. Mrs. Westbrook went to bed before ten o'clock every night. Her door would shut behind her. Giving her time enough to get to sleep, someone would drop a bunch of lit firecrackers from the top of the stairs. She would be awakened by the boom, throw open her door and everybody would get a laugh.

"The veterans had been dropping bombs, so what was a little firecracker to them?" Jones says. "At her age, you can imagine what all that commotion would be like when you're sound asleep. It's a wonder it didn't scare her to death."

Their plan was simple to everyone but the proctor with the free room and the $90 a quarter. He had to think about his position. So the simple strategy had to be revised. If he came down the stairs just behind the firecrackers, he would be expected to turn in the guilty parties. So instead of that, Jones would go to the other end of the building and use the steps there.

"I would run down the other stairs all out of breath and say, 'Mrs. Westbrook, what's happening here?' as if I knew nothing about it."

It went according to plan. Mrs. Westbrook survived and so did the proctor.

There was also the legal matter of a bootlegger that was operating out of Clark Howell. The campus was dry at that time and so were Athens and Clarke County. In a college town that today is dotted with an endless string of neon-lit bars and nightclubs, this is hard to imagine. But this was the late 1940s and Athens was a far different community.

No one had a still set up in their dormitory room, but one of the residents used to cross over into South Carolina and buy a supply of liquor that he would regularly resell for a profit right out of his dorm room. He had several partners in this underground corporation and they usually maintained an inventory of six or eight cases of booze that they warehoused right there on the premises.

Their price structure was situational—based more on demand than supply. Over the state line, they might pay $2.50 for a bottle of beer. Before a football game up the street at Sanford Stadium, they might sell that same bottle of beer for five dollars. After the game, it might go for as much as eight dollars a bottle. Their price tag might be even higher if there was a Bulldog victory to celebrate. They had been operating their little business for several years without any official intervention. Theirs was a thriving business that couldn't help but turn a profit. University of Georgia students always seemed to be thirsty for an illicit drink.

"Those older guys were used to getting a drink at night. They thought nothing of it," Jones remembers. Everybody around seemed to know about this activity—including Dean Tate.

Dean William Tate was the dean of men. His legend was already growing among University of Georgia people. For generations, he represented all that was good and holy about that institution. A decade later, he established himself as a hero in the way he personally stood up to angry students who were protesting the desegregation of the campus. Before the first litter of bulldogs named Uga was born, Dean Tate was the university's unofficial living symbol. There was no doubt that the all-seeing dean knew about the illegal liquor that was being sold.

Because he said so.

"Mr. Jones, there is liquor being sold at Clark Howell Dormitory and I know that you know there is," Dean Tate said in a telephone call to the surprised dorm proctor.

"I don't know that there is," Jones said.

"Well, I want you to know that I'm going to raid the place," he warned.

Getting off the telephone, Jones hurried down the hallway to what he suspected was the guilty room. These were older fellows, some of them were his friends. He knew they used to sell some booze but he wasn't really sure they were still in that line of work until Dean Tate called him. Walking into their room uninvited, he told them to sit down and shut up.

"You guys still selling liquor?" he asked.

"Why?" they said, figuring he might be a customer.

"Well, we're going to be raided," Jones announced.

This got their attention and they confessed.

"Then you need to know that Dean Tate is on his way and he's going to inspect this dormitory," Jones said.

They only had a few minutes to act but this crowd was cunning and creative. They had learned to plot strategy in a world war so under pressure they quickly concocted a plan. In those days, coal furnaces heated most of the buildings on campus. In the winter months the janitor stayed in the basement to shovel the coal into the furnace on cold mornings. The janitor always kept a mound of coal nearby, in case of an unexpected cold snap. The industrious entrepreneurs rushed their cases of illegal booze down to the basement and dug out openings in the coal. Covering their boxes with baseboard, the student salesmen shoved the liquor under the coal.

When Dean Tate arrived at the dormitory, he found nothing out of the ordinary—except for a good supply of coal for the winter. He looked around for the student proctor and put him on the spot.

"Mr. Jones, now do you know where the liquor is?"

Jones knew he could have gone to jail, but he also knew that he could not tell what he knew. This was home. He had to live there. No matter what the consequences, he could never turn in those veterans. He kept a poker face and said, "It's news to me."

Later, Dean Tate warned Jones that he was going to keep an eye on him and on the liquor venture in his dormitory. He knew, and he knew that Jones had to know. What Jones has never understood is why the dean made that telephone call, warning him of the pending raid. That remains a mystery, unless Tate himself didn't want to see those veterans on the street. Still Tate made it very clear: if anyone was ever caught selling liquor there, Jones was also going to be in trouble. But no one at Clark Howell was ever busted and business went on as usual.

Jones' business was to learn and study. Late in his college career he took on a job through his old mentor, Ed Beech, he became a theater monitor, visiting movie houses in Winder, Commerce and a number of other small towns around Athens.

Unknown to the local theater owner or manager, Jones would show up at the box office and buy a ticket to a movie. While he was there he would count the number of patrons in the house so film distributors could be sure that the figures being turned in by the operators were accurate. It was enjoyable and it gave him some extra spending money, but it was hardly profitable. Most of the time Jones had to split his wages with his friends since he had to depend on one of them for a ride to the theaters.

Without a car of his own, he usually had to use his thumb to get back and forth from Thomaston to Athens. Hitchhiking was a popular mode of travel in this more innocent time and on weekends when his friend Smith Haywood wasn't going to Thomaston, Jones would stand on the side of the highway and stick out his thumb.

"I always enjoyed hitch-hiking. It was an adventure. I would stick out my thumb and if a car stopped, I would smile and say, 'You going toward Monticello?' Folks usually would say get on in. People would talk to me about school or just about anything. They always seemed delighted to have me ride with them," he says.

Few of the rides he caught went straight through so this soon turned into a way for Jones to get a crash course in Georgia geography. He might catch a ride from Thomaston to Barnesville, another from Barnesville to Forsyth, one from Forsyth towards Jackson then others through Monticello and Madison. Sometimes, he would detour through Macon, Gray, Eatonton and Watkinsville. A trip home might take several hours so, needless to say, he didn't go that often, usually no more than once a quarter.

Life was good and so were his grades. Still living at Clark Howell, he volunteered to have foreign students as his roommates—particularly ones from South America. His jaunts there while he was serving in the Navy had left him with a fascination for that region so he took on roommates from Peru and Argentina. He also joined a campus organization for international students. For some inexplicable reason, he felt a kinship with people from that area and at the same time it allowed him to practice his halting Spanish. Years later, he would visit some of those former college roomies in their homelands.

Jones became a well-known figure on the UGA campus, being part of a number of varied activities—often in leadership roles. He became vice president of the Grand Old Party, a campus organization that brought together non-fraternity members. Three times, he had been offered a bid to join one of the Greek fraternities but turned down all three. He had neither the money nor the interest.

Jones was a business major, but he was also active in so many debating competitions that people thought he was in law school since the majority of the passionate debaters were studying law. Its leaders were usually law school students, too.

Preston Bentley, Jimmy's younger brother, was also a classmate of Jones at Georgia. He remembers when Charles decided he wanted to be president of the prestigious Demosthenian society, an organization that for years had been a breeding ground for future governors of Georgia. He asked Preston to run for secretary, joining with him on the same ticket.

"It seemed like he knew everybody on campus," Preston recalls. "We got elected easily."

Charles and Preston only had one class together at Georgia but they would occasionally see each other around campus. When they did, the two Upson County boys would sit down and talk about home. Bentley remembers an episode near Charles' dorm that impressed him, then and now.

"We were sitting there talking when this old black man came down the sidewalk. He was a janitor in Charles' dormitory, I believe. Charles stood up and said hello…and he shook the old man's hand. I had never seen a white man shake a black man's hand before. People just didn't do that back then. But Charles did. That moved me greatly," Preston Bentley recalls.

When Charles Jones was a junior at Georgia, some of his acquaintances invited him to join them in a very private meeting on campus. This unofficial group of students was going to discuss an increasing lack of school spirit involving the annual Georgia Tech-Georgia football game. They told him to keep it a secret.

After the war, the once bitter rivalry between the two in-state schools had grown somewhat dormant. At the time, neither the Bulldogs nor the Yellow Jackets were that dominant on the football field or in the Southeastern Conference of which each was a member. Attendance and spirit was waning in both Athens and Atlanta.

Jones and that small group of students decided it was up to them to do something to stir up things, to heat up those old school feelings. After talking over several potential plans, they created a plan for a late-night prank that was designed to rile up both campuses.

And no one was supposed to know.

"Since Tech's school colors were gold and white, we decided to get a couple or three gallons of yellow paint and at about 2 o'clock in the morning, we were going to decorate the University of Georgia campus. We planned to paint a big yellow X on the front door to the president's office and on the door to the dean of the law school. We painted up a car and down at the football stadium we planted grass seeds that spelled out 'To hell with Georgia' in big letters. Our little prank made the front page of the Atlanta Constitution. To retaliate, some people from Georgia went up and made a mess at Tech," Jones says, laughing at what they accomplished.

Friendly hatred returned quickly and so did the fans in the stands. By game day that season, temperatures on both sides of the field were elevated. Jones went to the game and says the Tech fans at Grant Field in Atlanta certainly were wide-awake. After the game, he went out to Little Five Points in Atlanta and watched gleefully as a group of Tech students burned a black casket that symbolized the University of Georgia. Their mission was accomplished, though none of them could take the credit.

Jones was twenty-two years old and on the verge of his senior year at the University of Georgia. Graduation was creeping up on him and so was the end of his Navy savings. Remembering his mother's lesson about getting the money to pay your way, he knew he needed to find something that would make some real money.

Trying to graduate as soon as possible, he was taking two five-hour courses in American and world history by mail that summer. He borrowed $250, and in the backyard of his parents' house in Thomaston he strung fencing and put together a series of chicken pens.

To everyone's surprise—including his own—Charles Jones was in the chicken business. It was fowl but profitable, the most profitable summertime venture he found—so much so that he still laughs about making a mistake by not continuing in the chicken business.

Investing that $250, he raised 500 chickens and in plain sight of the back door to Ben Jones' house. "Well, to be exact, I raised 492 out of 500," he says. He turned a 100 percent profit, too, After paying for the chickens, his feed and his chicken wire, he cleared about $250.

"I still say I should have quit the University of Georgia right then and raised chickens. I've never had such a good deal—before or after."

In the spring of 1950—six years after he had graduated from high school and less than four years after he had been honorably discharged from the US Navy—Charles Jones became a college graduate. He earned a bachelor's degree in marketing—the first person in his family to receive a four-year college degree. Doris Lawrence and Marion Bush were right. He could learn. Now it was time to be a grownup and get a job. He had always worked. Now he needed to earn a living.

He finished his class work in December of 1949 and took a job selling office supplies. He sold recording equipment and stamping equipment. Then remembering his fascination with politics, he enlisted the help of his old friend Jimmy Bentley and got a job at the state capitol. Essentially, he was working for the governor's office but officially he was working with the state's influential Department of Transportation. He reported to Governor Herman Talmadge but he filled out his time sheet at the DOT.

This put him squarely in the middle of two powers: the governor and the DOT. While the governor was elected by voters, Highway Commissioner Jim Gillis was the true seat of influence. If small town legislators could deliver a paved road, it ensured their re-election. So, hat in hand, they had to come to the DOT begging for a road back home. Those things translated into power and in politics, everyone respects power.

Talmadge was Georgia's governor by then, following in the footsteps of Gene, his colorful father. He had been elected to a two-year term in 1948. Two years earlier, Herman had claimed the office after the unexpected death of his father. The elder Talmadge died after being elected again but before his inauguration.

In a bizarre episode in Georgia's history, three men claimed to be governor in 1946. Sitting Governor Ellis Arnall was staying put. Newly elected Lieutenant Governor M. E. Thompson said the new state Constitution called for him to get the job. Herman Talmadge pointed out that he had received more votes than any write-in candidate on the ballot. It turned into a fiasco with reports of dead people voting, legislators being given spiked drinks and locks being changed in the governor's office.

The courts ultimately ruled in favor of Thompson, but only after Talmadge had held the state's highest office for several eventful months. The jurists said Thompson should have the position for two years, until a new election could be held. Going head to head in 1948, Talmadge defeated Thompson. In 1950, he was running for a full four-year term.

Jones was new to the DOT but he certainly wasn't new to Talmadge or his inner circle, including old friend Jimmy Bentley. Many of them had been classmates of Jones at the University of Georgia. Soon Jones was assigned to the governor and his re-election campaign. When the candidate was scheduled to speak in a community somewhere out in the state, Jones was among the advance crew that would go in and get the crowd ready. Charles was in and out of the governor's office on a regular basis. He was rubbing shoulders with the state's power brokers.

Hanging around the Georgia Department of Transportation, he was privy to insider discussions of major developments and major road projects all over the state—including the proposed route for an interstate highway that was going to run through Macon and the center of the state.

This was a heady atmosphere for a young man just out of college. It was also confining. He did not feel at home on the job or in Atlanta. It was too big. There was no way for a person to really belong.

D.C. McCarthy was ten or fifteen years older than Jones. They had become friends in the Navy and had maintained that friendship while Jones was finishing college and going to work for the state of Georgia. McCarthy worked for A. Stein & Company selling belts. His sales territory included Iowa, South Dakota and North Dakota.

Even before Jones graduated, McCarthy had told his friend in Georgia how much he enjoyed the travel, how interesting the work was and how much money there was to be made in sales. All of this began to sound more appealing to Jones as he became increasingly disenchanted with Atlanta and his position with the Department of Transportation.

Encouraged by his old Navy buddy, Jones took a job with Nardis, a women's apparel line out of Dallas, Texas. Working under a sales manager in South Florida, Jones would be selling women's sportswear, representing two different lines. One was Nordis. The other was Sidron—which was Nordis spelled backwards. His territory was the southeast.

The whole decision seemed so logical. Jones long had dreamed of seeing the world and keeping on the move. He was a people person and he could talk. His degree in marketing gave him the tools a person needed to sell. But just as his one-night expedition to Memphis had showed him, life on the road wasn't always what he dreamed it to be.

"I liked to take trips but being a traveling salesman was hard on you. You didn't have motels in those years. You had hotels. You didn't have fresh fruit in your room when you checked in. You didn't have a refrigerator in your room. You didn't have hair dryers or little bottles of shampoo. You didn't have air conditioning so your windows were always open, letting in the noise and the dirt. It taught me a lesson right quick," he says.

Very quickly, he turned into a "Road's Scholar," learning valuable lessons from the miles he covered selling himself and showing his wares. The lessons about the demands of being a salesman on the road he also filed away for later use but the lessons about day-to-day living he knew he needed to apply to his own life—and soon.

His career choices had proven to be mistakes, but it was not too late to correct them. He was a veteran and he was a college grad. He also was newly married. But inside he felt like he was still a little boy, one who had not yet celebrated his twenty-third birthday. "I was supposed to be a man, but I still felt like a boy," he says. "I thought all those things would appeal to me. But they didn't. Not even a little bit. I had learned about the need for roots, for finding a sense of place and the importance of participating and being a part of your school, your community. Those lessons were important to me."

Again, he began searching his soul and the classifieds. His brother Ben was selling shoes at Herbert Smart's Clothing Co., a popular men's store on Cherry Street in Macon. An old friend from Thomaston owned the shoe department and he had leased it to young Ben, who had taken it over after he was discharged from the Army. Ben had a knack for clothing. He seemed to be doing well and enjoying life there. Middle Georgia had been part of Charles' territory with Nordis and when he was in Macon making calls on local stores, the two brothers would get together and visit. Several times, they had walked up the street to the S&S Cafeteria for lunch.

"Walking down the sidewalk, he would speak to the mayor. He'd wave at this person and nod at this fellow. People knew Ben and he knew them. He seemed to belong. I liked all of that," Charles says.

Comparing Ben's settled life to his vagabond life as a salesman, Charles Jones figured it was time for him to find a permanent place to land. He was newly married to Emily Hancock, his high school sweetheart from Robert E. Lee. He knew that he needed to start thinking about a proper place to rear a family. Atlanta wasn't that place, he felt. It was too large a city for a person to make a difference in anything. Thomaston was too small. Maybe Macon would be a good fit.

"I knew I would cut a path wherever I went. Other people didn't know that, but I did. I didn't know what I would do, but wherever I went I knew I was going to make a difference," he says.

Charles and Ben began talking about going into the retail clothing business together. That seemed logical. Both of them understood that business and both of them were willing to work hard. Only thing was, neither had enough money to do it alone. At Herbert Smart's, Ben had catered to many of Macon's downtown professionals—its lawyers, doctors and dentists. They respected his knowledge of fashion and more than anything they liked him.

Dr. Marion Whitehead, a successful dentist in town, was one of his best customers and had become a good friend. Whitehead was willing to back Ben and Charles in their venture and the three of them began to seriously make plans for Macon's newest clothing store.

Talk continued for several months. They were working on a lease arrangement on a downtown location and making their final plans. Jones & Jones was about to become a reality. Then, on the eve of their plunge into business together, the Korean War escalated. Overnight, independent clothing stores found their sources for goods were drying up. Manufacturers soon would be filling the needs of the military—not small town clothiers, particularly new ones.

The two brothers thought it over and decided the time wasn't right to make such a move. They were forced to scrap their plans for a partnership. Charles again found himself in the market for a change. He turned to Whitehead for advice on what he could do. They had become friends. Marion and Elma Whitehead had been nice enough to invite Charles over to their house for dinner a couple of times.

The dentist did know of an established drugstore that was going to be available just down the street from their ill-fated clothing store. Whitehead also said he knew of an experienced druggist there in town who was itching to venture out on his own.

All of these things sounded appealing to Jones. People then depended on their druggist. They weren't just customers with insurance cards standing in line at a chain store. They were friends and neighbors. In many ways, the pharmacist filled the role that family physicians fill today. He not only provided the medicine prescribed by physicians. He also dolled out medical advice and suggested his own medications. It was a respectable profession and that drugstore would meet the needs in that part of town.

Glass's Drugstore was owned and operated by Albert Glass, who was getting ready to retire. Dr. Steven Wright had started the business years before and he was still a legend among the people in that neighborhood. The store was a well-grounded location with lots of history. Its clientele had depended on Wright and Glass for many years.

The store was located in downtown Macon, at 503 Broadway, at the corner of Broadway and Poplar. As a newcomer, that location meant nothing to Charles Jones. Poplar. Mulberry. Cherry. What difference could a few blocks make, he naively thought.

Typically, he did some homework.

Jones soon learned that Macon was a growing community. Before World War II, its population was around 70,000 but by 1950 it had spiraled to 100,000. The area around Bibb County was growing too, helped along by the Air Force base in Warner Robins.

Folks who lived in those adjoining counties, most of them rural, depended on Macon to be their shopping center.

When Middle Georgians needed something, they came to Macon to buy it. When they needed to bank, they came to Macon. When they needed to go to the hospital, they came to Macon. It once was a cotton town, the rail yards near the drugstore once vital to the city's economy. Now, like so many other post-war communities, Macon was looking for new ways to make a living.

Jones also discovered that Glass's Drugstore was the oldest operating pharmacy in Macon and that the city council met there many years before. Former owner Steve Wright had left Glass a prosperous business and Glass had done nothing to diminish that. It all sounded very promising.

Jones and Whitehead were establishing a three-way partnership. The third party was the druggist. He was experienced and he worked for Roy G. Williams Inc., a well-known pharmacy that was located just a few blocks away. Jones assumed he would know how things were in Macon, which would be a help in getting this store off the ground. Each of them was sure that the druggist would be the all-important man in the white jacket behind the counter filling the illegible prescriptions.

Though the three men hardly knew one another, each of them would fill a vital role in this newly-created partnership. The druggist had his degree and his license. The dentist had the capital. And though he was by far the youngest of the threesome and had never worked in a drugstore before in his life, Jones had the business savvy.

So on the second day of 1951, Charles Jones left the road and moved to Macon. He had $20 in his pocket, a month's supply of groceries in the trunk of his car and a University of Georgia diploma on his wall.

And he was going to need all three.

6

Doc Jones

His clothes said he was from the country and the shuffle in his walk gave away his age. Leaning heavy on his walking stick, the old man came in the back door of the drugstore then carefully made his way through the aisles that were busy with Saturday afternoon customers.

Velma noticed him first. She was working around the soda fountain and she watched as the white-haired man came in through the back door off Poplar Street. The old fellow had a sadness about him, but he also had purpose. He had been there before, she decided.

Velma had been around there for awhile, too. She was an old employee in an old store that had been given a new name. Velma and Mary had almost become permanent fixtures. They had worked for Albert Glass and they stayed on when at the beginning of 1951 the store became Charles Jones & Co.

The new owner told them to call him Charlie, that they were in this thing together. He was likeable enough, sure. But he was green and he was young. He worked hard though, she had to give him that. Velma was pulling for him. So was Mary.

Jones had taken over the drugstore only a few weeks before, but in their hearts Velma and Mary already doubted that he would make it. The store didn't even have a licensed pharmacist. Those first few weeks Jones had the place, Dr. Glass came in a few times and filled some prescriptions after the store was closed but they knew that was not the answer. Old Dr. Glass wanted to retire and if he had wanted to keep working, he never would have put the store up for sale.

After Dr. Glass quit coming in, they started taking prescriptions to another pharmacy up the street to get them filled. Nobody had to tell Velma and Mary how much trouble they all were in. They just knew.

Their new boss could see what was happening too. He wasn't stupid. Naïve, but hardly stupid. And while Charles Jones never let the two women see him, he was so upset at what was happening that several times he had sneaked away to the basement and vomited.

Watching that old man with black skin weathered by too many days in the Georgia sunshine amble through the store, Velma knew he was looking for something. He looked like so many of the folks who milled around that block on Saturdays.

Coming in from the country, most of them arrived early on Saturdays, so they could get a choice location on the downtown sidewalk. They brought vegetables they had gone out in the garden and picked that morning, ready to sell or trade. Depending on what season it was, they would offer bushel baskets filled to the brim with watermelons, butter beans, okra, yellow squash, homegrown tomatoes, cucumbers, or bell peppers.

The aromas were also enticing. Some of the folks built fires and boiled peanuts. Others threw slabs of pork ribs on a grill. If you weren't hungry when you got there, you were after you caught a whiff of what was cooking. By the time the stores opened up, the downtown sidewalks were transformed into an open-air festival and would be that way until the sun went down.

For one day of the week, that was Macon's town square.

Poplar and Broadway was somewhere between two blocks and two universes away from Mulberry or Cherry. On Mulberry, the steeples on the stately old churches cast dignified shadows and on either side of the street were the bankers in their leather chairs and expensive suits. At S&S Cafeteria, one of the city's homegrown businesses, a pianist played tasteful music while you enjoyed your meal there on Cherry. Retailers such as Dannenbergs had been in the city for generations and they were old, established, and proper. These were streets for Macon's ladies and gentlemen, folks of breeding, folks whose family trees grew tall and proud.

Weekdays, most of the shoppers around Poplar and Broadway were working class white folks, joined by a few low-level employees from the banks up on Mulberry. It was a wool hat neighborhood where most folks had mud on their shoes.

Folks walking through that neighborhood might be grabbing a quick sandwich at the Heart of Georgia Café before they went to see if Eddie Bashok had any bargains at his surplus store. They could be on their way to get a hair cut at James Braswell's Barber Shop or to see if Bill Collins could fix the rundown heels on their wingtips. They could be picking up a fifty pound bag of seeds at Karsten & Denson's or they could be shopping for a new set of whitewalls at Fitzpatrick's Tire Company.

At night, the atmosphere in that area took a totally different direction. It was rough and it was rowdy. There were juke joints and flop houses. Between the drugstore and the train station was an acknowledged Red Light District. It was not a place to take the kids.

Saturdays, it was mainly a country crowd. Country come to town, you might say. Many of them were African American like that old black man with the white head of hair. Easing into the drugstore, he seemed to be looking for something special, and Velma walked over to see if she could help him.

"I want to see the doc," he told her.

"Maybe I can help," she said, knowing there wasn't a doctor in the house.

"No, I need to see the doctor," he said.

Charles Jones was across the store dusting and cleaning. People had already noticed how industrious he was. What they had not noticed was that when no one was looking, he was reading the labels on the bottles on the shelves. He was giving himself a fast-course in their ingredients and in what they were supposed to treat.

Velma found him there, the old man right behind her.

"Charlie, this man needs your help," she said.

Smiling, Jones asked if he could help.

"Is you the doctor?" the old man asked in the vernacular of the day.

"I think I can help you," Jones said, avoiding the question.

"I want to see the doc."

"Just tell me what you need," Jones said.

The man said nothing. What could a kid in a white shirt and tie know?

Standing there, Jones began to feel embarrassed. He didn't know what to say or what to do. He felt helpless and inadequate. He couldn't lie to the old gentleman. He couldn't pass himself off as a druggist or a doctor, as the man kept asking to see.

"I'm not a doctor," Jones admitted. "But maybe I can still help you."

His cane in hand, the old man stood as straight as the years would let him. He told young Mr. Jones that he had been trading at that store most of his life, since Doc Wright owned the store. He was from Jeffersonville, out in Twiggs County. He had forgotten his money at home. But he said he would be back the next week.

Jones felt paralyzed. He wanted to help the fellow, but he didn't seem to know what he was supposed to do. All he could do was stand there and listen. The old man was about to leave and again the young store owner said he wished he could help. "I'll be back next Saturday," the white-haired man promised, starting back on to Poplar Street, the way he came in.

Watching that fellow leave, Jones felt like a little boy. He was married. He was twenty-three years old. He was a college graduate. He owned his own business. Kids were on the way. The world would have certified him a grownup. But right then he felt like a frightened little boy.

Over the next week, Jones felt as if he had aged from 23 to 66. He could not seem to get that old man off his mind. He suffered quietly. He wondered what became of the fellow and if he would really be back. He hoped the fellow would come again, so he would have a second chance.

When Saturday came around again, Jones kept his eyes on the door all day, watching for him. The old man never came and Jones has never forgotten him. He had failed the old fellow. More than that, he had failed himself. It was one customer and one day, but for Charles Jones, that was a watershed event in his life, and a scene he never wanted to repeat.

He had never seen him before and he would never see him again.

> That old gentleman was a saint to me, a great professor, and he didn't know it. I never got to see him or tell him all of that. He taught me so much. I can't see his eyes, but I can still see the rest of him right now. He was depending on me, and I let him down. That incident was like a spiritual experience for me. An awakening. I promised myself that from then on I was going to act like a man. You may look like a boy and talk like a boy. But if you've taken on the responsibilities of a family and a business, then you have to put away childish things.

That Sunday, after the old man had failed to return, Jones reexamined his own life and where he was in it. He did not like spending nights on the road. He knew he did not want the world he had found in Atlanta. He had decided long ago that he would not go back home to Thomaston. He was in Macon—at the corner of Poplar and Broadway.

"I didn't want to go back to where I was in life," he says. "This was where I was. Those were my circumstances."

The druggist, his would-be partner, had let him down. From the very first day in January, he was AWOL. When Jones called to see where he was that Monday morning, the druggist complained about his health, and a painful accident that he was being treated for under Worker's Comp. These were situations he hadn't talked with Jones and Whitehead about before the store had opened. Every day Jones would call and every day the man would offer new excuses.

Over and over, the druggist promised his new partner that he would be there tomorrow. But tomorrow was always the same as yesterday. Jones' patience was running low and his circumstances were catching up on him. Authorities were going to take away his federally registered narcotics permit any day, as they should given the absence of a licensed pharmacist. Even his regular customers were not going to keep coming back if he continued to send their prescriptions to another store to be filled. He wondered how long Velma and Mary would stay with him and he knew he couldn't make it without the two of them. Though he tried not think about such things, he did not know how much longer he would be able to keep the doors open.

Jones and the old man were together at a crossroads.

Come Monday, he knew what he had to do.

"I came in that day and put on a white jacket," he says. "The old man was looking for 'Doc,' and here he was."

Velma and Mary were surprised when they came to work and saw him wearing that white coat. Before they opened the store that morning, he gathered them together for an impromptu meeting. "When I got here, I told you we were in this together and for you to call me Charlie. Well, from now on, you can call me Mr. Jones or Doc—and I prefer Doc. We have to make this work, and we have to be more professional."

To folks around Broadway and Poplar, he did become Doc Jones—usually just plain Doc. Half a century later—long after he outgrew that white jacket—if older people in that part of town see Charles Jones they still throw up and hand and call him Doc.

"Who wants to get their prescription filled by a little boy named Charlie? Course, I couldn't fill prescriptions anyway, but if folks had problems they would see me as Doc. I wore that white jacket every day from then on. I still had that cute little baby face, but now I had some authority," he says.

Slowly, he began to feel as if he really was in charge. More importantly, he acted like he was. He had learned from that old man with the walking stick that when you hang the open sign in the front window, you had better be ready to do business. In the years to come, Albert Glass' old drugstore would change and so would its dynamic new owner.

Jones wasn't uptown on Mulberry but he made the changes necessary to do business where he was. He would serve you a cup of hot coffee and sack up a couple of bargains. He could sell you a locket to wear around your neck, a box of Valentine's candy in a heart-shaped box, a room full of furniture or a brand spanking new Olds 98. If you had ailments, he could sell you a package of living kidney pills. "You can't wait for God to come down with a burning bush and deliver it to you," he says. "You can't wait for your Daddy or your Mama to do it for you or your friends. You have to get up and push it yourself. I learned all of that in that little store. It was my classroom. That was where I got my Master's Degree in Business Administration."

Charles Jones & Company would hardly be thought of as your typical classroom, but the lessons came long before the profits. As a boy, he learned to work. At 503 Broadway, he was learning about responsibilities. For his first year, he struggled to pay the rent and meet the payroll. There was no room and no time for growth. But there were plenty of chances to learn.

"God loved me enough to put me in that situation where I had to learn two very important things. I had to grow up and become a man. Then I had to learn how to run a business."

And his first professor was an old man wobbling on a cane.

7

His Own Man

Ben Fitzpatrick called and said come on over, have a Coke with us. Putting the phone down, Charles Jones grumbled to himself that the tire man just didn't get it. If he knew how much Jones had to do in the store, he would know that he didn't have time for a bottle of Coke.

Fitzpatrick's Tire Company was on Poplar Street, across from the drugstore. Fitzpatrick and J. A. Smith were inviting Jones over more and more often. Just to talk. Just to visit. Both of them were first his customers, then his friends, finally his mentors. He couldn't turn them down so he told Velma and Mary that he would be right back.

Smith came into the store almost every day to buy Dutch Masters cigars—15 cents, two for a quarter. Sometimes he would buy a cup of coffee to go with his cigar, making himself right at home at a table in the back, puffing on his Dutch Master and reading a magazine.

When he first started trading with him, Jones knew him by what he bought, not who he was. It was Bill Collins, from the shoe repair shop down the street, who told him that Smith was the owner of the S&S Cafeteria chain. His cafeterias were serving food from Miami to Washington.

Like Fitzpatrick, Smith was a good bit older than Jones, who was still in his early twenties. Both of the merchants had been around that neighborhood for decades. Thirty years before, Smith had first gotten into the food business there on Broadway, opening Smitty's Barbecue. Now he was a rich man who enjoyed cheap cigars.

Heading over to the tire company, Jones was still feeling sorry for himself. He worked six long days a week in the drugstore and was back in there after church on Sunday to do the books. He put in many hours and many days. It would take him a while to realize that at one time in their lives Fitzpatrick and Smith had been where he was. They did understand how hard he was working. That was what impressed them about this new kid on their block, that and his obvious spunk.

"How are things, Charlie?" Fitzpatrick asked.

"Pretty good," he said, not letting on how tight things were.

Little by little, Jones was being accepted into a tight-knit fraternity of merchants that did business in a neighborhood that had never owned a pair of silk stockings. These fellows were old school in every sense of the phrase. They had their own personal styles and sometimes their edges were a little rough. There was not a college degree on the block except for Jones'. These men relied on experience and common sense that came with their birth certificates. These were not men whose goal in life was to be president of the chamber of commerce or to sit on bank boards. They were workhorses. They kept the show horses in their barns. But had you checked their financial portfolios, many of these men could buy and sell the fat cats with the big cars and big mortgages that matriculated on Cherry Street.

Macon was in so many ways a closed shop. It was not a transient community. People were born here, lived here and died here, knowing their obituary would be printed in the local paper. To be truly accepted, you needed to be a native son. Newcomers had to pay their dues, and sometimes that could take decades. Former Mayor Buck Melton says Macon was particularly that way in the 1950s when Jones came to town.

"Macon was then, and still is to some extent, a closed society. At that time, it would have been a big help for somebody to be born here, raised here and to have gone to school here. All of those things would be a big advantage. Macon was ruled by people who had a lineage here. Those people were the movers and shakers," says Melton, a longtime Macon lawyer.

As Melton notes, Charles Jones filled none of those categories.

"He likes to say he showed up with $20 in his pocket and he started that little business downtown. But he was likeable, smart, always had that enormous energy and was very driven to make things happen. Those things helped him overcome those other factors and he would become one of this town's most important leaders of the past thirty or forty years."

No one would have called Jones a city leader back on Poplar and Broadway. Nor would they have seen him developing into one. To Smith and Fitzpatrick, Jones seemed like a kid, yet they sensed in him a kindred spirit. He was an entrepreneur. He enjoyed the chase of a deal as much as the closing. He had drive. He had ideas. He had ambition. And when he saw someone else who had a good idea, he could usually figure out ways to make their idea even better. They knew these things about him for each one of them had tested him—and he had passed.

There was Henry Kaplan, from Kaplan's Inc., a furniture store that for generations had done business at 514 Broadway. At first, Kaplan would come into the store for one of Jones & Company's seven-cent cups of coffee. Coffee was a dime up on Cherry Street. Kaplan cherished those three cents so he would be in the drugstore every morning, waiting for the pot to brew.

If the drugstore was empty, he was pleasant. If it was filled with customers, Kaplan would make a scene. Usually, he would complain loudly about that day's coffee. It was too cold. It was too strong. It wasn't fresh. Velma and Mary got to where they hated to see him coming.

Enough was enough. Jones invited him to the back of the store.

"Kaplan, I don't know what your motive is complaining in front of all those people. But there are 35 or 40 people in here and I don't want you raising sand. You must have some reason for doing this, but I don't want you in my store. Don't you ever come back," Jones ordered.

Kaplan did leave. But the next day he came back.

"I'm sorry, Doc. I was just joking around."

From then on, they were friends. Jones had passed another test.

As he found he could keep his head above water, Jones began to see the opportunities waiting for him at Poplar and Broadway. This was not the place he chose to be. But he was there, and he began to make the best of that. The merchants who were his customers and neighbors could share their experience, strength and hope with him. Each one of them had a peculiar way of doing business and he wanted some of that. Finally, the student was getting ready to learn.

Visits with Smith and Fitzpatrick were part of that learning. That's why he dropped what he was doing and started across the street when Fitzpatrick invited him that afternoon. Dropping his nickel into the big red Coke machine at the back of the tire company, Jones grabbed his bottle out of the machine and found himself a chair. Fitzpatrick and Smith were already talking among themselves. Jones usually didn't have much to say. By then, he had learned to listen.

Outside the store window, a sixteen-wheeler rolled into the lot. The oversized truck seemed to catch Smith's eye and he got up from the table, leaving their discussion where it was and he walked outside. Fitzpatrick went with him and Jones tagged along. After the driver of the truck had finished telling Fitzpatrick's mechanic what he needed, Smith went over to him, stuck out his hand and struck up a conversation. They exchanged some comfortable chit-chat, and then the cafeteria owner got down to business.

"How you like this truck?"

"Pretty well."

"It's pretty new, isn't it?'

"Yeah, just had it a little while."

"How many miles to the gallon do you get?"

"Fourteen in town."

Smith kept on asking questions and the driver kept on answering. Smith was nosy. Now he wanted to know about the brand of tires the driver was running.

"They're Firestones, aren't they?

"Yeah, they are."

"Why do you use Firestones?"

To the surprise of Jones, the driver freely shared his opinions with the older man—who he had never met and didn't know. He told him all of his experiences with the truck and with that brand of tires. Jones watched and listened. For the life of him, he couldn't figure out what was going on. Two weeks later, he got his answer.

One afternoon, Smith was telling Jones and Fitzpatrick about this new truck he had bought. The company owned one truck but needed another big rig to drop food deliveries to his stores up and down the eastern seaboard. And the one he had bought was identical to the truck he discussed with that driver in the lot at Fitzpatrick's. It may have even been the same color.

Jones was flabbergasted, and he couldn't hide it. Why would Smith spend all that time with a mere truck driver? He asked the cafeteria mogul why he asked him all those questions when he could have gone to someone higher up the chain of command.

"Here was this very wealthy man and he wasn't so sophisticated or uppity that he felt he had to go to some high-level person with his questions. He went straight to the source, he said. That man was a truck driver. He wasn't educated. But he was an expert. What better person to ask questions about that truck and its performance? That, to me, was reality," Jones says.

For men like Smith, such practices were second nature. That was just part of doing business. You don't waste your time with the men in the suits. You go to the source, whether he has his name stitched on his shirt or a monogram on his sleeve. You don't check his pedigree or check to see how many diplomas he has on the wall.

A native of nearby Jones County, Smith never finished high school himself. He dabbled in the taxi cab business in Macon. Then he opened his first eating place, a barbecue restaurant, way back in the 1920s. From there, he slowly evolved into the cafeteria business. Within a decade, he was ready to expand. He opened his first S&S Cafeteria outside of Macon in Columbus, Georgia in 1936. Today, the company is still run by the Smith family. They own fourteen cafeterias in five states.

In the 1930s, Smith owned two eating places in downtown Macon. Sitting in one of them on Cherry Street, he would watch every day as the crowds gathered to eat at the Wysteria, a cafeteria across the street from him. That inspired him to buy that place from a man named Flournoy. Soon, Smith moved exclusively into that kind of serving style, ultimately opening cafeterias all over the region. He always kept his eyes open to what was happening around him. Even when Jones knew him, Smith made it a habit to ride around town and quietly count the cars in the parking lots of his competitors. Jones was taking this all in. "Mr. Smith always had a notebook and a pencil in his pocket. He would write the important things down so he wouldn't forget. I started doing the same thing—and I still do that," he says.

For his first few months on Broadway, Jones struggled to break even. There was his rent and there were salaries for him, for Velma and for Mary. When you counted everything up, he wasn't making as much per hour as they were—though he realized they were worth more than he was at the time. But finally, after his third month in the store, he was $160 in the black. That gave him a healthy dose of courage and he became confident enough to look for ways to stretch his wings.

Whatever he did, he soon learned that a drugstore was marginal. It could only make so much. He had to push, and push he did. Selling became a game to him, like it was in Uncle Robert's little store when customers would want to match him for a bottle of dope.

The old customers were still flocking in to buy some of Dr. Steve Wright's special over-the-counter products. Glass had continued to offer these products, even after Wright was gone. The best sellers were the L&K pills—L&K as in liver and kidney. The old owner had concocted this mixture and a wholesale house packaged them just for him. Jones continued to keep them in stock. Sold in small envelopes, a person could buy twenty-four of them for 35 cents. Jones never was sure what was in them. "But I think they would clean out a person's system," he says.

Every day, he was dealing with the salesmen who called on the store. They could smell fresh meat a county away, so like his neighbors on Broadway, they too were testing this unsuspecting merchant.

One of them was selling Jergens Lotion, and to hear that fast-talking sales rep tell it a drugstore should have bottles of his product on every shelf. Naturally, he had a deal. Buy six and you get one free, he offered. Jones bit, and now the salesman was reeling him in like a hungry Georgia catfish.

When the shipment arrived from the wholesale house, the six bottles were there but the free bottle was not. Jones tracked down the salesman to see what had happened to that offer. "Oh, didn't you know? You have to send your invoice into the office in St. Louis, then they'll send you that free bottle of lotion." The fast-talking salesman had left that information out of his spiel.

"The first time is your fault. The second is mine. I was learning," Jones says. "If Granny could go West with no water, no lights and no friends, surely I could survive."

Doc Jones was behind the counter now and while he couldn't fill a prescription, he could still give his opinion—something he is never without. Customers would tell him their problem and he would give them his solution. If they had a headache, he had something for them. If they were feeling run down, he knew just what to do.

He pushed vitamins and elixirs. He sold sex potions and love roots. He stocked Love Me Quick Perfume, dragons blood powder and a lucky root from India. There were the L&K pills, of course. At Charles Jones & Company, such items sold quickly. These were pieces of merchandise you would not find on the shelf at Chi-Chester's or Walgreen's or Roy Williams. You had to go see Doc Jones.

On the sidewalk outside on Broadway, he plugged in a juke box and cranked up the volume, using the music to draw a crowd. If he had a special sale going on, Jones would go out on the sidewalk himself and become a sideshow barker, luring folks inside with his non-stop chatter. On the afternoon before Valentine's Day, if he still had boxes of candy on the shelf, he would take to the streets.

"This is a seven dollar box of candy," he would scream, holding one of the heart-shaped containers above his head. "It's yours for four dollars. Your wife is waiting on it at home."

And he never shut off the lights with candy left to sell either.

Inside the store, he had anything and everything.

He would sell you a new car. ("What color do you want?")

Or a living room suite. ("You want that delivered?")

If a customer wanted it, he'd get it—as long as he could make a buck.

"It was a carnival," he says, "an entertainment center."

Looking around the store, there still were lots of items sitting around gathering dust. In the stock room, he discovered an assortment of items that Glass had never been able to move. Down in the basement, he found some more stuff. It was everywhere.

Jones had a plan, so he found a good-sized table and a clean white tablecloth. He put the covered table out in the store, in a spot where customers would have to go around it. On this table, he stacked up all this unsold merchandise he had been collecting.

On it, he put a sign: "Everything $1."

He didn't know how people would look at such a thing. He had studied advertising at the University of Georgia, but those classroom campaigns were not for him, they were for somebody else. As the lunch crowd began to gather that day, he watched customers milling around that sale table...picking up one item...putting it back...looking at the price...putting it back...then picking up something else.

"Hey, Doc, is this here a dollar?"

"Yes, ma'am, it's a dollar."

"What about this thing?"

"It used to be $3, but now it's just a dollar."

"Oh, lookee here. I've been looking for something like this."

Pretty soon, you could see nothing but the white tablecloth.

For Jones, this dollar sale taught him yet another lesson. It was not just merchandise or products he needed to know. More than anything, it was people. He began to closely study his customers—the ones who bought and the ones who didn't. He decided he needed to know and understand people if he was going to make it in business.

A salesman offered him a large supply of screwdrivers he could get —45 cents for a set of six. They had metal handles and were made in Germany. Jones bought a crate of them and starting displaying them near the cash register, so he would be able to reach them.

"If you came up to pay your bill from the soda fountain and I saw grime under your nails, I'd say 'You're a working man. Tell you what I'll do. I'll sell you this set of screwdrivers for a dollar and ninety-five cents. Look at 'em. They're imported. You know you can use them at home. And if you buy the screwdrivers, I'll throw in your lunch for free.' People would jump on it," he says.

People who came up to the cash register to buy cigarettes would get another offer. "They're 23 cents…but I'll sell you two packs for 45," he would say. If they said yes, Jones knew they liked a deal. That information he would file away for next time they visited his store.

If you didn't have grease on your hands and you didn't smoke, maybe you needed some jewelry. Jones started picking up inexpensive costume jewelry from sources all over the country and soon it was moving out of the store as fast as he could move it in.

"If somebody paid their check with a twenty dollar bill, I would tell them that their lunch was free if they bought this dollar and a half necklace. They usually did, too. We started building a reputation. If there was a special occasion, folks would come into the store looking for just the right gift—whether it was boxes of Norris chocolates or costume jewelry," he says.

Charles Jones operated that store for nearly five years. He now compares that experience to the rigors of basic training in the Navy. "I had to learn to swim," he says. "Things happened for the best. I wouldn't have said that then, but I know it now."

By the end of his time downtown, he was a man in a hurry. His father, years before, had told him of the distinct stages in a man's life: the one that comes before you get married, the one that comes before the children are born and the one that comes before the children start to school. Ben Jones said a man ought to make his mark before the kids go to school, so he would have more time to spend with them.

His twin girls, Jan and Judy, were born in late 1951. Charles, his wife Emily, and their two girls were living in the Massey Apartments, which had a hard and fast rule against young children living there. He knew they were living there on borrowed time.

Besides, he was getting itchy for a new challenge. He long ago learned that the profit margin on a store such as his was small and usually precarious. You could make a living, but you couldn't make a very good one. Jones wanted more, for himself and his family.

Jones was born with ambition. The energy he was always blessed with was boiling over. He couldn't help thinking back on a one-hour course he had taken near the end of his time at the University of Georgia. It was about finding a job. The professor had lectured the students about finding a need and filling it. Telling no one, Jones began his own study of Macon, to see what it needed. Once he figured out what that need was, he would set out to fill it.

One evening, about closing time, Jones began his daily ritual. Old Dr. Glass had warned him about the danger of getting robbed. He had advised Jones to forget about the safe. Leave it empty, then leave the door open so a potential robber could plainly see that it was empty. He suggested that Jones keep the money somewhere else. Ever since, he had been putting his money in sacks and hiding it on a shelf behind the rows of medicine bottles. That plan had worked well thus far.

That's what Jones was doing when J. A. Smith came in. His visit was unusual. He didn't usually come by the drugstore at that time of night. It was supper time—a busy hour at his cafeteria up the street. Smith was always there, pouring iced tea and making sure the line kept moving.

"You want a cup of coffee," Jones asked.

Smith said no, that he had something on his mind.

"I want to see you for a few minutes," Smith said.

They sat down and Smith started to talk. He told Jones how his business was growing everywhere. Then he talked about his plans to expand even more into Florida, especially in the high-traffic areas of the state. He told him about a new restaurant he was opening in Ormond Beach, near Daytona Beach. He told Jones how many people it would seat and how much it would cost to build the place. He talked about how much it could clear every month. He said they would close their old location near there and consolidate everything into this brand new restaurant. And he wanted Charles Jones to be his partner.

By that time, Jones was taking a $250 a month draw at the drugstore and working six long days every week to do that—not counting the hours he put in on Sundays. He and the family had just moved into their first house, borrowing the down payment on a $10,200 home. Their budget was tight. If the household funds didn't last until Friday, they dined on potted meat and Vienna sausages. It was a rule they wouldn't violate.

Now Smith was saying they would pay him $15,000 a year to run this new restaurant. Jones didn't need a calculator to compute that would mean his income would increase nearly five fold—before the IRS got its share.

"Good God! I mean Gabriel had blown his horn. I thought I was fixin' to go to heaven. The very idea. In my low estate, here was this successful businessman telling me that he wanted me, and that I would make all that money. I was elated," Jones says.

With both of them furiously scratching numbers on a pad, they continued to talk about how the place would operate and what Jones' responsibilities would be. What kind of money they thought it would make. What his share of the business would be. They talked for some time that night and said they would get back together again the following week. Jones wanted time to mull over the offer and the numbers.

Jones thought about Smith's proposal all week, and he was flattered. But as he crunched the numbers, the math did not compute. Instead of an equal partner, he concluded that he really would be about a 15 percent partner. That bothered him. He knew he could be stubborn and he knew that in the drugstore he enjoyed doing things his way. He liked it that way. He relished being independent.

"I knew I could control something about what happened here. I didn't know what would happen down there in Florida. This was a known and that wasn't, I decided."

Jones turned down the offer and the two businessmen shook hands. Smith continued to be a regular customer at the drugstore—buying 15 cent cigars and drinking seven cents a cup coffee. Many years later, they would do business together more than once, butting heads and making money. Finally, in the fall of 2001, Charles Jones was among the mourners when J. A. Smith died at the age of 99.

The value of Smith's offer went beyond a job and Jones is still grateful: "Mr. J. A. Smith paid me one of the greatest compliments he could have paid me. He believed in me. That told me that I needed to see through my eyes what he saw through his. It told me I had value—something that I badly needed to hear at that time in my life. I guess in me he saw a man that would work, that was honest and that was a merchant—which was a very big word to him. By making me that offer, he gave me confidence that I would make it—whatever I chose to do."

8

Ambassador Motel

The ash on Billy Watson's cigarette dangled like a participle at the end of a sentence. The more he puffed, the more it teetered. This was big business they were discussing and all Charles Jones could think about was the ash growing on the end of that cigarette.

Jones was doing his best to keep his mind on what they were talking about. His future could be at stake. Yet he could not take his eyes off of that cigarette. And the longer they talked, the longer the ash on the end of that cigarette grew.

This was a big meeting for Jones. His friend Steve Solomon had arranged this appointment with Watson, the executive vice president of Macon Federal Savings and Loan Association. Watson agreed to see the brash young drugstore owner as a favor to Solomon. And now all Jones could concentrate on was the ash dangling on the end of that cigarette. Watching it expand, he kept wondering when it was going to fall into the banker's lap.

Jones was distracted, all right. Numbers were bouncing in the air. Facts were being tossed around. His most private dreams were being exposed. This was something he had worked on for a long time. In the midst of business, it dawned on him: Watson didn't even realize that ash was there. He kept puffing and figuring, and that ash kept on dangling. The banker was asking pertinent questions. Some of them Jones wasn't prepared to answer.

"Why do you want to build a motel?" Watson asked.

That one he could answer.

Jones said he had been studying the issue for a long time and that he had concluded that Macon badly needed a motel—something the town didn't have at that point.

He began telling the veteran loan officer of his nightly checks on the motels located on the edge of the town. He pointed out that they were usually full and he said he had the numbers to back that up. He added that he had some inside information that a major four-lane highway was going to be built around Riverside Drive. He wanted to build the first motel out there, to take advantage of this additional traffic that soon would be flowing through the area. "How do you know about that highway?" "Mr. Bill, I used to work at the Georgia Department of Transportation," Jones explained.

That piece of information would prove correct. Jones' timing was more than just a little off, however. This was 1955, and it would be more than fifteen years before Interstate 75 sliced through that part of the town, bringing with it the Snow Birds passing through in their annual search for Florida Sunshine and the tourist empire of Mickey Mouse. But neither of them knew these things as they sat in Watson's smoke-filled office. Then came a simple question that Jones couldn't answer. "You got your plans?" asked Watson, still puffing on that cigarette. No, he didn't, he said. Jones had few concrete plans, just this growing germ of an idea that he had been carrying around in his head for months and months—maybe years. He told Watson that he would have some more defined plans to show him soon and they set up a second meeting.

Jones and Watson were first introduced by a fellow who regularly traded at the drugstore. The customer worked for the Noland Company, a local plumbing supply outfit, and he was in and out of the store often, picking up packs of cigarettes and cups of coffee. On one of those stops at the store, Jones was talking to him as he paid his bill. He casually asked the fellow where he would go to borrow money in Macon. "You need to meet Mr. Billy Watson," the man said. "He heads up Macon Federal."

Not long after that conversation in the store, the customer introduced Jones to Watson. So when Solomon called and said he had a friend he wanted to bring by his office, Watson had an idea who this Charles Jones fellow was.

Solomon knew Watson very well. He had done lots of business with Macon Federal over the years. Solomon owned one of the city's more successful truck and car businesses so, unlike Jones, he and the banker ran in the same circles. Their meeting that day would turn out to be the beginning of a profitable relationship for both Jones and Watson.

When they got back together for their second meeting, Watson had more questions, mainly how much money Jones wanted to borrow. He gulped when the merchant said he would need $35,000. Now that ash was really in a precarious situation. "Mr. Jones, Macon Federal has never financed a motel before," he said. "We don't know very much about that kind of business." "I know that," Jones said. "But you do loan money for houses and houses don't produce revenue. A motel will. I have a choice. I can build a house for $35,000, live in it and pay for it for the rest of my life. Or I can build this motel, move my family into it, and it will pay for itself."

Watson was way ahead of him. He had already considered that important fact. But he listened closely as Jones talked about friends of his who were home builders, building new subdivisions all over town. A typical house in one of those developments might have three bedrooms, a living room, a dining room and a kitchen. A builder might borrow $35,000. Jones said his proposed motel was going to have six rooms upstairs and twelve rooms downstairs and would require that same amount of cash. "And my rooms are going to make money," Jones repeated, showing confidence he didn't know he had.

Watson nodded, balancing another ash on the end of yet another cigarette. He liked what he was hearing and he was starting to like this optimistic young man whose endless supply of energy seemed to match his supply of ideas. Jones continued to describe his plans and his dreams.

Watson finally admitted to Jones that he was leaning toward a positive answer to his request. First, however, he would need to run the whole deal by his loan committee. If they approved, he said, Jones would get his $35,000. It would be a fifteen-year deal at six percent interest.

More than a week passed. Every day, Jones went through the motions at the store. For him, that was a long ten days. He grew more nervous. Finally the phone call came. He had his loan. "In those days, Mr. Bill didn't write you a check himself. He just gave you a commitment for the loan and you went across the street to C&S Bank. They would give you the money and handle the account. They had never heard of me, but they had my money waiting on me because none of this put them at risk. Macon Federal was taking the risk. Strangely enough, I eventually became a member of that bank's Board of Directors, something I never dreamed would happen that day when Mr. Bill sent me over there," Jones says.

Jones' move into the motel business didn't come overnight. It was the culmination of several years of thinking, driving, and walking. His parents had opened a motel in Thomaston so he had a limited knowledge of the hospitality business. Closer to home, the city of Macon did not have a single motel doing business within the city limits. There were a few out in Bibb County. That fact had set Jones to thinking.

Taking a cue from J. A. Smith, he began a daily tour of the motels outside of town. He would close up the drugstore as early as he could and start his prescribed route. There were not that many to check. There was the Pinebrook Motel on Vineville Road,

Courtesy Courts on Gray Highway, and the Magnolia on Seven Bridges Road. He got to know them all.

Every night, Jones would make his rounds. Motel by motel, he would count the cars in the parking spaces and check the license plates to see where the customers were coming from. He kept judicious notes. He probably came to know more about those businesses than the people who were in them.

Like most towns then, the traditional business travelers still checked into Macon's old downtown hotels—the Dempsey, the Lanier, or the Georgian. That's where the restaurants were. That's where you could buy a pair of socks or a tube of tooth paste if you needed them. If you wanted such items and you were staying in a motel, you often were isolated on a highway outside of a town. At those hotels, Jones would stand outside and count the number that were turned out, floor by floor. He wrote down those numbers, too.

Remembering his own brief experience on the road as a clothing salesman, Jones figured he could lure many of this clientele to his motel—if he ran it right and if he pushed it.

This was the era before the interstate highway system had been built so trips were still long and tiring. Cookie-cutter motel chains with free shampoo in every room and fast food restaurants with their golden arches and drive-through windows had not yet taken over America's roadsides. Many travelers—particularly the businessmen—planned their trips so they would be in a place where they could check into those downtown hotels where they knew the desk clerk and the bellman by name. It was habit and it was practical.

Families on the road would stay behind the wheel of the car until they got tired, hoping to find a place to stay that was reasonable, safe, and clean. Toll free numbers had not been installed so if you called ahead to a hotel or motel, you were not only paying long distance fees you were choosing blindly unless you were personally acquainted with that place of lodging, its owner, or its manager. When people did stop, they would sometimes have to knock on the door and rouse the motel owner out of bed. Before checking in, they would want to check out the room and the rates for every motel was different. Many times, they would see the room, say thank you, and then get back on the road in search of a cheaper rate.

It was a personal business and Jones was a personable guy.

"I knew I liked people and I thought they liked me. This was something I thought I would be interested in, too," Jones says. "It was serving people, making them comfortable, talking with them and meeting with them. That was the emotional part of me—not the intellectual side."

The question soon became where to locate this proposed motel. Using that advance knowledge he thought he had garnered from his brief stint at the state DOT, Jones centered his search around River Street—which later became Riverside Drive.

Chain operations would look to professionals for advice. They would commission high-priced market surveys and hire traffic counters to help them before they put their money on a single piece of property. Jones did these things by himself. He canvassed that area door to door and on foot.

Considering the explosion of growth and development in that area today, it is hard to imagine how naked it was in the early 1950s. Instead of shopping centers and neon signs, there were pine trees. Those pines had to be lonely because there were few people out there for them to talk to. Over a period of months, Jones got to know most of the people who lived on that roadway—from Pierce Avenue all the way out of town.

Up one side of the road and down the other, Jones knocked on doors. Folks got to know him and he made friends with many of them. He wasn't asking them these questions as a faceless developer. He became a buddy, a neighbor. People got used to seeing him around.

After the resident answered the door and they exchanged some pleasantries, he would ask them what they had heard about this four-lane highway that was coming through there. Was it still going to bypass the old Highway 41 route? What did they think would happen when it did come? He began to find out who the major land-owners were and what plots of land might be coming available soon. He found out what the going cost of land was out there, not by checking at the courthouse but by asking folks who lived around there. His knowledge grew, and it was based on shoe leather, not science.

Even armed with all of this knowledge, his confidence was shaky. Down the road, he would swing million dollar deals with swagger and style. This deal was much more personal. He was putting Charles Jones on the line—not just cash.

Dave Thornton calls it buyer's remorse.

Thornton and Jones are two of the oldest developers in Macon these days, but in the early 1950s, they were both new to the game. It was Thornton who eventually sold Jones the land for his first motel in 1953. Jones had found the property on one of his many trips up and down Riverside Drive. Even then, he wasn't sure. One day he was. The next day he would waver. As Thorton says,

> You have to remember, this wasn't too long after World War II. During the Depression and during the war years, people didn't have the money to do anything. You didn't build houses or buy businesses. The Korean War came right after that and things were also slow. By the time we're talking about, money was everywhere. Everything was cheap and you had GI Loans making it possible for people to buy new homes. You could get 100 percent financing on some deals. But we didn't know all of that then. We were still real cautious. We had been raised that way.

Jones had fears and apprehensions. "I was born cold and hungry," he likes to say, "and I never want to go back to being cold and hungry." Fears or not, he went on and bought the property that fronted Riverside Drive, near Pierce Avenue. He had few real plans, but he had a stockpile of vision—a trait Thornton recognized in him many years ago.

"Charlie is an entrepreneur," Thornton says. "That's something you can't teach. It's innate in a person. I don't know his background in high school and college, but I would imagine he had all kinds of involvement's, adventures and money-making things going on."

A native of Florida, Thornton was also a late-comer to Macon. He came to town to attend Mercer University. Except for a tour of duty in World War II, he stayed. He says he didn't learn all that much at the university, but that it did teach him how to make a living. Thornton has been active in the real estate business in Macon for more than five decades. He still thinks about a Mercer professor who talked to his class about the difference between dabbling in the stock market and dabbling in real estate:

> He said investing in the stock market is putting your money in the hands of strangers. You have no input. You've got no control over that company or those shares of stock. When you get into real estate like I have and like Charles has, you can change the value of a piece of property. You can apply your own visions. You can pick out pieces of property that you can make an impact on through building, through development, through rezoning. Even back then, Charlie had a vision that he tied together with an inborn entrepeneurship. That's inborn, like a kid who can throw a baseball 98 miles an hour. If he was teaching a course in entrepreneurship, I'd like to sit in on it.

Jones had finally settled on land owned by Lee Johnson, a former Macon city council member who had developed nearby Woodland Hills. Johnson had left available some commercial property on Riverside. That was the land on which Jones wanted to make an impact by building his motel. That was in 1953—two years after he moved to Macon and three years before he would be ready to break ground on his vision.

Until he had his meeting with Watson at Macon Federal, Jones had shared his ideas with no one. Not J. A. Smith. Not Ben Fitzpatrick. Not even his family. He kept his own counsel. He was Lucky Lindy again, flying solo. This would become a Jones trademark. Only on rare occasions would he take in a partner, remembering his experience with the missing pharmacist in the early days of the drugstore.

Typically, he first accumulated his materials—his knowledge of the area motels, his knowledge of land and property in that part of Macon, his experience as a traveling salesman and his experience as the ring master at the drugstore. He prepared like a lawyer getting ready to go to court. He needed everything to be in place.

Jones was moving deliberately so a headline in the *Macon Telegraph* caught him off guard. It said "Jones to build motel." He didn't know where that information came from but it was something he was not ready to talk about. Overnight, this motel became a topic of conversation all over town. "Most people were saying, who's he?" Jones jokes.

He was moving purposely slow, but with Watson's commitment for a loan Jones was able to begin some baby steps. He found a contractor—a choice that would prove to be a disappointment—and he began to put his plans to work after all those years. It came time to get the proper permits he would need to start construction.

Jones went to city hall and asked to see Bill Brannon, the city's building engineer. Brannon was a retired Army colonel and very authoritative. Jones was twenty-seven years old but still was intimidated by Brannon and the process. Someone pointed out Brannon and Jones told him he was there to apply for a building permit for a motel on Riverside Drive.

"Where are your plans?" Brannon said.

"I didn't bring them with me."

"Well, you have to have your plans. You should have known that."

Jones was saying he would come back another day with his plans. Then he started to think about those fast-talking salesmen he had to deal with down at the drugstore, how some of them had flimflammed him in the beginning by promising things and never delivering. Something told him to stand up to Brannon, to be a man. "Mr. Brannon, if I come back with those plans what else am I going to need before I get my permit?" "You'll need a check for twenty-five dollars and you will need a formal request for your application," the city official said.

Jones came back with what he thought were the necessary papers. He did not have professional blueprints or an architect's rendering. He just had two written pages of plans for his motel. Brannon took the papers, looked them over briefly and turned them down—just like that.

"He took his pencil and drew a big X on them," Jones says. He gets emotional even now remembering how the officious bureaucrat treated him that day.

"Mr. Brannon, who's your boss?" Jones said.

His voice was clear and so was his intent. He wasn't going to accept that kind of treatment. The official could have turned him down constructively. Instead, he drew that big X on plans that for Jones represented years of dreaming and saving. "The Appeals and

Justice Board," Brannon answered, "but they haven't met in 11 years." "What else do I have to do?" Jones said.

Once more, Brannon talked about a twenty-five dollar check.

"Then we can call it a deal."

Jones demanded a piece of toilet paper—anything he could write on—and a counter check. Brannon explained that he did not have to do those things that day, that he could send them in later.

"I do have to do it today," Jones said, curtly.

On a piece of paper he was given, Jones wrote out a request asking that a meeting of the Appeals and Justice Board be called for the purpose of approving a motel on Riverside Drive. He said that his check for twenty-five dollars was attached.

"Yours very truly, Charles H. Jones," he wrote at the bottom.

He handed the papers back to Brannon and left. His problems with city hall were not over, however. Jones planned to use Norwegian brick in the construction of the motel. Brannon explained that those bricks had never been used before in Bibb County. Using that brick was important to Jones since they provided several options in how he finished the rooms of his motel. Brannon was slow giving him an answer.

Meanwhile, Jones got an unexpected phone call from Kenneth Dunwoody, Sr., the chairman of the Bibb County Commission. Dunwoody also happened to be the owner of the Cherokee Brick & Tile Company, the local outlet for Norwegian Brick. Jones commented,

> We had never met personally, but he said he understood that I had been having some problems with Bill Brannon on the Norwegian Brick. He said the board was going to meet and that he was having lunch with Mr. Brannon. He told me to stay out of it, that he would get back to me. I don't know what he did. I wasn't privy to their meeting. But when Mr. Dunwoody called me back, he

said, "Go by city hall and pick up my building permit—which I did immediately.

The permit was waiting when Jones got to city hall that day. Jones and Brannon would work together often in the years that followed. There would be no more rancor and no more misunderstandings. Jones never brought up those early conflicts again and neither did the retired colonel. "I won't say I loved him, but I did learn to like him," Jones says.

Slowly, things came together. Even with constant delays and serious problems with construction, the Ambassador Motel was taking shape. While workers were busy on the motel construction, Jones was still busy on Broadway, continuing to put in long hours and long days. "I had energy like a bull," he says. "I didn't think there was anything I couldn't do."

He would need that energy, too. Using the contacts in High Point, North Carolina that he had developed through his furniture sales at the drugstore, he started to shop for furnishings—the bed frames, the tables, the television sets, the bedding, and the carpeting. Their prices were not that good so he went to a wholesale house in Atlanta that was owned by the father of a classmate at the University of Georgia. Their prices were better so he did business with them. Meanwhile, the cash register was jingling and the pressure was growing.

Remembering how warm and dusty it could be in hotel rooms that were not air-conditioned, he was determined to have a unit in every one of his motel rooms. He finally bought Victor's, a brand of air-conditioners they sold at Davison-Paxson, a Macon department store owned by the Macy family. He paid retail. "I had to buy from them. I had credit there," he explains.

The pressures were on him but they really were not financial. He knew the value of the land before it was improved. He knew that if the motel failed the building could easily be converted into offices or apartments. Those factors made the $35,000 investment very sound and the risks were minimal.

The pressures Jones was feeling were more personal than financial. This country boy from Molena was stepping out front. If he failed, everyone would know it. More importantly, he would know it. Failure was a word that Miss Marion never included among her vocabulary words so it was one Charles Jones never used. "I had faith in myself and in God. He wouldn't let me fail," Jones says.

It was summer by the time work on the motel building was completed. Now all that was left was setting up the furniture and finishing the last minute touch-ups in the rooms. Moving his wife, their two daughters, and their nine-month-old son into six rooms on the top floor, Jones opened the doors on the Ambassador Motel in July of 1956.

It was a back-breaking time for all of them. All day, Charles worked at the drugstore, hurrying to the Ambassador in time to greet the guests checking in late in the day. Once folks were in their rooms, there was ice to deliver, grass to be cut and windows to be washed. It was always something.

If Jeff didn't keep him awake crying, Charles would be awakened by the ringing of the bell at the office. Sleepily, he would go down there and turn on the lights. He was glad to check in an overnight guest. He was not so glad when the person would say no thanks, that they were looking for a five dollar room.

"I lost 15 pounds those first few months," he says. "It was non-stop."

Macon had its first motel and it was an instant success. Not forgetting the promotional skills he had developed at Charles Jones & Company, he worked on ways to give his new project that push he knew it would need.

Remembering the promotional tricks he had learned on Broadway, he retrieved several packages of those German screwdrivers and put them in the trunk of his car. In what spare time he could find, he went all over town. Then he rode up and down the federal highways leading into Macon. He would stop in at every service station along the way.

Greeting the owner or whoever was on duty at the gas pumps, Jones would tell them about the Ambassador, that Macon finally had a motel. "Tell folks about us if they're looking for a place to stay," he would say "I'd give them a card and a set of those screwdrivers," he says.

He got to know the guests personally when they stayed at the Ambassador. He learned the salesmen's schedules and when they would be back through Macon the next time. He held rooms for them on those dates, just in case they needed them. If they showed up late and the motel was full, he made arrangements for them at the Dempsey—on him. He introduced the salesmen to one another, so they could have some company at dinner if they wanted it. He got together with his regular customers at the swimming pool and shared a soda. Guests were not just staying at the Ambassador. They were staying with Charles Jones.

His sincere, personal interest in his customers helped make the Ambassador a success from the day that it opened—even without that interstate highway that Jones had predicted. This was the early days of motel chains and Holiday Inn put in one of its earliest franchise operations down the road from Jones. For a number of years, it was Jones referring his overflow to the big guys instead of the other way around. Word of mouth was a powerful advertising tool and business at the Ambassador continued to grow. Finally, in 1957, he found a buyer for the drugstore and became a full-time member of the hospitality industry.

By that time, he had hired some much-needed help at the motel. There was someone to check in guests, someone to change the sheets, someone to cut the grass, and someone to shine the shoes of the guests. Jones continued to be his own fix-it man, however. It was a chore he enjoyed.

There were hours when they were frantically checking in guests but there were many more hours when there was little to do around the motel. For a person who enjoyed work and working as much as Jones, that free time at first proved to be disconcerting. Then, with time to think, new visions and new ventures began to materialize.

Living on the grounds of the motel was convenient but demanding. You were never off duty. There were overnight check-ins and there were always maintenance problems that would develop in the wee hours. The personal relationship he had developed with his regular guests gave them the license to drop by and invite him to share a soda or to visit and Jones had started closing his office drapes so they would think he wasn't there. Finally, he created a back door so he could slip out without folks seeing him.

Having the Ambassador Motel as both his business and home address was also costing him money, he decided. His growing family was taking up six motel rooms. The math was simple. If the Jones family was living somewhere else, those rooms could bring in around $900 a month. He was able to build a house in a comfortable neighborhood near the motel and use the money he made on those rooms to make the monthly mortgage payments—and still have money left in his pocket. "I made money by moving out," Jones laughs.

With Watson's support, Jones began buying and repairing duplexes throughout the area surrounding the Ambassador. Watson also approved a loan so the motel could be expanded for the first time. A second expansion followed in a few years.

With income from that rental property, Jones was able to buy a farm in Monroe County and he began harvesting timber from it. There was something about land that was always enticing to him.

He had only lived on a farm for the first eight years of his life, but its appeal has never left him.

At the time he bought that farm, it was the most money paid per acre in the history of Monroe County. But there was more to that deal than that. For Jones, it was another one of those learning experiences that he seemed to find at every turn.

Jones paid $125 an acre for the first section of land and Mr. Martin, the owner, came back to him offering the adjoining land. It was 480 acres and Jones insisted that he did not have that kind of money. Martin kept coming back and finally Jones succumbed. "I didn't have to pay any money down or anything, just sign the note," he says. Later on, he was curious. Why did Mr. Martin keep coming back to do business with him. Why did he make it so easy for Jones to do business with him. Years later, he finally had the chance to ask him about that and Martin spelled it out. "Because you never told me my land was worth less than what I was asking," he said. "You need to know, there was this big real estate man who came to me about four months before you did that first time and wanted to buy that land. We stood up on that hill and that fellow said, "Your land ain't worth a hundred and twenty-five dollars an acre. It's worth eighty-five dollars an acre. You didn't do that. You never diminished me," he said.

He hadn't seen that as inventive or smart. Jones had just done what came naturally. Growing up, his father had told him "If everybody else is coming through the front door, you come in the back." He figured that meant do business your way, not everybody else's. "That was my first big purchase, and to this day I have never tried to diminish somebody else. I pay them what they ask. If we can't justify their price, then we pass on the deal. I figured that the best way to be greedy is to not be greedy," he says.

Wanting to share his success with his family, he invited his father's brothers and their wives to come down to Macon and stay at the Ambassador—on the house, of course. Once more, he could sit and listen at the stories he had heard so often. That became an annual event and it grew into an outing for his first cousins.

Etta Haney, one of those cousins, came to the first gathering. Jones had leased a bus and the uncles and cousins were going to pile on it for a trip to New Smyrna Beach, Florida, where he owned another motel. She knew her cousin was doing well in Macon and she appreciated the way he wanted to share it. At the same time, she was worried about the fast pace he was keeping.

"Charles, don't push too hard," she suggested.

"I have to Etta, I have to have a challenge. I can't keep the norm."

Other ideas were taking shape and by 1961 Jones had developed Riverside Plaza, his first shopping center and the second in Macon. His holdings in the Riverside Drive area of Macon were growing and expanding. Almost overnight, he became a force in business that others in town could no longer overlook. "I had a plan," he says, looking back on those early frantic years. "I was making lists of things I wanted to do that year and things I wanted to accomplish in the following years. I kept a list that went five years out. I still do that, too. It's like playing checkers. You always plan your moves before you make them. I knew what we owned and I knew what I planned for those particular pieces of property. Yes, I had a plan."

But opportunities would come that Charles Jones never anticipated.

9

Timmy Turtle and the Lions Club

R. G. Laterno's airplane landed on Griffin's unpaved runway and word of his arrival spread as fast as the visitor's two-engine plane. Not many people flew their own plane in 1936, so folks in Thomaston were buzzing. Grownups were duly impressed and so were the young people, including nine-year-old Charles Jones. It was a night he would long remember.

Nearly seventy years later, he still remembers this man coming to town to speak to the Baptists. Jones went to the meeting—mainly to hear something about that airplane. He left church that night remembering much more about the man who flew it.

Jones and his brother split their church time between the Baptists and the Methodists. On their own, they had joined the Baptist church, taking no chances when a fire-breathing evangelist gave the congregation a last-call to the altar. They still went to Sunday School with the Methodists. They were attracted there by the Sword Drills—a Christian competition that could send you racing through the Bible, praying that you would locate John 3:16 before your classmates did.

On this particular Sunday night, they sat on a hard Baptist pew, ready to hear this high-flying businessman share his personal testimony. Laterno's business was heavy equipment, the big pieces that could move as much earth as a driver asked them to move. He lived in Pennsylvania, with one of his many plants located in Toccoa, Georgia, and his customers were all over the world. He had a bald head and a friendly face. More than the way he looked, Jones recalls his message. It is a talk that even today can move him to tears and make his voice quiver as he tells about it.

Standing at the pulpit, Laterno started telling folks about his personal life. It was a pretty routine life at the beginning. He told about growing up, going to school and getting married. He talked about going to church and going to work. Then he told them about a deal he had made with God. "I got down on my knees and I told God that if He would let me be successful, that I would give him 10 percent of everything I made," Laterno said, as if he was describing a deal he had closed with another businessman.

There was more to his story but the bottom line was that God delivered. The man started making lots of money. He bought a bigger house because now he was running with a bigger crowd and they expected him to have a bigger house. He drove bigger cars because his new friends expected him to drive a bigger car. He was still making lots of money but now he needed lots of money to keep up that lifestyle that the world expected him to have.

Then, without warning, the economy slowed down. His business was no longer making lots of money. He had to cut expenses somewhere, he decided. Deal or not, he decided to cut down on that 10 percent he had been setting aside for God. Instead of ten, he was giving seven, then five. Finally he cut it out all together. He was keeping all of the money for himself. One morning he woke up and he had no company at all. He was bankrupt. "And it's easier to get back on your knees when you're bankrupt," he said.

He made God another offer and God didn't refuse. "Lord," he prayed, "I really messed you up. I did not keep my word. If you will let me up, this time I will give you 90 percent. I will keep only 10."

Once more, the man and his business prospered. He kept his word this time, giving 90 percent of all he made to godly efforts.

He kept only ten. You can only eat so many meals, he said. You can drive only one car at a time. You can live in a simple home. You don't need a big house.

This message moved the nine-year-old sitting on that hard Baptist pew in ways he could not imagine. Later, he read stories about the visiting preacher, but he never again heard R. G. Laterno speak. Yet, after all these years, Jones still remembers the effect Laterno's message had that night. "It had an impact on me that I will take to my grave," Jones says.

This man who flew into town in his own airplane was keeping only 10 percent of what he earned, and he still had enough money to buy that plane. His message wasn't lost on the young boy. This businessman was giving away 90 percent and he also was giving freely of his time to be with them that night in that small Baptist church near the center of Georgia. R.G. Laterno understood the value of giving and of being a giver.

A young person in elementary school might not connect those things with community service but an older person did. So when the invitations for him to get involved and do more in the community than run a motel came his way, Charles Jones remembered R. G. Laterno. He said yes.

The more he did, the more he wanted to do. He had an inner drive even he doesn't fully understand. With the Ambassador Motel flourishing and his real estate investments increasing, Jones was even busier than he was when he was hawking candy on the downtown sidewalks. He still laughs about planting sod on his front lawn at home by the light of a flashlight. Other folks came home and did such things by sunlight. He was too busy for that. Friends took up golf, but he preferred an occasional game of tennis, knowing you could line up a tennis match after hours under the lights.

Jones, his wife, and their three children were active in the Vineville Presbyterian Church. Their daughters, Jan and Judy, had been the first twins born in that church in more than thirty years. They had started to church there when Jones was embarrassed to put his measly dollar in the collection plate. Trying to hide that fact, he would wait until the end of the year when he could put in all of his money at once. A thoughtful minister had set him straight on the issue, encouraging him to give whatever he could and not to worry about the amount of money he was dropping into the basket on Sunday morning.

Later the Jones family were among the founding members of the Northminster Presbyterian Church. Jones was a deacon, elder, and moderator. He helped the new congregation get off the ground by opening the doors of the banquet hall at the Ambassador for services on Sunday mornings and by underwriting the purchase of land for a permanent church building.

Jones would have told you flat out that there was no time left in his busy day for anything else. His old friend Billy Watson lived by a different clock, however.

Jones was down at Macon Federal to close a deal on some duplexes he wanted to build when out of the blue Watson asked him if he was a member of any civic clubs. Watson probably knew the answer to that question. Outside of business, Jones wasn't involved in anything but church.

Six months later, Watson asked again. "You belong to a civic club?"

"It's never entered my mind."

Watson was not going to drop the matter. He was sending his friend a message. He thought it was time Jones did something other than make money. The third time he mentioned it, he asked Jones if he had heard about the Macon Lions Club. "I've read about them in the paper and we went to their Christmas program down at the City Auditorium," Jones said. "The kids enjoyed it."

"Well, I'm going to nominate you for membership in the Lions Club," said Watson, a longtime member of the club. "We don't have any hotel people in there right now. You can only have two people from the same category."

Jones asked what kinds of activities the club was involved in and who its members were. He was stalling. He didn't let on to Watson but the idea intimidated him. Joe Parham, the editor of the *Macon News*, was a member. Julius Golson, the superintendent of schools, was in there. Steve Solomon, the car dealer, was a member. Jones could not imagine fitting in with such men. On Broadway, he had never rubbed shoulders with many people of their ilk. He didn't know what he could contribute to that kind of circle.

"I appreciate it, Mr. Bill. But I'm just too busy," he said. This didn't stop Watson.

"I know you're busy," the banker said. "We're all busy. But you need something else to do besides work all the time."

Nothing was settled and not long after their talk, Watson called Jones on the phone. He told Jones to get down to his office, that he had nominated him for membership in the Lions Club.

"They've accepted you, and I want you to join."

Nothing he was going to say would change Watson's mind. Jones was told to be at the YMCA at noon on the following Tuesday. This was not an invitation. This was an order and Jones did as he was told. He joined the Lions in 1961. By 1964 he was president.

Men like Parham and Solomon became his colorful running buddies. The three of them would be joined at the hip in a variety of groundbreaking activities that would translate into fun for them and progress for the city. Jones or Solomon would start some kind of project and Parham would report it in the afternoon newspaper. They were an ongoing team.

The civic club became a vital part of Jones' future. "I like to tell people that I am a product of the C&S Bank, the *Macon Telegraph,* and the Macon Lions Club," he says.

Around this same time, Jones also got a phone call from the devoted founder of the Timmy Turtle Nursery for Mentally Handicapped Children. With his connections in local real estate, she thought Jones could help them find a new home for the facility. For him, this led to a rewarding connection with her effort and with the children the nursery helped. He was first a member of their board and later its president.

Timmy Turtle needed a new home. It cared for ten or twelve mentally challenged children at a time when public schools made no place for them. Looking for a new location, supporters thought they had found the ideal spot and it was only a few blocks from the old site. Representing the group, Jones went before the city's Planning and Zoning Commission. To his surprise, neighbors of the vacant lots showed up and protested the building of the nursery. "I was shocked. The board turned us down," Jones says. "We were only moving a few blocks. I couldn't believe it."

Parham wrote an editorial in the *Macon News* that blistered the neighborhood for protesting the relocation of Timmy Turtle and its handicapped children. That day, Jones got a phone call from Sanders Walker, one of the principals in Fickling & Walker, a major real estate and insurance company in the city. He said he owned four lots near Mercer University. "I don't know if they'd be adequate, but my mother and I would be pleased to donate them to the nursery," he said, asking for anonymity.

Of course the lots were adequate. Having a site gave Jones the license to hit the streets looking for further assistance. Unions donated labor. Cherokee Brick Company donated bricks. Georgia Power gave a refrigerator and stove. Within four months, a dedication ceremony for the new home of Timmy Turtle Nursery was being held

"It was a reminder that when we lose, we really win," Jones says.

Everyone involved in that project participated in a commitment to something bigger than himself or herself. They weren't looking for acclaim. They only wanted to help a group of children who needed them.

"They couldn't plead for these things for themselves. They were only little children. They depended on a greater force than themselves. Those of us who had healthy children who were able to run and play and learn owed them anything we could give them," Jones says.

As he often does, Jones threw himself into that building project. When he could steal a minute or two, he would drive toward Mercer and check on the progress of the work. He was usually in a hurry, and on one trip he was in too much of a hurry. He was doing 45 miles per hour in a 25-mile-an-hour zone on Pierce Avenue when an officer of the law pulled him over for speeding. The state was cracking down on speeders and the Georgia State Patrol was suspending the driver's license of anyone caught going more than 15 miles over the legal limit—including Mr. Jones.

Jones had to give up his license for 60 days. He lived nearby so he could walk to work at the Ambassador. At other times, that meant he was leaning on friends to take him to business appointments—even his Tuesday Lion's Club meeting. His mistake was telling Parham about what had happened. Parham filed that information away for future foolishness.

Jones pulled no strings. Nor did he ask anyone else to pull strings on his behalf. He walked it for sixty days. As the end of his suspension grew near, he figured the Georgia State Patrol would merely put his license in the mail and the postman would deliver it to its rightful owner.

On this particular Tuesday, Jones still was still not a legal driver. He hitched a ride downtown and walked into the Lions Club meeting. Parham was there as usual. So were a number of officers from the State Patrol office in Perry, Georgia along with several local lawmen in full uniform. People were eating and talking and the regular meeting was about to begin when Parham walked up to the podium. He had a special presentation to make.

"As many of you know, Charlie Jones has been ripping up and down our city streets in a reckless manner. He has been guilty of breaking the laws of our city and our state," the rotund newspaper editor began. "But in spite of his personal failings and his total disregard for the law, the State of Georgia is willing to give this criminal one more chance."

That said, one of the visiting State Patrol officials came over to where Jones was sitting and personally returned his driver's license. Though that may have been a happy day for him, Jones laughingly swore revenge on his old friend Parham.

At the Lions Club, they were joking about Jones' reckless driving but around town they were talking about this energetic businessman who had suddenly emerged as a major player in local affairs. The Ambassador Motel had become a haven for out-of-town guests and a center for in-town meetings. People in that part of Macon were shopping at the A&P that anchored his first shopping center on Riverside Drive and his land holdings seemed to grow every day.

His reputation had spread to the Greater Macon Chamber of Commerce, an organization that had to be attracted to a developer who had that much drive. Jones had met local realtor, Thad Murphy when the Northminster Church was expanding. When he called and asked to come by and see him, Jones assumed the realtor wanted to talk about real estate. Murphy, president elect of the Chamber of Commerce showed up representing the chamber and he wanted Jones to get involved with the organization's tourism committee.

His invitation struck a chord with Jones. He had already been thinking that the interstate highway was still expected to come through Macon, forcing commerce in the area into a regional approach to business. In the back of his mind were other motels, not just in Macon but throughout the area. "That growth was going to be an opportunity that we had to be ready to take advantage of, to the north, south, east and west. We had to consider the role Warner Robins played in the local economy, what kind of situation our school systems were in, the role of Mercer University. I valued those things highly," he says.

Jones may have been an outsider and at this point he had lived in Macon less than ten years, but he had become a student of Macon history. He read the history books. He talked to natives who lived here. Locals took such things for granted. Jones did not. Such facts were important to him—personally and professionally.

So when Murphy came to see him, he was way ahead of them on this issue. They didn't know this and neither did he but their invitation to get involved with the Greater Macon Chamber of Commerce was going to be important to the organization, to the community, and to Charles Jones.

Less than four years later, a similar group of chamber officials would come to see Jones. Bill Ott, editor of the *Macon Telegraph*, Pink Person, realtor, and Buck Melton, attorney, came to his office to ask him to become Chamber president. The new kid in town was being recognized.

"He always had that driven personality," Melton says. "When he tackled a job, he didn't just sit on a board or a committee. He could never stay on the sideline. He had to be involved, to be a part of things. He was willing to spend a lot of time and energy working for a worthwhile cause. We had some interesting times."

It began with Mr. Bill's unyielding nudge for his protégé to do more than make money. With his work for the Lions Club and Timmy Turtle, he was building confidence and contacts. His community involvement really blossomed with his acceptance of a committee assignment for the Chamber. Charles Jones was building a strong foundation that would be topped with change, progress, and growth—for him and for the community.

In the years that followed, Jones would help bring a forgotten people home, soothe ruffled feelings during an explosive racial crisis, go after world class industry, and secure a medical college when would-be experts said it could not be done.

As Melton said, it would be interesting times.

10

Medicine Man

Two decades had come and gone since the end of World War II, but despite minor cosmetic changes, the fiber of 1965 Macon was much the same as it was in 1945. Sears, Davison's, and Dannenberg's were doing business downtown as they had for generations. The Nancy Hanks still blew its whistle coming out of Terminal Station as it carried passengers from Savannah to Atlanta. The Dempsey bragged about being the area's premier hotel. The Lanier Hotel still told stories about Jefferson Davis staying there 100 years before. The Peaches were playing baseball and fans were still buzzing about Pete Rose's graduation from Luther Williams to the big leagues. Segregation was hotly defended, so much so that passengers had boycotted city buses and the YMCA had shut its doors to avoid being integrated.

Changes were on the horizon and so were the 1970s—changes that would dramatically affect the people of Macon, the way the city did business and the way the community prepared for its future. Some of these changes could be seen in advance. Some of them took the city by surprise.

The changes were many, including:

• The ribbon would finally be cut on Interstate 75 in early 1967. Its opening would end years of bickering among the locals that had brought threats from state and federal officials that the interstate system would bypass the city all together.

• The Macon Coliseum, with nearly 10,000 seats, would open in 1968, making it possible for the town to attract Elvis and ice hockey.

• The old city hospital would be renamed the Medical Center of Central Georgia and move into a new facility in 1968, just three years before the opening of another new medical campus—the Coliseum Medical Center.

• Capricorn Records was making music and turning Macon into a rock 'n' roll Mecca. Owner Phil Walden was excited about the promise of Otis Redding and the Allman Brothers. (By the end of the 1970s Redding and Duane Allman were dead and the record label was bankrupt.)

• The *Macon Telegraph*, one of the oldest businesses in the city, was sold to Knight-Ridder Newspapers. For the first time in the city's history, the two daily newspapers were not under local control.

• Macon's public schools were integrated in the early 1970s and Mercer University voluntarily desegregated.

• The Nancy Hanks would make its final run up the rails in 1971, ending an era in a city so historically dependent on railroads.

• Macon Mall would open in 1975 and many established merchants would leave downtown for the shopping center.

• In a city that cut its teeth on cotton and textiles, Bibb Mills was being seriously threatened by foreign interests who were as much a threat to that industry as the boll weevil had been to King Cotton earlier in the century.

Old and new were butting heads every day in ways no one could have anticipated at the end of the world war. Many of these conflicts were brought about by changes in the world at large. Some of them were inspired by a changing Macon.

Traditional leaders in the city did not seem to know how to deal with these growing conflicts. The older men were tired. They had paid their dues. The younger ones were reticent about getting involved. The newer people who had moved into the community were not sure what their place was or if they even were wanted. Some people would have preferred that these painful issues just go away. They were content to maintain status quo, never anticipating the changes that would occur by the end of the century.

The city's social structure was changing and so was its political structure. The city needed leadership that would deal with the old and the new, leaders who would confront rather than ignore.

And then along came Jones. Charles Jones came out of nowhere. In a town where native sons were revered, he was a relative newcomer. Macon had been his home address less than twenty years when he began to emerge as a community leader. He made things happen with the Timmy Turtle program. He got to know a lot of people through his work with the Macon Lions Club. He had slowly gotten involved with the Greater Macon Chamber of Commerce through its work in tourism. He soon moved into the Chamber's leadership rotation, serving as a vice president.

Whether he knew it or not, others had been watching him. Still in his late twenties and early thirties, he was about to be become a key player in Macon's efforts to deal with change. It was not a position to which he aspired. "I don't think anybody sets out and says 'When I grow up I'm going to be a leader.' It is not something you aspire to and it is not something you plan for. Leadership is an evolutionary thing," Jones says.

Those who observed him may already have figured out that Jones was not the type of person who saw a position on a board or committee as an honorary title. He wanted action and he expected action. Socially, he could be shy. Thrust into a situation where action was needed, he was anything but shy. Show him a China shop and he could be a bull. Often impatient with others' inability to act, he usually stepped out of the pack and became the chairman or the director. It was and is part of his makeup. Old friend Buck Melton noticed that trait years ago. "When Charlie tackled a job, he didn't sit just sit there on a board or committee. He had to be involved and he had to be part of it. He was always willing to spend a lot of time and energy working for the cause—whatever it might be," Melton says.

Like Jones, businessman Ben Porter is not a native son. But over the past four decades in Macon he has successfully owned a number of radio stations as well as working in management at Charter Medical Corporation. He says Jones always approached leadership as a calling. "I have an awful lot of friends who are great people. They were born, bred and raised here, but they have never found it appropriate to give of themselves to make the community better, to make things happen. Charlie is one of those unusual guys who feels an evangelical calling to make things happen. That is what he's done all his life," Porter says.

Jones puts himself on the line.

"You've got to make tough decisions to get things done and that's going to make somebody mad, somebody unhappy, somebody dissatisfied. Charlie has never backed away from that. I've never known him to do anything he didn't think was the right thing to do for his interests and for the community's interest. And he doesn't mind being overbearing in the broad sense of the term to get it done," Porter says.

That bullheaded courage would serve him well with the old Macon City Hospital Board. Accepting a position on that panel would be his introduction to local conflict and controversy. And Porter is right. Jones backed away from neither.

Macon City Hospital was founded in 1895. It was a privately run hospital until 1915 when the city took over operation. It was expanded in 1931 and again in 1952. The city council took its oversight of the hospital seriously, managing every micro it could find. City councilmen habitually meddled in the most mundane issues such as where the hospital bought its milk and dairy products and what price they were paying for these products—an issue that eventually led to a lawsuit. Councilmen got involved in hiring and firing, especially if one of their relatives or political supporters needed a job.

The facility, even the newest wing, was in terrible disrepair. Buckets were lined up in the hallways to catch water flowing from a leaky roof. Bills went unpaid and medical supplies went unordered. Sections on the grounds looked like a junkyard with discarded materials stacked up for the taking. The city of Macon owned the facility, but no one was really in charge.

These were things Jones faced in 1965 when he joined the hospital board. It was a volunteer position, but for more than two years it became his full-time job. When the hospital found itself without a chief administrator, Jones moved his office into the hospital, running his own business out of there as well as the hospital. Some of the challenges he discovered were major, but some seemed almost trivial. "Sheets were a big problem," Jones remembers. "Sheets were disappearing in substantial numbers. I started to ask questions about the process. I found out a person went to the laundry to get clean sheets and they left the dirty ones somewhere else. Finally, I suggested we just make it a rule that when you went to get a clean sheet for a bed, you had to turn in your dirty ones before we would issue you one."

There were seven different entrances to the facility and if the hospital was going to be secure some of these doorways had to be closed. That created a stir, and so did a decision to limit visiting hours. Visitors were regularly getting in the way of physicians trying to make their morning rounds so early visitation hours were eliminated. Ministers who were used to dropping in on members of their flock early in the day were upset. A compromise was reached for the preachers, but mornings were given back to the doctors and staff.

Most of the things Jones was doing made good business sense. For too long, the hospital had been run like a game or a toy. Even the local medical community took notice, veteran physician Waddell Barnes says. “He didn’t try and be a M.D., that’s right. Charlie is talented, very talented. But the thing that made the difference was his commitment to the hospital. Not for the benefit of Charlie. Not for the benefit of his kinfolk or friends. He was willing to overlook a lot of things if it honestly helped the hospital. Everybody knew that, and it made a lot of difference,” says Barnes, now retired with an office in sight of the modern medical center.

The hospital board continued its search for a new administrator, but at every turn there was a roadblock—usually the same one. Prospects they were considering wanted to know who was really in charge of the hospital: the administrator or city government.

That was the first question asked by Damon King, who at that time was chief administrator of the Hall County Hospital in Gainesville, Georgia. In the spring of 1968, he became the top candidate for the Macon job. King suggested that board members from Macon come to Gainesville for the interview. That way they could see first hand the hospital that he was running and could judge for themselves how he was running it. Jones was among the group that came.

“That’s how I met Charlie,” King says. “He offered me the job, but I wouldn’t take it. To me, it was structured for failure, not success. I told them I wouldn’t take the job as long as the city was involved. The way it was designed, every major decision had to be made by the city, and politicians have an entirely different agenda than running a good hospital. It was not just Macon. It was that way everywhere.”

King says such a management structure eventually affects health care. Politicians, he says, do not have patient care at the top of their list. Nor do they demand efficiency. Studying the operation under the old regime, King told Jones and the board that he would not consider the job unless the hospital was taken away from city control and put under a private That said, King figured he would never hear from Macon again.

But King didn't know Charles Jones.

King's statement became a challenge and a rallying cry for Jones and the board. Hospital professionals already had told the board that the Macon way was not the best way. So, coupled with professional opinions and King's response to their job offer, board members began to lobby locally for a change of management for the hospital.

Later in 1968, the change finally came. The legalities completed, a hospital authority was created. This new group of citizens would be given total control of the facility, which was renamed the Medical Center of Central Georgia, knowing it would be providing care for a thirty-two county area. Jones thought his work was done.

Privately, he was not sure he could afford to continue as a member of the authority. The demands of the hospital had taken their toll on his own business so he badly needed a break in service. Despite that, he did accept an appointment to the newly created panel. He was the only member of the old Board.

Though he was among the appointees to the new authority, Jones sincerely hoped his days out front were over. An old friend from Gordon Military College had other ideas. Johnny Mitchell was dean of admissions at Mercer University, working closely with Dr. Rufus C. Harris, the highly respected president of the Baptist institution. Mitchell and Jones had renewed their friendship once both turned up in Macon. Like Jones, Mitchell became a member of the newly seated authority. He thought the hospital authority needed Jones' experience and energetic leadership.

No sooner had the gavel sounded opening the authority's inaugural meeting than Mitchell raised his hand and nominated Jones as its first chairman. He was elected overwhelmingly. Jones' first order of business as chairman would be to change the mind of Damon King, who was still running that hospital in North Georgia. That, Jones soon learned, would not be easy.

Jones and King are both plain spoken and can be pushy. Having them working so closely together would prove to be volatile. But though they butted heads and matched egos, they were an effective team. Before any of those things would come to pass, Jones had to recruit this man who had unceremoniously turned them down several months before—even putting it in writing at their request. What happened next is classic Charles Jones.

King was attending the American Hospital Association's annual meeting in Atlantic City, New Jersey. Late one evening, he got back to his hotel and was told he had an urgent message waiting. That scared him. King feared something had happened to his family. When he retrieved the message, it told him to call Charles Jones in Macon, Georgia. It said it was an emergency. Dialing the number, King waited for Jones to answer.

"Damon," said Jones, almost breathless. "We've got our authority. So will you come to Macon now?"

Jones went straight to the point. No small talk. Just business. King, however, was not so rushed. "Charlie, I'll be glad to talk about it now."

"Well, can you be here tomorrow?"

King was in a hotel room more than a thousand miles away. He had meetings and workshops left to attend. He still had a job in Gainesville and the hospital there had bought his plane ticket to Atlantic City. It was time for bed—not Delta. Jones didn't care about such trivial things. He wanted him there by the following day—preferably ready to go to work.

Typical Charlie, King says. "I mean, he has no patience whatsoever for procrastination or waiting around. He wants it done yesterday. And he keeps on rolling. If I were to describe him, I would say he is the most driven person I have ever encountered—and I'm a fairly driven person myself. We share a lot of the same characteristics," King says.

Relentlessly prodded by Jones, Damon King finally did accept the position at the Medical Center in Macon. With Jones, the board and King working together, an ambitious new facility would soon be built. Under King's leadership, most of the problems of Macon's old hospital were solved, one by one. But these solutions did not occur overnight. "Charlie would remember how bad it was. The whole place was dirty. It started at the front door, literally. I started by teaching people to mop and wax the floors. A hospital, first of all, has to be clean. Charlie was a good ally, particularly after he realized that I was capable of running the hospital."

Renovations began. So did the endless clean up. Anyone coming in the front door of the hospital could see that changes were being made. Word spread—which is just what the hospital needed to happen. On the medical side, the hospital was modernized department by department. Among those changes were a cardiac unit and a revived obstetrics department. Both departments opened in the early 1970s. Just as important were the internal changes—ones the public and the patients could not easily see. At the top of that list was a major building program.

Waddell Barnes says Jones helped the hospital clear an unusual hurdle. Barnes says,

> [W]e had an elderly architect who thought she was due this particular project. She had never drawn a plan for a hospital in her whole life. Well, Charlie and I—along with several others—decided that this very nice lady had no business drawing those plans. She had already done a

substantial amount of work on the project so we had to pay her something like half a million dollars. Charlie was the real impetus behind making that change despite that so-called waste of money. It was a courageous thing to do.

Over the past three decades, the Medical Center of Central Georgia has matured into a nationally recognized facility and a valuable asset for Middle Georgia. Medicine itself has become an economic tool for the city and the Medical Center is Macon's largest employer with 4,345 employees. King continued as administrator at the medical center until 1997. He now serves as president emeritus, working for the Central Georgia Health System.

King stayed on despite a relationship with Jones that was often rocky. Each of them shared the same goal: a better hospital. But their personalities and style often clashed. It took several bitter confrontations before the two men learned to co-exist.

The success at the Medical Center drew attention to Macon and to Charles Jones. His developments were paying dividends for him and for the city. His drive and leadership had cleaned up a community eyesore.

The Greater Macon Chamber of Commerce, meanwhile, was trying to meet a multitude of challenges. There were problems with downtown flight. There were simmering racial issues. There was economic development. There were political issues. In short, there was plenty to do.

It was time for the Chamber to put its leadership in place for 1972 and there was a knock at Jones' door. Bill Ott, Pink Persons, and Buck Melton came to formally ask him to offer for president of the chamber. Melton says Jones was the right choice at the right time. "Obviously, Charlie is smart as a whip," the attorney says. "I mean, he's thinking all the time. He sees way ahead of most of us and sees all the possibilities. He's got unlimited enthusiasm. He doesn't let any obstacles get in his way. He will go through you or around you to get something done."

Melton says Jones has never been a person to sit around a board table and endlessly discuss a situation, no matter how complex or controversial it may be. Jones, he says, is always ready to go and ready to act. It was that way in 1971 when the three men came to his office and asked him to become the Chamber's volunteer leader. "Charlie has guts and courage," Melton says. "So when we asked him to take that job, he was smart and ready to go."

11

Race

Singing hymns and chanting slogans, the mostly black crowd had marched through town for several blocks—all the way from Macon's City Hall. They were too upset to be tired—too upset and too anxious. They were on a mission. They knew where they were going. They didn't know what would happen when they got there.

A single man waited for them on the sidewalk outside of the Greater Macon Chamber of Commerce. With a smile on his face and his right hand extended, Charles Jones came out to meet them. He welcomed them. He called some of them by name. He invited them to come on inside.

Looking at one another skeptically, they followed him, still not knowing what to expect. No one knew what to expect that morning, including Jones. Late the night before he had gotten off an airplane from a busy trip across country. He had been in Arizona for several days so he had not had time to pick up the tension that Macon was wearing like a morning fog.

Someone called Jones at his home just before 9 o'clock that morning and frantically told him that he had to be at the Chamber office by 9:30, that he was presiding over a very important meeting. There wasn't time for him to hear all the details of what had happened in town over the past few days and nights but he heard enough to know that the whole community—white and black alike—was tense.

It was 1971 and Ronnie Thompson was the mayor of Macon and he was building his well-earned reputation as "Machine Gun Ronnie." All over the state there was an epidemic of racial unrest. Black Columbus police officers had ripped the American flag patches off their uniforms and the city had been hit with a rash of fire bombs. Albany had installed a curfew. Macon was trying to avoid such outbursts but everyone knew it wouldn't take much for the city to explode—figuratively if not literally.

Race had been an emotional issue across the South for decades. Feelings boiled when black soldiers came home from World War II and began to expect some of the freedoms they had been fighting for overseas. They surfaced in 1954 when the United States Supreme Court ruled school segregation went against the law of the land. In the turbulent years that followed, strife spread throughout the region. There were bus boycotts in Montgomery, confrontations in Albany, lunch counter disputes in Atlanta, church bombings in Birmingham, name-calling mobs at the University of Georgia, and the murder of civil rights workers in Mississippi.

In 1968, trying to mediate a strike of garbage truck drivers in Memphis, the Reverend Martin Luther King Jr. had been assassinated on a balcony outside of his motel room. The threat of violence was real. Bitter feelings were building all over the country and in Macon the colorful mayor's shoot to kill order had turned an unwanted spotlight on Middle Georgia.

Every town had its racial issues, be it public accommodations or public schools. Macon's schools had been integrated only two years before and it took a federal court order to break that barrier. Issues such as these had led up to that morning's march on the Chamber of Commerce. Local black leaders were buoyed by a number of NAACP figures from around the state and around the region. The group had demands, and they wanted to be heard.

Jones was quickly brought up to date when he hurried into the Chamber offices that morning. He was the Chamber's president-elect. Local attorney Buck Melton was president but he was out of the city. Board members had chosen Jones to lead the meeting even before he left Phoenix the night before. Still fuzzy after the dramatic time change and never a person who enjoyed doing business first thing in the morning, he was at home having breakfast when he got the call to rush down there. Now he was walking into a room filled with concerned faces.

"Macon is all upset," Chamber official Billy Mitchell said.

"What are we going to do, Charlie?" one fellow asked.

"What do you mean?"

"I mean, what are we gonna do?"

"I don't know what *we* are going to do, but I will tell you what *I* am going to do. When I see that group coming down the street, I'm going out the front door and meet them. I'm going to welcome them. Because I don't know any other way to act."

His attitude set the group back on its heels. Knowing Jones' tempestuous reputation, they expected him to react far differently. What they really wanted him to do, no one knows. But smiling and welcoming the protesters was definitely not very high on their list. Pushing him further, someone asked what he intended to do when the black marchers came inside the buildings. "I am going to offer them seats around this board table," Jones said. "We are going to stand up. We will treat them as guests."

Moments later, someone said the marchers were in sight. And Jones did just what he said he would do: he met them outside and welcomed them to the Chamber of Commerce. People on both sides of the issue were dumbfounded. Inviting the group of protesters inside, he offered them coffee then told them to find a seat. "Make yourself at home," he said, playing the host.

With white businessmen and a few elected officials lined up around the walls of the boardroom, Jones started the meeting. He was informal, but there was no doubt whose meeting this was or who was in charge. Looking at the marchers, he said the community wanted to know what they were thinking, what was on their mind and so did he. By the time the third person around the table had his turn, some of the comments were growing personal.

"Wait a minute," Jones said, stopping the man at mid-sentence. "I'm presiding and there are a few things I'm not going to allow. Lower your rhetoric if you're going to talk. Talk like you would like to be talked to."

This was new territory for most of the black people at the table, especially the locals. They weren't used to speaking out in front of white men in suits. Even with all that had happened, they weren't comfortable when it came to being specific. Jones had to encourage them.

"Put it on the table," he said. "Tell us what you're feeling."

One by one, people did.

"How would you feel, if every time you went into Davison's or Belk-Mathews there was a white hand sticking out to take your money?" one person asked.

"I wouldn't like it," Jones said, thinking only a few seconds.

Turning to the head of the downtown merchant's association, Jones asked if that organization could do something about that problem by noon the following day.

"Give us some black hands to take folks money," Jones requested.

The merchant leader said they would.

"And how would you like it if every time you went down to city hall to pay your taxes there is nothing but white hands reaching out to get your money?"

Again, Jones said he wouldn't like that.

Mayor Ronnie Thompson was not at the meeting, but the vice mayor was. Jones asked if city leaders would get together that afternoon and do something about that issue. The official said that was reasonable, that they would make a decision right away.

The same question arose about the staff at the Bibb County courthouse and a county official agreed to consider a change. Jones didn't stop there. He told everybody that the meeting would reconvene the next day and that all of the groups would report back on what they were doing. No quibbling. No debate. He was clear to everyone that change had to come and it had to come right then. Not long after that, the meeting ended. To everyone's relief, the tension that was there early that morning was subsiding.

Jones still does not think what he did that morning was all that unusual. He says it happened so fast that he did not have time to plan. "I had to act with my heart," he says. The strategy he used that morning was unusual for 1971, however.

Angers were diffused when the president-elect of the city's chamber of commerce didn't wait for the marchers to wave picket signs or to storm the door. He met them with a smile on his face. He welcomed them. He didn't ask them to stand up while the white business people sat in the formal meeting chairs. He invited the black leaders to take the chairs. He invited them to have a seat at the bargaining table. More important than the symbols, Jones made it comfortable for people to share their feelings. And finally, there was action—not promises, but action.

Thirty years later, descriptions of such meetings do not have the impact they did in 1971. Neither white nor black under the age of forty understands the unwritten behavioral codes on both sides. Cities such as Macon have come a long way in the intervening years. Now, though neither Macon nor the country are without any number of racial divides, simple things such as the color of a hand that takes a person's money are no longer thought about. And in too many cases, they are taken for granted by today's youth.

Virgil Adams is in his mid-forties so he does not take those times for granted. He was a teen-ager in 1971, a sophomore at Macon's Central High School. He was a member of the first court-desegregated class to graduate from the previously all-white school. His memories of growing up in the city are still vivid. He remembers the separate water fountains at the train station. He remembers the spare room in the back of their house that his family rented out to black baseball players on the teams coming to town to play the Macon Peaches. Black players could not stay in the all-white hotels with their teammates or come in the front door of local restaurants.

Adams remembers being a five or six year old child, playing in the front yard of his family home on Riverside Drive and hearing the roar of motorcycles. As they thundered down the street, he was frozen. It was the Ku Klux Klan, on its way to a public rally at Central City Park. The youngster could see the white of their hoods. "It was the probably the most scared I've ever been in my life. I had heard about the things they had done and would do. And they were coming right by my house in Macon, Georgia. I remember those motorcycles. Some of them had sidecars. The only time I had seen sidecars was on TV, shows about the Germans in World War II. They had their hoods on, but they were pulled back on the sides of their faces. I can remember my mother and grandmother rushing out and telling me to get back in the house," says Adams, now a successful Macon attorney. He recalls the fear he felt as a teen in 1971:

> I remember vividly that shoot-to-kill order. Ronnie Thompson did so much to damage Macon's image. It was real. When it got dark, you needed to be off the street. Parents wouldn't let us out of the house at night for fear of us being locked up, beaten by police or shot. That was the clear message. If you were black...especially if you were young and black...and, even worse, a black male...when the sun went down you needed to be off the streets. You were going to be arrested, and you potentially could be shot. That was the message.

Adams came back to Macon after graduating from college and law school, hoping to affect changes in the community that is his home. He remembers shopping downtown in the stores people were talking about in that meeting at the chamber more than thirty years ago:

> Blacks were a large segment of the population at that time but those numbers were not reflected in the hiring practices of the city, the county or the downtown businesses. Downtown businesses made a lot of money off the black community but they had no black employees in their stores. Black leaders at the time were saying, look, if our money is good enough to spend with you and for you to take, then our people are good enough to be working in there. They wanted to see people working in the banks, in the courthouse, in city hall. They wanted to see somebody who looked like them in the places where they did business.

Cities all over the South were confronting such issues in those years. It was not the first confrontation in Macon nor would it be the last. Jones, in fact, had been faced with serious racial questions while he was a member of the Macon City Hospital Board. That meeting, too, began with a telephone call. Only that one came late at night. "I was asleep. It was after midnight… The phone rang and somebody said they needed me at a meeting, that it was an emergency. I asked what kind of emergency and they said we had to talk about integrating the hospital. I went on down, but I couldn't figure why we were having to do that in the middle of the night," Jones says.

They were meeting at the Medical Center and when Jones arrived the entire hospital board was already there waiting on him.

He listened to the discussion for thirty or forty-five minutes, still trying to figure out why they were doing this after hours. He could listen no more. He had to talk. "What choices do we have?" he asked.

"Choices?"

"Yeah, what choices do we have other than to integrate?"

"None," the chairman said.

"Well, then what are we doing here now? I will vote to integrate the hospital but I will not do it in the middle of the night. I will do it in the daylight tomorrow. Right now, I'm going home. I have to have eight hours of sleep. If I don't, I can't make a living." With that, he stood up and left.

Jones looks back on that private late-night meeting and still wonders what was being accomplished, other than to mask what they were doing and what was being said. "I often think what my Granny would have said about that, or my Daddy or my Mama. I was determined that we would make that decision in broad daylight," he says.

Jones was chairing the hospital authority when R. J. Martin was appointed. Martin, the principal at Ballard-Hudson High School, was the first African-American to sit on a significant board in either the city or the county. Members of the authority frequently had lunch at the hospital together before their meetings so when Jones decided to have a dinner for the members at his home, he thought nothing about inviting Martin and his wife to be among his guests. Some of his other dinner guests that night were shocked, reminding Jones that desegregation usually ended at the end of the work day and certainly did not extend into a person's home.

For Jones, who came out of the country and out of his generation, race was a different issue than it was for many of his peers. The cotton patch, he says, was always integrated. He grew up working and playing with the black neighbor kids, just as many rural people did. They picked cotton together, and bell peppers. They played ball together. But of course, they did not go to church or school together. "This black family lived on our place. John the Baptist was there as far back as I can remember. He did work for my Mama, helping out around the house. He was a friend to everybody in my family, especially me. I would eat breakfast with he and his wife all the time. I spent a lot of time with them and I got to wondering why there was such a disparity between our life and theirs. I wondered even then how I would feel if it was reversed," he says.

Jones was in the Navy when President Harry Truman integrated the military and he saw the early affects of that change. Then, as a merchant on Broadway and Poplar, he was reminded of that disparity that he had seen working around John the Baptist in the cotton patch. "Those Saturdays down at the drugstore were like 4th of July picnics. People came in from the country and brought the crops that they had grown. I got to know many of those people. I remember them coming into the store, their money wrapped up in handkerchiefs. I never did break many twenties, but I sure did give change for a lot of ones. Those people were good friends and good customers. I remember this one woman who would buy a single tin of snuff. I knew she didn't have much, and I would slip some candy in the bag for her kids. Sometimes, if they needed it, I gave them medicine for their children…stuff like that," Jones says.

Those years at the drugstore, his were the white hands taking the money from the black customers. So he understood what the protesters were saying that day at the chamber of commerce. And in his heart, he knew how he would feel if the roles were reversed and he was on the other side of the cash register. His own background made Jones comfortable in dealing with the situation at the chamber of commerce board room more than thirty years ago.

"Those black men that day were doing what it took to make the system respond. And when human beings are involved, our system ought to respond quickly and with compassion. It never occurred to me what other people were thinking that day. That was my time to act. I didn't ask to be in that place, but it was my time to be there. I couldn't stand there and say that it wasn't right for black people to feel that way, not to expect a black hand reaching across the counter. That was not part of my humanity."

The people in that room at the chamber were doing just what his Daddy had done many years before when he decided the children around Thunder deserved to be picked up every morning by a school bus. The elder Jones saw a need and he petitioned the county. The people around that board table were doing the same thing. "And the message that been coming out of city hall and the courthouse had failed. The failure revealed itself that morning. There was no point in going down there and trying to reverse a crusade that was justified...and it was justified," Jones says.

Charles Jones received some puzzled looks from some of his chamber colleagues that morning along with some hearty handshakes from the protest group. The following year, Mercer University presented him the Algernon Sydney Sullivan Award as the community's "Man of the Year in Race Relations." That plaque still hangs on the wall of Jones' paneled library at home. But old awards are as forgotten as the deeds that earned them. This concerns Virgil Adams.

To him, young black people today need to do more than remember those years. So do white youth. They need, Adams believes, to appreciate those times, those people and those experiences. Having Adams tell of his personal experiences is one thing. Having Jones, a white man, tell his side of the same story is another.

Says Adams: "Young black people hear all the time from blacks my age and older about the way things were and what blacks went through back then. What they don't hear as much is that other side. They need to see that there were white people who spearheaded some of these changes. People who were willing to step out and tell other whites that something wasn't right. That is a piece of the message young people need to hear. So when they hear the name of a Charlie Jones, they say, 'Oh, okay, that's the guy I read about.' This other side is important. It's a big deal. It makes a statement about the man."

12

Ocmulgee

Charlie Jones had made his best pitch. Come home, he implored the Indians. Come home to Macon. He was the closer and he had nailed it. Others presented deals and promises. He talked about Georgia being their spiritual home, their holy ground. He put the invitation into emotional terms, promising to transform the trail of tears into a trail of cheers. Leave Oklahoma, he said. Come home.

Even though more than 150 people were crowded into the meeting room at Tulsa's Alvin Plaza Hotel, it was quiet as Jones returned to his seat. Around the room that day were more than two dozen representatives of the Inter Council of the Five Civilized Tribes: the Creek, the Seminoles, the Cherokee, the Choctaw, and the Chickasaw. Calling them the civilized tribes wasn't a derogatory term. The Congress of the United States had given them that label years before. Scattered among them were fourteen visitors from Georgia—from state officials to college administrators—even Macon's infamous mayor, Ronnie Thompson.

Everyone had listened politely as Jones and his friends talked, spelling out all that would be done for the Creeks if they came home to the banks of the Ocmulgee, the river that meanders through the city of Macon. Then Sister Bessie Sore Thumb stood up.

She was old and she was revered. She wore the historic regalia of her tribe. She was respected and so were her words. She had the floor and many of the visitors assumed she was going to thank them for coming and for making such generous offers. All eyes were on her as she started to speak. Bessie looked straight at Jones. "I speak for all the Creeks when I say that this white man speaks with a forked-tongue," she said. "He lies. What he has said you cannot believe." Bessie Sore Thumb did not talk very long but her words seemed to put an arrow through the heart of Charles Jones and his dreams.

Now everyone in the room was looking at Jones, watching for a glimmer of reaction from the visiting businessman, the obvious leader of this group from Georgia. Pushing back his chair, Jones calmly got to his feet. First he thanked the aging Creek for her words. Then he responded to her allegations. "I didn't live 100 years ago, Sister Sore Thumb. Neither did you. But I am sincere when I say that I am sorry for what we did. We were wrong. But I hope you can forgive us for what our forefathers did to your people. We want to make up for that," Jones said, recalling the horrible decision to drive the Indians out of their homeland in the Southeast.

Like the Indians who gathered in Tulsa for that meeting, Charles Jones was a product of the same Georgia lands. He had been born in Upson County, a political division sliced out of former Indian territory in 1822.

A monument that stands at the Indian mounds in nearby Rock Eagle has this inscription dedicated to the forgotten people who centuries ago settled this area: "Tread softly here, white man; for long ere you came, strange races lived, fought and loved."

In a written history of Upson County, where Jones spent his teen years, the author talks about the Creeks. "Not a print of his moccasin survives but Creek Indians were the area's earliest inhabitants."

Growing up, Jones had paid little attention to this common heritage but in 1957—when he was first appointed to the board of directors of the Ocmulgee National Monument Association — he began to study the history of not only the mounds but of this part of Georgia. It was a history washed in the blood of the Creeks and other tribles. For Jones, it was the beginning of a lifelong fascination with a people he came to love.

Standing near the Ocmulgee mounds, just across the river from downtown Macon, a visitor is on land that once belonged to the Lower Creeks but now belongs to the US government—the authorities that ripped that tribe away from its native soil and banished them to Oklahoma. Little more than two centuries ago, there were few white men in sight. This was the edge of the Great American Frontier and the only civilization were the Indian villages that dotted the countryside.

Near this site nearly 1,200 years ago stood a green-sloped pyramid that served as the principal temple for a large village and a ceremonial ground. At that time, it was home to a group of Indians that came to be known as the "Master Farmers." They introduced innovative agricultural practices and a new religion similar to the pyramid-building Indians of Mexico and Central America. These people were gone by the time the first European explorers came through the area, replaced by an important village of the Lower Creek nation. Fort Hawkins was built around that same area in 1806, so settlers could do business with the Creeks.

When Jones first walked over the 683 acres of the national monument, you could look to the west and on the horizon were the tops of modern buildings in downtown Macon. But it was still easy to imagine another time when fancy dancers stomped their feet and voices droned and chanted, paying homage to the corn god, the eagle deity and the ivory-billed woodpecker. Jones found himself overcome as he realized how new to this area his people were in comparison with the Indians who called this place home at least 10,000 years before he did.

His world was new. Theirs was not.

As he became more and more consumed by his studies of the early Indians, he became more involved with the Ocmulgee Mounds. He became chairman of the board of directors—a panel that included his old pals Joe Parham and Steve Solomon along with Susan Myrick, a local writer that years before had been a consultant during the making of *"Gone With the Wind."*

Around this same time, Jones became more active in the Greater Macon Chamber of Commerce, particularly interested in tourism. In his mind, he began to mesh together his obsession with the Creeks and his sometimes civic and sometimes personal desire to attract more tourists and more visitors to Bibb County.

Those thoughts grew into his dream of an Indian Homecoming.

"I thought they had a divine right to come back," Jones says.

In 1971, Jones was elected president of the Chamber of Commerce. He would assume that position in 1972. Over the intervening months he began to mull over his goals for that term. He gathered local leaders together for focus groups and he hired an outside consulting firm.

From those sessions came these five goals:

- A medical school for Mercer University.
- A new industrial park.
- A homecoming for the Creeks.
- Unity between Macon and its surrounding neighbors.
- Attract new industries.

But while Jones may have seen that homecoming as a divine right, history saw it otherwise. His dream of bringing the Indians back to Georgia was blocked by more than a century of pain as Jones soon learned through his studies.

The history of Georgia and the Creeks walks a parallel line. It was the Creeks that gave General James Oglethorpe permission to build Savannah, setting the stage for the land grab that ultimately evicted them from their homes. Through the American Revolution, the two peoples coexisted but after the war, the Indians became unwilling pawns in the government's lust for land.

Not long after the inauguration of George Washington as president of the new republic, he arranged a meeting with Creek chiefs in New York. At that conference, the Indians signed away all their land on the Oconee River, inspiring a rush of white settlers into Georgia.

During the 1800s, the white man's government wanted more of the Indian land and authorities began to systematically break the spirit of the Creeks and the other nearby tribes. Treaties were signed and promises were made. Neither was kept. The Indian issue was important in Georgia and in Washington. President James Monroe delegated Wilson Lumpkin, a prominent Georgia lawyer, to help designate the boundary of the Creek treaty in 1818. A year later, he served in a similar role for the Cherokee Treaty of 1819.

In 1825, Lumpkin was involved in the planning for railroads in Georgia. He studied land from Chattanooga to Milledgeville, at that time the capitol of Georgia. Along the way, he became acquainted with most of the Cherokee leaders and became convinced that the tribe ought to be removed to lands beyond the Mississippi River. Later, as a member of Congress from Georgia, he worked hard on the issue of Indian removal, maintaining it would be good for both the state and the Cherokees.

When Andrew Jackson was elected president, Lumpkin was still a member of the United States House of Representatives. Their views on the Indian problem were similar. In 1830, Congress passed the controversial legislation that authorized the removal of Indians from Georgia and the southeast.

A year later, Lumpkin came home to run for governor, an office he held from 1831 to 1835. Once elected, he ignored a legal ruling by the Supreme Court that said Georgia's laws were not valid in the Cherokee territories. He carved up their land and created 10 new counties north of Atlanta. Parcels were available through a state-run lottery. Time and time again, the state passed laws that cut away at the fiber and soul of the Cherokees, the Creeks and their leaders. After his four years as governor, Lumpkin became a United States Senator where he continued to work for Indian removal.

Lumpkin's friend and political ally, William Schley, was elected governor of Georgia in 1835. While the Cherokees were all but gone from the state, the Creeks remained a political issue. When bands of Indians angry at their treatment by authorities started terrorizing settlers in the western area of the state, Schley helped organize state militia units and went to Columbus to join them personally. The governor set up headquarters in Columbus and supported General Winfield Scott whose federal troops continually routed the Creeks on both sides of the Chattahoochee River.

Thus began one of this country's most distasteful decisions. Indians were to be forcefully removed to Oklahoma on a bloody walk that has become known as 'The Trail of Tears." Members of various tribes were herded into Fort Mitchell, a compound high over the Chattahoochee. It was located on what is now Alabama, overlooking Fort Benning, one of the foremost military installations in the world. Peaceful Indians were herded into corrals like livestock. At Fort Mitchell today there are plaques listing the names of the displaced Creeks. An eternal flame burns in their memory. In the fall of the year, Indians gather at that site for a stick ball game and to tell the old stories.

The march from Georgia to Oklahoma spanned from 1836 to 1839. It was long and deadly. Those who could not keep up were left for dead. Families were separated. Survivors were tired, sick and angry. Bad weather was ignored. Soldiers ordered the Indians to keep moving. More than half of the Indians who left Alabama died along the way.

Indians have passed down oral stories of that ruthless move from generation to generation, telling the tales in graphic detail. There are even songs with eerie morbid lyrics. For the Indians, it is a sad history. For the white man, it is a painful, embarrassing decision that was never righted.

Jones was determined to do something to bring people and time together. As he investigated, he found there was a town in Oklahoma known as Okmulgee where the Creeks had clustered. Except for the letter "k," it was a namesake of the river once fished by their ancient ancestors who were herded west like cattle being taken to market. To Jones's surprise, there had been no contact between the Creek Nation in Oklahoma and the state of Georgia—much less the city of Macon. "That just seemed ridiculous to me," Jones says. "After all, this is their ancestral home and to me Macon should have meant as much to them as Israel does to the Jews."

Jones began sharing his far-fetched dreams with Parham, Solomon and Myrick—his friends in Macon. The more he talked, the more others became interested. For several years, Jones and his friends had talked about taking a train to Oklahoma so they could meet the Creeks who once had been their neighbors. That idea never came together.

In the fall of 1971, Jones was invited to Arizona to meet with Ramada Inn's corporate planners. They wanted his company to build and own a motel in Forsyth, Georgia, near the campus of Tift College. He was about to be the chamber president and he still chaired the monument board. It seemed to Jones that these things weren't a coincidence, that he was destined to do something about this dream he had carried around for several years. So on his way back from Arizona, he scheduled a stop over in Oklahoma. That was when he first met Claude Cox.

Creek Indians called Claude Cox chief because he was. On top of his head sat a cowboy hat that would hold much more than ten gallons, one that would have made John Wayne envious. On his feet was a pair of cowboy boots with toes so pointy that a kick to someone's backside could be lethal. He was in charge and he knew it.

In 1970, Cox had become the first elected chief of his tribe. For too many years, the white man had decided who would lead the five tribes that were still under federal jurisdiction. Richard Nixon had changed that. He was the elected president of the United States and Claude Cox became the elected president of the Creeks. Cox would lead the Creek Nation for more than 20 years, a wise leader who skillfully maneuvered between his own people and the government bureaucracy.

Cox had worked with a lot of people but he had never run into anyone just like Charles Jones. The stately Indian leader and the cigar-chewing Georgian didn't know it then but they were beginning an unlikely friendship that would continue until the chief's death. Eventually, Cox would make this fast-thinking visitor an honorary member of the Creek Nation. But when they first sat down together in the Muskogee Creek Council House, Cox couldn't understand how or why Jones wanted them to come to Georgia.

Jones insisted on calling it their home, but the Creeks knew nothing about this place called Macon. Jones claimed it was the tribe's divine right, but the stories Indians had heard about their removal were anything but spiritual. Jones said they would be welcome, but Cox told him about federal laws that said it was a capital offense if a Creek was caught crossing from the west bank to the east bank of the Chattahoochee. Cox listened. But he said little. "I came to realize that to go fast, he rowed slow," Jones says.

Jones spent three days in Okmulgee. He ate their food and it was sometimes an adventure. He visited their simple church. He met the chief's family. And he never stopped inviting them to come home. Perhaps Cox did not believe anything would come of

Jones' outrageous plans or perhaps just to get rid of him, the chief finally agreed to a high-level pow-wow back in Macon. Jones said he would get together the key people and they would meet at the Ocmulgee National Monument.

Between September and December, Jones was busy talking on the telephone and writing letters. Before Christmas, Chief Cox and his wife were in Macon, joined by Bill Ames, an official with the US Bureau of Indian Affairs in Tahlequah, Oklahoma.

Jones was the consummate host. He arranged meetings with local officials. He served them dinner in his home. He was on call to take them wherever they wanted to go. More than anything, he wanted Cox to have private time on the land where his ancestors had lived, quiet time to reacquaint himself with his ancestors.

Jones and Cox went to Indian Springs, twenty-five miles north of Macon. It once was owned by William McIntosh, the half-breed Creek chief who in 1821 signed the treaty that deeded five million acres of Creek lands to the United States government. A tribal council later sentenced McIntosh to death. Later about 100 warriors set fire to his house and when he ran out they shot him down.

The Creeks finally deeded the remainder of their land in Georgia. For their property, they received $27,491 in cash, $5,000 in blankets and other goods and $10,000 to be devoted to educational purposes. They also were promised homesteads in Oklahoma along with other inducements designed to lure them west. When they arrived there, the land was bare. There was no food or shelter to be found.

Jones and Cox stood on the rock where McIntosh signed that infamous treaty. They also dined on the grounds, to the chagrin of some local people who later asked Jones why he brought *those* people to the dining room. More than anything, Jones wanted to be with Cox when he visited the mounds near the Ocmulgee.

At the Indian mounds, they visited the council house, one of the oldest public buildings in America. Cox was so tall that he had to duck to go through the door. Inside there were no chairs, just carved out areas where the council members once sat. The chief was quietly counting. "We have the same number," Cox said, breaking the silence. "What's that chief?" Jones said. "We have the same number on our council," he said. There was a kinship, a connection. "It was spiritual," Jones says, "for the chief and for me."

While Cox was in Macon, the governor of Georgia was speaking at the former Hilton Hotel. He sent word that he wanted to meet the chief. Jones arranged for them to meet and Cox presented then Governor Jimmy Carter a keepsake. Their picture made next morning's *Macon Telegraph*. Four years later, Cox was still chief of the Creeks and Carter had been elected president of the United States.

Cox felt a strong connection to the area. His people had been expelled 150 years before and there were no Creeks living nearby but with the land he felt a kinship that he could not explain. So the chief began to listen to Jones and the others who continually were bombarding him with ideas and offers.

There would be an Indian presence at the mounds. There would be a trading post where they could sell their handmade goods. There would be jobs. There would be homes. There would be full scholarships for Indian students at Mercer University. There would be a new life on the old land.

Before he went home that December, Cox was talking openly about as many as twelve Creek families moving into the area by the spring of 1972. That idea was more than history. It was economics. "We are talking about putting in a Creek Indian Trading Post here in Macon because a lot of tourists come through here on their way to Florida to visit Disney World," Cox told the *Macon Telegraph*. "A trading post here would help our people in many ways. We've got people in need of employment and we're going to try and work through this program of arts and crafts."

The visit by Cox led to Jones and an entourage of Macon leaders going to Oklahoma in February of 1972. The Tulsa World even wrote editorials about the visit. The editorial said the distinguished visitors from Georgia were trying to persuade the Creeks to return to their homeland—and the newspaper was not surprised. "The (Indians) conquered a wilderness West of Arkansas. They introduced advanced agriculture, commerce, printing, modern political institutions and public education to this part of the frontier. They took a leading role in the creation of a new State, then helped nurture it into the Space Age. No wonder Georgia would like to have back some of her original citizens."

They wished well Oklahoma Creeks who accepted jobs or scholarships in Macon but told the visiting officials they could not wish them unlimited success in their recruiting campaign. "Good people are Oklahoma's most valuable product," the editorial said. "And we would not like to see them exported."

It was a recruiting campaign, too. Jones had primed members of the group on how to behave and what to say, recalls John Mitchell, who went along to offer the tribes at least ten scholarships to Mercer. "Charlie coached us to be gentle, and not to drink much fire water," says Mitchell, now a retired Mercer University administrator. "He was a dynamo. Unless you have heard him, people can't imagine him when he's on his feet. Not many folks can match him when he's the Lead Dog."

Jones had assembled the power brokers he needed to sell the Indian leadership on their offer to expand the invitation to the other tribes. The mayor of Macon was there along with the chairman of the Bibb County Commission and the commanding general from the Warner Robins Air Force Base. There were representatives of the parks service, the chamber, the state department of industry and trade and a representative of the governor.

Thompson told the tribal leaders that "The area there is a loss without you." Mitchell offered scholarships to Mercer and the support of the university. Jones said the relocation project was an attempt to rectify past injustices: "No people in the history of man were ever mistreated any more than the Five Civilized Tribes now residing in Oklahoma."

Though Indians had been relocated to other places over the years, this was the first attempt to relocate them to their native area, Cox said. "Through the Bureau of Indian Affairs, we have relocated many of our people to Los Angeles, to Dallas and to other places. But it has always been either north or west or south."

Bessie Sore Thumb offered her concerns about the proposal, which Jones talked about that day in the hotel meeting room. He elaborated on what he said to her in an interview with the Tulsa World: "If I were an Indian, I wouldn't believe anything the white man said—period. But insofar as the truth is inside me, I invite you to come on home."

The council believed in him. After the visitors from Georgia left the room that day, the Executive Council of the Five Civilized Tribes approved the other tribes' involvement with Jones and the city of Macon. The resolution was adopted on February 9, 1972.

"WHEREAS, Macon, Ga. Is the ancestral home of the Creek Indian Tribe of Oklahoma and the site of the Ocmulgee National Monument, and

WHEREAS the Auxiliary Board of Directors of the Ocmulgee National Monument and heads of various institutions, agencies and business leaders of the area are cognizant of the injustices perpetrated upon a great people—the Five Civilized Tribes—most of whom now reside in the state of Oklahoma, and

WHEREAS, in an effort to rectify these injustices and wrongs to the Creek people and members of the other Five Civilized Tribes, the Auxiliary Board of Directors urges interested members of the Creek Tribe of Oklahoma to return to their ancestral home in Macon, Ga., and

WHEREAS, as an inducement for the Creeks to return to Macon, the Auxiliary Board of Directors, composed of leading businessmen, government officials, and interested citizens of Macon, have agreed to give employment not only to Creek Indians but other members of the Five Civilized Tribes, and

WHEREAS, Mercer University offers ten free, four-year scholarships to members of the Five Civilized Tribes, and also offers scholarships in business, vocational and technical schools located in the area, and

WHEREAS, the National Park Service, working with various agencies and business leaders of the area, has agreed to establish a craft shop at the Ocmulgee National Monument and pay salaries of the Indian workers in the shop as well as pay for all utilities and rentals until such time as the Creek people are in position to assume this responsibility, and

WHEREAS, the Creek Indians would have exclusive rights to sell Indian made crafts.

NOW THEREFORE BE IT RESOLVED: That the Executive Committee of the Five Civilized Tribes in a special called session held in Tulsa, Oklahoma, February 9, 1972 voted to go on record by resolution expressing grateful thanks and sincere appreciation to the citizens of Macon, Ga., for this gracious offer to the Creek people and other members of the Five Civilized Tribes.

BE IT FURTHER RESOLVED: That the Executive Committee of the Five Civilized Tribes further voted to go on record assuring the citizens of Macon, Ga., the fullest support of the Five Civilized Tribes in this endeavor."

More than twenty years later, Charles Jones still remembers that decision and the homecoming that followed as one of his proudest accomplishments. It was a community's effort but it was his dream. Down the road, there would be setbacks and out and out failures, but Jones still believes it was good for the psyche of the Creeks and the people of Macon. "Both sides learned to forgive and to understand," Jones says.

By May 1972, the first wave of Creeks arrived in Georgia. As promised, there were cheers—not tears. Some went to work at the monument. Some enrolled at Mercer University. Locals were enthusiastic and they were curious. Newspapers all over Georgia wrote stories about the homecoming. Once the welcomes were over, there were obstacles. Unlike Oklahoma where Indians lived in great numbers, they were a novelty in Georgia. More than 150 Indians came in the coming years and they would face obstacles.

In a 1980 interview with "Brown's Guide to Georgia," Gerald Harjo remembered what it was like for the Indians who moved here in 1972. Harjo, a Creek, came to Macon with Ervina, his bride-to-be. She was a Cherokee. The program initially was for only Creeks but Jones made an exception for her. "The people in Georgia are amazing," he told the magazine. "They were so receptive to everything when we got here. We just couldn't believe it. They were treating us like stars or something…asking us for autographs and all that. In Oklahoma, it's like, 'If you've seen one Indian you've seen 'em all.' At first we thought the people (in Macon) were crazy. We thought these white people were just putting us on." Not everyone thought the Indians should be treated like stars.

An author who had written about Indians and the Ocmulgee River thought it was a sacrilege to have the Creeks there as tour guides and merchants. Russell Chalker, a retired school superintendent from Carrolton, Georgia spent fifteen years researching "Pioneer Days Along the Ocmulgee." He welcomed them back, but not in that context. "I can stand there at the Old Fields and visualize that thing and appreciate it more in the silence than I could hearing somebody beat a tom-tom," Chalker told the Atlanta Journal.

The University of Georgia archaeologist who helped unearth the mounds in the 1930s told the newspaper that the Indians who were coming back to Georgia bore little resemblance to the ones who left there in the 1830s. "The Indians who are coming are already acculturated by the white man," Dr. A. R. Kelly said. "They are very little like the original Creeks."

When the Indians did arrive, there were surprises that no one would have expected. Harjo had been promised a job at the Ocmulgee National Monument. He was led to believe that he would be a guide at the historic site where his forebearers had lived. When he reported for work, he found he was going to be cutting grass, running a lawn mower instead of tour groups. Harjo made more noise about the lawn mower than about that assignment:

> I could have cut grass in Oklahoma," he said in the magazine interview. "I wasn't just some uneducated sonofabitch who couldn't do nothing else but cut grass. I had been to college, Jack! I didn't have to come all the way to Macon, Ga. to cut grass. I raised hell about it. Then they moved me up into the office. I worked there as a guide for three summers. A lot of people came out to the mounds and I showed them around. Everything was fine. There was a trading post where some of us worked and I instigated some dances at the park.

Harjo was one of the Indians who received a scholarship to Mercer, where he finished his undergraduate degree. For a while, he was on the faculty at Macon's Central High School, an instructor in art and American History. Like so many of the Indians who came to Georgia from Oklahoma, he eventually left the area.

"The newness wore off," Harjo said in 1980. "They forgot about us."

There were also changes in the leadership and philosophy at the park. The Indians who remained in Macon found the promises of the past weren't being fulfilled. Jones was no longer president of the chamber and the leaders who followed didn't share his dreams or visions. Today, few people ever talk about the efforts to bring the Creeks home.

One of the young Indians who accepted the invitation in 1972 might have had the right idea. Ben Checotah was laying bricks when he answered an ad in Oklahoma and came to Macon looking for a new life. He's gone now. But for a time, he was content in Georgia, learning about a background he didn't know he had.

Checotah often told a story about being at a fancy banquet in Macon where Jones was introducing him around, trying to make him feel welcome in the strange social surroundings. Putting his arm around the young Indian's shoulder, Jones leaned over and asked Checotah if there was anything else he could do for him.

"Yeah," he said. "Give us back our land."

A generation has passed since Charles Jones met the Indian chief with the oversized cowboy hat and invited him home. Chief Claude Cox is dead. The Creeks who came back have drifted away. Jones is proud of being an honorary member of the tribe and will put on the ceremonial headdress Chief Cox gave him if you ask. He regularly sends money to the church in Okmulgee and will read any literature he can find about that era. Even now, he can get excited telling someone about how Macon needs to consider building an authentic Indian museum.

Jones' dream has become as much a part of local history as the stories of the Creek Nation. The Ocmulgee Mounds are only a short drive from the traditional center of Macon, nestled between two interstate highways. It is a memorial without a pulse, catering to the dead instead of the living. The only Native Americans there are found on the pages of books and the spirits that some say still walk those hallowed grounds. As far as the existing monument is concerned, a visitor can speed through Macon on Interstate 75 and never know it is there. "It is," Charles Jones says, "a well-kept secret."

The leaders of the tribes in Oklahoma haven't forgotten. In the late 1990s, work began on the Fall Line Freeway, a state four-lane that would connect the state's secondary cities. It would slice across Georgia—from Augusta to Macon to Columbus—and would link together South Carolina and Alabama. On either end, work was progressing but not in Bibb County.

Macon businessman Ben Porter—like Jones a former chamber president—was trying to work out a workable route through the city but discovered two stubborn stalemates: wetlands and the Ocmulgee Monument. Environmentalists did not want to build a bridge that would disturb the wetlands and historians did not want a highway built that close to the Indian mounds. "We weren't going through the Indian property but the road would be about a mile to the south which was still too close for them," Porter says. Knowing his relationship with Chief Claude Cox, Porter enlisted his old friend Charles Jones. "We thought he would be the right person to plead our case to the Indians."

A meeting was arranged in 1997 and the Georgians took off for Oklahoma. There was Jones, Porter, a county commissioner and an engineer from the Georgia Department of Transportation. Just as they had when their neighbors went before the council in 1972, the people from Macon had a deal to propose to the Indian chiefs. "We had a very nice meeting," Porter says. "Here's twenty or more gray haired leaders of the tribes sitting in a semi-circle. The engineer makes his case. The county commissioner tells how the community needs this road. I make a little speech asking for their cooperation. We were saving Charlie for last, because he's such a good preacher."

Once more, Jones was the cleanup hitter and once more he hit one out of the park, Porter believed. Nearly a quarter of a century had passed since Jones first talked to the tribal council. He told them about his close friendship with Chief Cox and the Creek Nation, how they would always occupy a special place in his heart. "He used his best evangelical style," Porter recalls. "It was one of the best talks I've ever heard and those Indian folks were nodding their heads the whole time. Charlie was pleading with them to withdraw their opposition. We all were pleased with ourselves. When he sat down, I thought we had our road."

Now it was the council's turn to talk. One of the older chiefs stood. "This white man speaks eloquently," the Indian leader said. "He said things that that make our hearts move. He says all he wants is just a little bit of our land. It is just like it was in the 1830s. That white man told us all he wanted was a little bit of our land. We listened and we said yes. We signed his paper and the next thing we knew we were walking to Oklahoma."

Approval was never given and the road is still not built. "I believe they set us up for the whole deal," Porter says. "But Chief Jones made a great speech."

13

Citizen Jones

Word came down and the message was crystal clear. By order of the governor, there was to be no selling. This was more than a polite request. This was an executive mandate. Treat these folks like guests in your own home. Welcome them. Wine them. Dine them. Fill their bags with pricey gifts. Smile and shake their hands all you want. But do not pressure them.

Governor Jimmy Carter was playing host to CEOs from around the world and he wanted people down the line to follow his rules. And though he had the pious countenance of a Southern Baptist Sunday school teacher, *or else* could be pretty tough with Mr. Carter.

The visiting executives were part of the annual Red Carpet Tour and Macon would be one of their stops. The Red Carpet Tour was a journey sponsored by the Georgia Chamber of Commerce. During a single busy week in the spring, key business leaders from around the country and around the world are shown the best the state has to offer. Destinations are rotated among Georgia cities, but the tour usually includes a visit to the Masters and the azaleas in Augusta.

City by city, Georgia shows off, hoping that these influential people from faraway zip codes will go back home and suggest that their companies move their offices and factories to Georgia. Immediately, if not sooner.

Having such movers and shakers come to town made folks in Macon move and shake. Cities had to wheel and deal with the Georgia Chamber of Commerce to be sure the Red Carpet group spent quality time in their particular community rather than make a mere stopover. Macon was excited when they found out the group would be having their evening meal at the Macon Hilton. The downtown hotel was still new and proud locals wanted the visitors to experience it. And if Macon was going to put its best foot forward, they wanted to be sure the shoe was shined real good.

The Greater Macon Chamber of Commerce collected souvenir gifts for the goody bags intended for the visitors. That evening's program was meticulously planned. All of this was geared to send a positive message about Macon. Charles Jones would serve as the emcee at the dinner. He was president of the chamber, but more important than that he was quick on his feet and quick with his gab.

Jones was comfortable with that assignment. But there was still the matter of the governor's marching orders. No selling, Jimmy said, which didn't set well with Jones. Call him a motel owner. Call him a developer. Call him chamber president. Call him a city leader. Call him what you want. At his very core, Charles Jones was (and is) a salesman. The Good Lord just made him that way. If he finds himself standing at a lectern in front of a room filled with potential customers, the man's gotta' sell. The governor himself would be there next to him on the dais so it would be a slap in Carter's face if the master of ceremonies were to lapse into a sales pitch. Jones knew he would need to be on his best behavior.

Everything that evening moved according to plan. Cocktails weren't stingy. Salads were crisp. Steaks were tender. Waiters were attentive. The formal presentation went off without a hitch. Everybody was smiling, including Jimmy Carter.

Jones followed the agenda as written. The script said for him to introduce his good friend, the governor. As Carter finished his remarks, Jones returned to the microphone. It was time for the last call, time to say good night. Well, almost. There was still time for a parting message so Jones began his benediction.

> Before you go, I need your attention for just a moment, folks. This is personal. I need you to do something for me. When you leave our city and our state and you get home, you're going to be busy. There will be phone calls to return and meetings to attend. You may remember the azaleas and the golf at Augusta National, but you'll forget all the good times you had in Macon and the good times we had with you. But I want you…when you get home…every morning when you get up, when you sit on the edge of your bed and you put on your shoes. When you bend over to tie your shoes, you will be in a prayerful position. And right then, I want you to shut your eyes and say, *"Oh, God, what can I do today to move my headquarters and my company to Macon,* Georgia?"

As the visitors left town that next morning, they were still talking about what Jones had said. Even Carter was impressed. His no-sell edict aside, a year later—at a similar gathering—the governor suggested Jones do a repeat performance as the emcee.

Those prayers Jones called for must have been offered for the Lord certainly smiled on the city in the years that followed. Companies did move to Middle Georgia. Big companies, some of them from around the world. Important companies with good-paying jobs. It was an era of industrial growth still unparalleled in Macon's history and Charles Jones was right in the middle of it as president of the local chamber and the Macon Bibb County Authority.

One by one, the industries came, most of them in the early 1970s. The Government Employees Insurance Company (GEICO) relocated to Macon. Brown & Williamson Tobacco Corporation built a plant in the city's new industrial park. YKK Incorporated came all the way from Japan to make zippers. Thirty years later, those companies still are four of the ten largest employers in Bibb County accounting for more than 8,000 jobs.

Jones is not one who waits for prayers to be answered, attorney Buck Melton says. Jones can't stay on his knees that long. He wants to be up and moving. Melton, a former mayor of Macon, knows firsthand the impatient energy that Jones exudes.

"He has never wanted to sit around and wait for people to show up and ask can we put up a plant and hire 200 people in Macon? He has always wanted to go out and work to make that happen. He is just a driven personality. We all worked hard in the 1970s to get YKK, GEICO and Brown & Williamson and Charlie was a big part of making those arrangements and selling those people on coming to Macon," says Melton, a one-time candidate for governor of Georgia.

Arranging and selling were full-time jobs, too. Says Melton: "Charlie is thinking all the time, way ahead of most of us. He's sees the possibility of something and he doesn't want any obstacle to get in his way. So many people want to sit around the coffee table and talk about a situation. Not Charlie. He says, 'Let's go. Let's get it done.' People like a person like that. Sure, he might go off on wild goose chases on occasion. Most of us do. But his instincts about how to get from here to there are always good. He's full of courage and guts. Very few people get involved in something and say they want to be the chairperson. Charlie does. He's always ready to go."

Macon was a city that needed a strong dose of Charles Jones. Macon needed a dose of his energy. For years, it had been stagnant in so many ways, sitting dormant while its neighbors wiped the cobwebs out of their eyes and dealt with a changing world.

From the outside looking in, Macon seemed to be blessed. It was dead center middle in the state of Georgia. It was criss-crossed by a busy Interstate highway system. It was a straight shot to the Atlantic and rail service offered connections north, south and east. It was a quick hop to Hartsfield International Airport without the headaches of Atlanta traffic. It was home to Mercer University and Wesleyan College as well as Macon State College, a state-run two-year institution. It was a commercial hub for that part of the state. It was close to Robins Air Force Base, an influential military installation that is Middle Georgia's largest employer with 19,000 workers. Outsiders wondered what was holding Macon back and people in the know advised the city to look first at itself.

In a 1980 article in *Business Atlanta*, Macon architect Gene Dunwoody talked about his hometown's conservative attitudes. "Historically," he said, "it has never changed rapidly from the inside. It has always changed in reaction to something. And the city is ever mindful of its history. Traditions are hard to break. I call it the 'big old country town' syndrome."

Macon had never dealt well with change. Even as her textile world crumbled and railroads eliminated passenger service, the city tried to perpetuate its social mores and its traditional economic system. It hung on to old-fashioned segregation with a vengeance and the emergence of Ronnie Thompson as mayor had besmirched the city's reputation even further. The city still quarreled with the county, each squelching talk of consolidating city and county governments that had been erupting since the 1940s. Founding families still felt their voices deserved to be louder and more dominant. Never considered a wealthy town, Macon's economic base for too long had depended on federal and state jobs. As a younger generation not schooled in the city's old ways began to emerge as leaders, these men and women were more concerned with what tomorrow offered. To them, the past was just that—past.

Dunwoody talked to the magazine about Charles Jones taking over the chamber in 1972. "When Charlie was elected president he called in everybody and I mean everybody. The chamber conference room was packed. Then Charlie stands up and says, 'Men, we've have been washing each other's laundry too long. Now we're gonna wash somebody else's.' With that, he started telling folks what we were gonna do. And by golly, folks did it."

Before Macon could flourish, Jones realized problems on the homefront had to be solved. Successful people thought because they were doing well that everybody in town was doing well—and they weren't. Bank presidents weren't speaking to other bank presidents. City officials were suspicious of county leaders and were given the same trust in return. Folks in surrounding communities avoided the city folks. People in town were condescending to country people who were only welcome when they came to town to spend their money. Blacks and whites lived separate lives, a carryover from the segregated world into which both races had been born.

There was an epidemic of tunnel vision, and Doc Jones had to treat it. "We have 150,000 people living in this county, almost a quarter of a million in the metropolitan zone and not all of them are doing fine," Jones said at the time. "And I'm tired of seeing our best talent go elsewhere to make a living. Leaders have to think about everybody: the poor, the rich, the black, the white, everybody. We've got to keep growing. We have no choice."

Around town, Jones issued the same challenge he offered the Red Carpet visitors: What are you doing to help Macon grow and when are you going to do it? He was approaching industrial growth the way he approached his own development company. He thought. He acted. Then he worried about the consequences. He made personnel changes and he modernized the way the chamber operated internally. He cajoled people in politics. He started to work on ways to bring people together. He was a top that wouldn't quit spinning.

Harping on the area's need to work together, Jones organized a meeting of leaders from throughout the Middle Georgia region. At lunch that day were county commissioners from Twiggs, Jones, Monroe, Peach and Crawford. There were all levels of officials from Warner Robins, Milledgeville and Perry. There were leaders from Bibb County and from the city of Macon. Members of the chamber board of directors showed up. They convened at the Holiday Inn on Interstate 475. No one had to ask who was in charge. It was his lunch and his program, and nobody knew what to expect. Including Charles Jones.

Looking around the room, Jones tried to put himself in the place of the folks who had come from the smaller towns. For him, that wasn't so difficult. It had been less than twenty years since he had arrived from Upson County to open up his drugstore at Poplar and Broadway. Doing business there, he had experienced the differences between life on Poplar and life on Cherry Street. He knew these people from the small towns didn't trust the city slickers and he knew that many residents of Macon tended to look down on their neighbors with addresses that began with RFD.

Jones tried his best to keep the meeting informal and homey. Wanting everyone to feel comfortable, he welcomed his guests before lunch and he welcomed them again as they started to work on their desserts. He reminded them that he had come there from Thomaston himself.

Looking at the Macon contingent, Jones asked for all of those that were born in Macon to stand. Three stood up. Then he asked all the people who lived in Macon but had been born in some other contiguous county to stand. About ninety percent of them stood. "Now look at each other," he said. "I want you folks from out in the country to know that the folks involved in Macon are country folks too. We are all playing on the same field. We have everything in common. We've got to push all that old stuff aside now. We've got to come together for Central Georgia. The things we're talking about doing are bigger than Macon, Georgia."

Not even Jones knew how big they would be.

14

Zip

How he happened to sit where he did that night, no one remembers. It was one of life's unexplained coincidences. All people today remember is that Cloyd Hall, a hometown boy, was seated next to a businessman from Florida who wouldn't have been able to locate Macon on a service station map.

Hall, an aide to Governor Jimmy Carter, was making polite dinner conversation. Somewhere between their salad and their dessert, the other man casually mentioned that he was helping a large international firm locate an industrial site somewhere in the southeast. He was careful not to identify the company, keeping its name confidential as is the custom with such ventures.

"Have you considered Macon, Georgia?" Hall asked.

That simple question asked miles away from Georgia would change the future of Hall's hometown. It wasn't long before word of their conversation was passed to Macon. Charles Jones was soon in contact with the search firm that Hall's dinner guest represented. Still no one would identify the industry, not even in a whisper. The only thing Jones knew was that it was big and that it was from outside of the country.

Jones considered himself a raw rookie in the game of industrial recruiting. He had been thrust into that role when he moved into the presidency of Macon's Chamber of Commerce. An eternal student, Jones set out to learn all he could about this new assignment. He enlisted the help of a prominent teacher: Lewis

Truman. A retired Army general who was serving as Georgia's Commissioner of Industry and Trade, Truman helped Jones in many ways. One piece of advice he offered was that the city would need to acquire an industrial site that it could offer companies that were looking for a new home. Truman even identified a piece of land between Macon and Forsyth, not far from Interstate 75. Jones, however, set his sights on more than 250 acres of land across the Ocmulgee River. At one time, it had been the county farm. But Jones had other plans for this 450-acre plot that came to be known as Ocmulgee East.

The stretch of land not far from Interstate 16 would prove very important to the economic future of Middle Georgia. But at that time, no one could have predicted how well known that property would soon become—not even the effusive Mr. Jones. Before long, real estate planners on another continent were discussing that undeveloped piece of land in Bibb County, Georgia, USA.

YKK had never heard of Macon and the people in that Georgia city certainly knew nothing about YKK. YKK officials were familiar with Georgia, however. They were already considering a site east of Atlanta. Founded in Tokyo by Tadao Yoshida, who started the company in 1934, YKK was one of the world's foremost manufacturers of zippers.

By 1960, YKK was ready to enter the American market. The company first set up shop in Lyndhurst, New Jersey, opening a corporate headquarters and a small assembly operation. Ten years later, YKK made the decision to expand its base and set up its first zipper manufacturing plant in the United States. Because most of its manufacturing customers were in the southeast, YKK representatives quietly began to explore available real estate in Tennessee, North and South Carolina, Alabama, and Georgia.

YKK, of course, was the company that man from Florida was representing. YKK knew about Macon before that city knew about anything about manufacturing zippers. Before the Japanese industrialists ever met face to face with Macon officials, they had quietly done homework of their own. Unknown to anyone, they had visited the area, learning first hand how much time it took to drive Interstate 16 to the Port of Savannah and Interstate 75 to the international airport in Atlanta. They had personally walked the rolling land of the old county farm. They preferred to first take an anonymous visit to Macon, without the presence of local glad-handers.

By the time, YKK's representatives met with Jones, attorney Buck Melton and the other Georgians they were ready to talk serious business. Jones also was doing his homework. He learned the choice had come down to two locations in Georgia: Macon and Rockdale, near Atlanta.

On a visit to YKK's headquarters in New Jersey, Jones, Melton and Bud Moss coyly tried to find out details of the Rockdale offer. Conversations between the groups were like two prizefighters bobbing and weaving. The Japanese had information Jones wanted and the Macon businessmen had information the YKK representatives wanted. It turned into a game, one that Jones relished. It was a game he played deftly.

"How much is that land at that other location?" Jones asked.

"A thousand dollars an acre," the official said.

"Why that's what our land is," Jones said, pulling a number out of the sky.

Jones represented no one but the Macon chamber. The land itself belonged to Bibb County and he did not officially have the authority to speak for them. But that was not the time to worry about such small details. Hometown issues could be worked out when he got back to Georgia.

When YKK made its first official visit to Macon, Jones pulled out all the stops. He invited the Japanese officials to his home and he hired limousines to get them there. Neighbors thought the President of the United States was coming when the limos came through the front gates of his graceful white home that to his guests must have looked like Tara.

There was another round of gamesmanship when the YKK officials walked the proposed industrial site with Jones and a group of locals. The Japanese seemed to feel at home. The rural rolling land appealed to Yoshida. It reminded him of his own home in Kurobe, Japan. He noticed that when he got off the airplane. But naturally there were lingering questions to be answered, including one major inquiry.

"What about water and sewerage?" they asked.

"It's right here," Jones answered without a blink.

In reality, there was no water and no sewerage.

Bibb County officials were furious about what he had said. Jones, they yelled, should have consulted with county government before he made such a sweeping promise. Feathers were ruffled, but this deal was too important to quibble over. When all was said and done the utilities would be there, just as Jones had said.

There were also social questions to be confronted. On a visit to Japan, Jones asked Yoshida—he called him Mr. T—how many Japanese workers would be moving to Macon when the plant opened. Yoshida estimated there would be around fifteen.

"That's not enough," Jones said.

"What do you mean," Yoshida asked.

"There are no other Asians living around the area so they won't have anyone to socialize with," he said. "You need 75 or 80, at least."

A personal bond began to develop. Listening to their new friends in Macon, YKK officials had decided to secure 54 acres—seven times more than they had contemplated in the beginning. YKK's leaders liked the site, but land was land. They chose Macon because of the enthusiasm they experienced there. They felt welcome. Jones and his colleagues wanted YKK, and the Japanese people knew they wanted them.

Negotiations continued. It was one question after another with the Georgians usually the ones expected to provide the answers. On his way to Japan for one of their final meetings, Jones was growing typically impatient. He wanted action and YKK officials continued to haggle. Always, it seemed, they had one more question.

Sitting on the airplane, he remembered an unusual piece of advice he had read in a paper Rufus Harris, the president of Mercer University, had written about doing business in Asia. Harris had advised that a person had to be clear when he had gone as far as he would go when negotiating with Japanese businessmen. It was information Jones filed away for later, not realizing how soon he would need to put it to use.

When the Macon contingent arrived in Japan—before they had even left the airport—YKK officials posed yet another question. Jones doesn't remember what they asked. That's not important now. But he does remember his answer.

His answer was no—a final no.

More questions and still Jones's answer was no.

"My answer is no, and I can get back on that airplane and go back home if I have to," Jones said, making his stance very clear.

Yoshida politely accepted Jones's answer.

In the fall of 1972, YKK signed a letter of intent to build a 2.75 million square foot facility in Macon. Around 1,600 people would be employed in the massive plant. YKK would become the first tenant to build in Macon's new Ocmulgee East Industrial Park and the first Japanese industry to settle in Georgia. A short time later, Texprint Inc., another Japanese firm, followed YKK to Bibb County. Since then, more than 300 Japanese companies have moved into the state.

In late 1972, eight of the people most involved in the lengthy negotiations left Macon for Japan to sign the final agreement. Jones led the Georgia delegation, taking with him an assortment of gifts to present to their new friends. The Georgians were given VIP tours of the YKK operations in Kurobe and were amazed at the scope and size of the plant.

The date of the signing in Japan was interesting: December 7, 1972.

15

Hat Trick

The only thing folks in Macon knew about zippers was that they were an important accessory on a fellow's trousers. Tobacco, now there was something folks in South Georgia could understand. They could grow it and they could smoke it.

Like tobacco, politics was a traditional Southern crop and the two were about to be blended together in the personage of a United States senator who was a home-grown product of that same Deep South soil.

Charles Jones had been spending time on a deal involving people who spoke another language and did business in a culture different than his. Now he was about to be negotiating with a company that understood the influence of both agriculture and politics.

Like YKK, Brown & Williamson arrived shrouded with secrecy. Macon knew it was under a faraway microscope again but they did not know whose it was. Understanding how that game was played, city leaders prepared a package of information for the unknown firm.

By the time they knew what company it was, the giant tobacco company was looking at property on the highway to Warner Robins. Brown & Williamson soon began to refocus its interest on the Macon industrial park as well as a site near Huntsville, Alabama.

Jones was growing in confidence and so was the community. Macon was writing a new chapter in its history. The Creek Indians had been brought home. A Japanese industry had been landed. Jones says these things told the outside world that as a community Macon was not only prospering but changing.

"Sure, there was greed involved, but it also showed that Macon was growing and progressing in other ways. To accept the Indians, to accept people from Japan who didn't look the same or speak the same language, the city was growing as a people," he says.

Confident or not, Jones and his team of supporters knew that they first had to go against the offers being dangled by their neighbors to the North. Alabama did not tax materials that were stored in warehouses. Georgia did. That was a political hurdle so Macon officials started working on affecting a change in the Georgia State Constitution. There were other issues in the way, but ultimately the choice would come down to the state of Georgia and the state of Alabama. It was time for Melton and Jones to play their high card.

Their ace was the late Herman Talmadge. Talmadge was Georgia's senior senator and a major player in Washington politics—particularly in the field of agriculture. He was a former governor of Georgia and after being elected to the United States Senate he had followed a long standing Georgia tradition by being assigned to the Senate Agriculture Committee. It was in his blood, for early in his father's mercurial rise to political power in Georgia, Gene Talmadge served as Georgia's Commissioner of Agriculture. By 1972, Herman Talmadge was chairman of the Senate Agriculture Committee—one of the oldest standing panels in that body. Even today his portrait hangs in the room in a Senate office building where that prestigious committee meets.

The name of Talmadge would be magic with Brown & Williamson. Melton had talked this strategy over with an attorney who represented the tobacco company and he privately agreed that Talmadge would be effective, that the senator was a personal friend of Brown & Williamson's CEO. Now all Macon needed was to secure Talmadge's support.

Jones put in a call to Herman Talmadge. They had known one another for many years, since a very young Jones had introduced the campaigning Talmadge at a political rally in Thomaston.

Jones finally reached the senator at his home in Lovejoy. The Senate was in recess and Talmadge, home from Washington, was resting at his farm, a comfortable drive up Interstate 75 from Macon. The senator invited Jones and his friends to come to his house so they could sit down and talk. To Jones's private chagrin, Talmadge said come early—which to the senator meant somewhere near dawn.

Talmadge may have been awake, but the sun wasn't when the group left Macon that morning. A bus was hired and eight or ten people got together for the short trip to the Talmadge farm near Atlanta International Raceway. When they arrived in Lovejoy, they discovered it was the senator's birthday. His wife, Betty, had a favorite cake baking in the oven.

The visitors were escorted into the living room where chairs had already been arranged in a circle. Even at that early hour, Talmadge had been working the phones. He was sporting a man-sized cigar—an appropriate ornament given the reason for their visit.

Pleasantries were exchanged and hands were shook. It was the senator's unmistakable drawl that signalled it was time for them to get down to the purpose of their visit.

"Well, what can I do for my friends in Macon," he said.

Jones told him about their preliminary discussions with Brown & Williamson, and how they badly needed his help to close the deal for Macon.

"They won't do anything unless you bless this decision," Jones said.

"I'm sure going to bless it so what we can we do?"

Jones suggested a phone call to the CEO.

"What else do you want me to talk about?" Talmadge asked.

"Nothing," Jones said. "There's nothing else."

Through his lawyer friend, Melton had secured a direct phone number for the Brown & Williamson CEO. A call was placed and before long the tobacco official was on the line. Talmadge took the phone.

"This is Herman," he said, keeping it personal.

The two men knew each other well. No introductions were needed. They had worked together often on issues that came through the Agriculture Committee. The conversation was personal and it was brief. Talmadge told him that it was personally important to him that Brown & Williamson locate its plant in Macon.

That was it. End of conversation.

By the next day, Brown & Williamson officials were calling from Kentucky. They wanted to arrange a meeting in Atlanta at the Stadium Hotel, down the block on Capitol Avenue, between Georgia's state capitol and the old Atlanta Stadium.

When the Macon people arrived that day the hotel conference room was almost full. Nearly 150 people were crowded into the meeting hall. There were several representatives of the tobacco company and a number of state officials. Macon was well represented by Jones and a crowd of other political and business leaders. Governor Carter was present and so was Talmadge, Georgia's senior senator.

As the discussions progressed that day, it soon became clear that the Brown & Williamson plant was coming to Macon. There were technicalities still to work out on both sides, but the deal had in effect been struck that morning at Talmadge's farm. The senator had celebrated a birthday. Macon had much more to celebrate.

In an era when cities and states must also compete with other countries around the world, recruiting industries has evolved into an intricate cut throat effort. Professional consultants are employed, armed with big screen TVs, elaborate video productions and the ever-present Power Point presentations. Everything is slick. Everything is rehearsed. A city might be selling a product instead of itself. Inducements often include under the table deals, waivers on taxes, and other expensive and unethical methods. With all of those changes in approach, it is interesting to look back at a simpler time when the effort came down to a team of amateurs and old school power politics.

Put simply. Georgia had Talmadge. And all Macon had to do was light his cigar. Closing the deal with the Government Employees Insurance Company (GEICO) proved more personal than political. Officials from GEICO came to Macon to look around. Locals did not know if this trip was serious, a courtesy call or a ploy to drive up the ante on prospective deals with other cities. GEICO was already being recruited heavily by people from Tampa, Florida. Tampa's offer was already on the table.

While representatives of the company were touring Macon, Jones met with a key GEICO official one afternoon hoping to see what the city's prospects were. As they talked, the man began to tell him about how he had a son in college who planned to go to law school. He injected the fact that some of the people in Florida had told him how his son could go to law school there.

Jones listened intently. Already he had sensed that all things being equal, this official wanted the company to move to Macon. Only one thing was blocking that decision and Jones began to think he knew what that was. A lot of business offers and promises were being tossed around, but having his son enrolled in a nearby law school seemed to be the most important issue to the official and his wife.

"When is your son going to be here so we can meet him?"

"He's here with us now," the GEICO official said.

Thinking on his feet, Jones invited the man, his wife and his son to come to his house that evening—so the young man could talk with him and Buck Melton, a graduate of Mercer Law School. Jones said he would have someone drive them out there. That afternoon, Jones hurriedly added others to that evening's guest list. This was going to be an important meeting and he knew it. His guest list would be vital.

Johnny Mitchell remembers Jones's frantic phone call.

"He was talking real fast, telling me how this man's son wanted to go to law school and that we had to do something. I kept baiting him. 'Charlie,' I said, 'what if the boy can't read and write?' He ignored me and said for me to get some folks together and be there at 6 o'clock."

To the surprise of the GEICO executive and his son, there was a house full of guests at Jones's home for the impromptu gathering. The guest list included former Macon Mayor Ed Wilson, the dean of the Walter F. George School of Law at Mercer University, and Mitchell, the university's admissions director and a close ally of Jones. Relaxing in Jones's backyard, they all got to know one another better. It was friendly and low key. There was talking and there was drinking. Jones made sure that the young man had an opportunity to talk with the head of the law school.

After awhile, Jones walked over to where the dean and the prospective student were talking. Jones began to talk about how the young man would need to know where Mercer's law school was, when to register for classes, and what courses he would need to take. It was not if he was coming but when he was coming.

"He's going to do just fine," Wilson promised. "He's going to get the right courses. I'm going to handle him. I'll take care of him."

Right then, Jones knew Macon had herself another new industry. "Forget the contract," Jones says. "It was done." The Walter F. George School of Law had itself a new student too. Mitchell may have teased Jones about the young man's learning skills, but the executive's son eventually finished number one in his Mercer law school class.

Mitchell says you could sell tickets to watch Jones close a deal. "Charlie would tell those folks from GEICO, Brown & Williamson or any other outfit that came to town that if they could find any community better to live in than this one, to call him—collect! 'Then tell me where you are and I will move there with you,' he'd say."

His sales pitches paid off, too. During an amazingly short span of time, Macon secured three world-class industries, outbidding several communities considerably larger than the medium-sized Georgia city. They received some high-powered support—including much-needed assistance from the Georgia governor's office and the United States Senate. However, the real sweat and effort came from civic-minded people such as Charles Jones.

Macon residents who have come in late can not truly understand what the community was like prior to that era and how rapidly the community progressed. They can not fully appreciate what those people accomplished economically and socially in that short period of time. They should appreciate, for the success of those people nearly three decades ago continues to pay dividends on the pay checks of thousands of Macon area workers.

Figures provided by the Macon Economic Development Commission and the Greater Macon Chamber of Commerce underscore that impact. Statistics show that in 2001, GEICO employed 3,700 people, Brown & Williamson employed 3,000, and YKK employed 1,100 people. So in hardly a year, Jones and his team of volunteers helped attract industries that today translate into jobs for nearly 8,000 people in and around Macon and Bibb County. Even now, those companies make up three of the area's top five employers.

Melton says their ability to work as a team made the difference.

> There was a lot of activity in plant location in those days so I don't think we got more than our share, but we did get three pretty good companies. We made it a point to give them what they wanted. There had been a sense that we were not moving ahead in terms of getting new jobs, new industries and a new tax base. We had a good team of people who worked really hard in those days. We went and knocked on a lot of doors to let people know we wanted to grow. We had some really good people who were trying to get things changed and Charlie was right in the middle of that, Melton says.

Action was so furious that sometimes they were stepping over their own feet. Near the end of 1972, a GEICO official sought out Jones with a sincere apology. His company would not be able to make the formal announcement they were locating in Macon in December as planned. The announcement would have to be postponed until January, the insurance man said.

Jones was relieved. He didn't say so, but delaying that event was perfectly all right with him. During December, he would be in Japan for the signing of the contracts with YKK.

It was that kind of year: a hat trick.

16

Takin' Care of (Personal) Business

Three times he had scored for Macon, but Charles Jones was having trouble scoring for himself. He had taken his city to the penthouse and he was in danger of being relegated to the basement. He had been a major part of an effort that brought 8,000 jobs to town and there were times it seemed as if he would need one of those jobs for himself.

While Macon was flourishing and Jones was making his share of positive headlines, his own company was quietly floundering. At a strategic time in the national economy, he had been tending to civic duties, leaving his own interests unattended. The oil crisis was taking a bite out of tourism so his four motels in Macon and Forsyth were lighting the vacancy signs much too often. Construction was also at a standstill because of the energy crunch. Across the board, Jones was in trouble. His personal life was no better. His marriage to his hometown sweetheart was crumbling and he was living alone, away from his four children for the first time.

Compounding his problems, he had entered into what would prove to be a lengthy transaction involving the United States government and British Petroleum Oil Company. At the center of the deal was a massive office building on Eisenhower Parkway. Sinclair Oil had built it in 1969 as a data processing center. Before the building was even finished, Sinclair was bought out by BP. There was no need for the credit center in Macon since BP already had a computer operation up and running in Atlanta. For nearly six years, the vacant building had been a white elephant grazing on Highway 80.

In the beginning, Jones thought the BP deal would be relatively simple and quickly profitable. Before it was finalized, this convoluted arrangement brought Jones in front of an abusive federal judge and threatened to bring him to his knees.

"Through it all," Jones says, "I thought if we could hold out and keep going that we would eventually win. I just didn't know if we would be able to hold out and keep going."

In early 1974, a prospective tenant was in town talking to Jones about office space the developer had available. The two men had done business several times before and so the visitor asked Jones a private question. He wanted to know if Jones had heard what federal agency was shopping around for 70,000 square feet of office space. Jones didn't know the answer, but he filed away that question.

That fall, Jones noticed a legal ad in the *Macon Telegraph* that said the federal government wanted to lease 70,000 feet of air-conditioned office space for data processing and other office uses. The site had to be in a city and it had to be available for occupancy no later than the first of May 1975. There was an October 25, 1974 deadline on the request—only six days after Jones was reading the notice. Jones sat tight and a month later a second ad appeared. Now the requirement was for 60,000 square feet and the deadline had been moved back to March. Keeping all of this to himself, Jones again did nothing.

He did not react until he found that a government official was inquiring around town about the availability of local utilities. The federal representative had filed a solicitation of needs with the chamber and a number of local real estate firms. Such solicitations were routinely filed all over the country so once more Jones did nothing. He did not turn up the heat until he noticed the latest specs in the newspaper ad specifically called for a site in Macon, Georgia. Responding to a phone call from Jones, the government representative visited him on November 15—a month before the government's latest deadline.

By then, Jones had thought of a piece of property he thought would be an ideal location for the General Services Administration to locate. The vacant British Petroleum building on Eisenhower Parkway was available and had been for some time.

Jones figured the BP site would fit the government's needs since it had been originally built as a computer center. BP was not interested in a lease, however. They wanted to unload this unused property. The government was not allowed to buy property itself. It had to lease. That meant Jones would have to buy the building and work out a lease with the GSA. He had hardly a month to make those things happen.

Contacting BP officials in Cleveland, Ohio, Jones learned that BP wanted $1.4 million for the vacant building "as is," and $1.2 million for the 110 acres that adjoined the building. Looking down the road, Jones figured he would need that land for future expansion so he considered it a package. BP had set a deadline of 4:30 P.M. on December 6, 1975. It was a deal Jones thought he could swing, but he knew he would need help.

Knowing Melton was adept at putting together complicated deals, he called the attorney and asked him to work with him on the purchase. Jones's interest in the site was news to Melton. He told the developer that he wasn't the only one looking at the BP building.

"My gosh, Ed Wilson (the dean of the Mercer law school) is with me right now and Mercer University has an offer in for the BP building to house its law school," Melton informed Jones.

Jones did not want to enter into a bidding war with the university. They were his friends. He called Mercer President Rufus Harris and told him that while he was also interested in the property he would not do anything to jeopardize their plans for the law school. Mercer administrators quickly discussed the situation and decided the law school could find other locations in town but that a data processing center with $30 million worth of computers would be a valuable addition to the local economy. Jones was told that Mercer was withdrawing its bid.

With Melton as his attorney, Jones put in his own bid at 4:20 P.M.—ten minutes before the appointed deadline. Following his lifelong routine, Jones did not haggle over the price. His bid was exactly what BP was asking. He did include an escape clause that would allow him to be released from the purchase terms if the GSA did not lease the building.

Other offers were on the table, but BP went with Jones. They wanted a buyer that would act with dispatch and dependability. Jones always figured the fact that he didn't dicker with them over their asking price also had something to do with their decision to sell to him.

As soon as the deal developed, Jones knew he would need to resign from the industrial authority so he informed Executive Director William Durrett and Bud Moss of his decision in early December. The authority was enthusiastic about the prospects of a new industry coming to town and offered to help Jones with his financing. He declined, figuring critics would question the propriety of the authority doing business with its former chairman. Local banks had already assured Jones that he would have interim financing until a final mortgage could be arranged.

Discussions with the government went well at first. As expected, the GSA would need to renovate the building and a lease was executed so that work could begin. Then, on the last day of January in 1975, a rival for GSA's affections appeared. It was Huntsville, Alabama. Huntsville maintained the data processing operation ought to go there since they already had unused office space being paid for by the government with a three year and 10 month lease still under contract. With the Alabama bid now on the table, Jones had to refigure and lower his previous bid.

Meanwhile, his option with BP was running out. Jones would have nothing to offer the government without that arrangement. By then, others were interested in the site. Officials at BP called the government and asked who the feds wanted to do business with.

Under the circumstances, the GSA said, there was only one party they should sell the building to: "That Charlie Jones fellow from Macon." That did not make sense to the people at the oil company who may have considered Jones a minor player in a small town.

"Well, he's got this," the government official explained. "He will put on his boots, he will leave his office, and he will go out there to that building and get his hands dirty. He will put a hard hat on his head and he will get that building converted. He won't have to ask anybody else to do it for him. These other people you're talking about will go through an organizational chart and they won't get started until it's past deadline."

Hearing that, officials at BP—desperately wanting to move the unused site—cooperated with Jones by lowering their sales price so the Macon developer could compete with Huntsville.

Neighbors in Macon and the state also rallied around Jones, considering his plight a code red on the industrial front. He had the support of the Greater Macon Chamber of Commerce, Forward Macon, the Macon-Bibb County Industrial Authority, Georgia Bank, and First National Bank. Governor George Busbee was in his corner along with a number of state agencies. A unified front was being put together and Busbee even provided a state airplane so Jones and Melton could fly to Washington to seek help from senators Talmadge and Sam Nunn along with Congressman Bill Stuckey. Former Congressman Carl Vinson, still a powerful name in Washington circles, was making calls on their behalf from his home in Milledgeville trying to lure the civil service computer center to the area.

By April 1975, more than a year since he had entered into the deal, Jones signed a lease with the federal government for the BP building. It was a $3.75 million deal, good for Macon and good for Jones. At that time, it was considered to be the largest individual real estate transaction in Bibb County history. Jones himself was due to reap more than $5 million in fees over a 15-year period.

Only it wasn't over yet. With backing from a cadre of Alabama officials, Huntsville Associates—a limited partnership that wanted to lease the building it owned in the Alabama city to the government—filed a lawsuit in federal court. Their suit against GSA Administrator Arthur Sampson claimed that GSA specifications had put them at "an unfair competitive advantage." Jones, it appeared, would not be banking any of those prospective fees very soon.

In the beginning, Jones felt confident. As a businessman, he understood that, as in sports, there were winners and losers in any real estate deal. Only Huntsville wanted to change the rules after the game was over.

"We knew and they knew that between Macon and Huntsville, one would win and one would lose and before the decision was made, we were willing to abide by the results of the decision. Now we think it is a little unfair on the part of our neighbors and friends in Alabama to cry foul after the fact, when they agreed to the rules of the game before the decision," Jones said at the time.

Jones was not concerned about going to court. "I have a lease and I am moving to meet the terms of my contract," he said. "I will meet my obligations and I expect the government people to meet their obligations."

The arrangement would not be so simple. The case was assigned to a federal jurist in North Alabama. With Melton handling the case, Jones assumed that all of these exchanges would be a formality, that the issue would be ironed out without any major slowdowns. For the city of Macon, 300 jobs were on the line. For Jones, he was gambling his sizable investment and his reputation. Ahead were numerous trips to Ohio to meet with BP officials and many trips to Washington to meet with political leaders and government bureaucrats.

It came down to Georgia versus Alabama. An optimistic Jones was either naïve or stupid. "The government itself tends to be fair, generally speaking, in the way it executes the law so I had to think if we could hold out that we would eventually win. Holding out was the problem. I didn't know how long I could be stretched. It was an expensive proposition—financially and emotionally. Buck, he was tenacious. Every time we'd get two feet back, he'd try to go two feet forward if we could," Jones recalls.

Jones was depending on the law. What he could not predict was the belligerent attitude of that federal judge in Alabama who was going to hear the case. To Jones and Melton, the judge sounded more like a chamber of commerce flak for the city of Huntsville than he did an impartial jurist in a somber black robe. Melton was assuring Jones that this judge had no jurisdiction over him since Jones was a resident of Georgia. Federal marshals had shown up in Macon with legal papers to serve on Jones but Melton had kept them at bay as long as he could.

Jones was grabbing a much-needed weekend of rest on the Georgia coast when Melton called and said they had a court date in Birmingham and he had better hurry back to Macon.

"You told me I didn't have to fool with that," Jones said.

"I know," Melton said. "But we have to go. It's an order and he is a federal judge."

Arriving in Birmingham the night before their court appearance, they checked into a hotel. When Jones arrived at the federal courthouse the next morning, he walked into a legal ambush. He was immediately served with three boxes of legal documents. Melton told his explosive friend to sit there and keep his mouth shut, that he would do the talking.

"I sat there staring at the judge," Jones says. "I couldn't say anything out loud so I said it all with my eyes. You know you're wrong. You know you don't know me and you know what you're trying to do is wrong, even though you are a high-and-mighty judge. Those were the vibes I was sending."

Meanwhile, that high-and-mighty judge was plastering Melton at every turn. The judge was swatting away Melton's motions as if they were South Georgia gnats. Things were not going well. To the Georgians, that morning session seemed to last for days. Finally, the judge recessed for lunch.

Melton wasn't hungry. He was livid. They had less than two hours for him to prepare, but Melton knew what he had to do. He explained to Jones what his strategy was and how risky it would be.

"I've never done this before, Charlie. But it's the only thing we can do," the veteran lawyer said, spelling out in laymen's terms what he intended to do when they got back to court that afternoon. By hand, Melton began furiously scribbling on a legal pad. When he was finished writing, he found a courthouse clerk that would type it for them. The document was written, typed and signed by both Melton and Jones just in time for the afternoon gavel.

Melton rose and addressed the court. His voice was clear. "Your honor, I have never done this in the practice of law before, but I have a statement here that has been signed by my client and by me as his attorney. In essence, I am asking that you recuse yourself as the judge in this case."

The terminology was new to Jones, who at that moment could not fully grasp the implications of such a request. A federal judge is all-powerful in his courtroom and for a lawyer—an out of town lawyer at that—to make such a statement was a legal risk for both lawyer and client. Melton was not only questioning the judge, he was challenging him, alleging that he had interests in that case that went beyond the written law. If Melton were successful, the case would be relocated to another courtroom and another judge. If he failed, Jones would be back in front of this same judge under circumstances no lawyer would welcome.

The judge listened, then calmly said he would take Melton's request under advisement. When court recessed for the day, the two Georgians started back to Macon not knowing what was ahead. "I was nervous, but I was very proud of Buck," Jones says. "He was a fighter."

Neither of them knew what to expect or when to expect it. But only a couple of days passed before Melton called. He asked Jones if he was sitting or standing. "It doesn't matter. Just let me have it," a weary Jones said.

The news was good and bad—with the emphasis on bad. On the positive side, the judge had acknowledged the choice of an Alabama courtroom could be deemed prejudicial. The bad news was that he was agreeing to hear the case himself, somewhere in North Georgia. Lawyer or not, Jones knew this wouldn't work. So did Melton, who said he was asking a higher court for a ruling on his request for the judge to step aside.

An emergency judicial committee was being convened in New Orleans. This group of jurists would make the final call on Melton's motion. Melton went to Atlanta for the first hearing. He told Jones to stay home, that it would be a day filled with non-stop legal procedures. That evening, he called Jones and said for him to be in court in Atlanta the following day. With his family at his side, Jones was in the courtroom at 9 o'clock that morning.

Jones tried to hide his fears from his sons and daughters. His children were young. They didn't need to know the depth of what was at stake, that far more than the BP deal was in question. The future of he and his four kids was also being threatened. Jones tried to temper his despair. He knew that he had done all he could. If he had misinterpreted this arrangement, he had only himself to blame. The legal decisions were out of his hands.

They sat and waited and finally a judge sat down behind the bench. The committee had ruled in favor of Melton's request. The Alabama judge was finally out of the picture. The Georgia court now had jurisdiction and a federal judge from Georgia would hear the case. Jones was relieved. Now the playing field was level.

The court ultimately finally ruled in Jones's favor, paving the way for the GSA to move into the building in Macon. There was little time to celebrate when the decision finally came. Other problems were looming—problems that offered other kinds of threats.

While the legal issues had been languishing in court, the conversion work had begun on the BP building and bills were piling up daily. Jones had been forced to enter into contracts for money he didn't have. His bankers were getting edgy. With the 1976 oil crisis in full bloom and gas prices soaring, Americans were not traveling as much as they had in the past. So, like others on US highways, Jones's motels had been hanging out too many vacancy signs. Interest rates were soaring sky high and his cash flow was drying up. To make matters worse, no one could forecast when his deal with the government would be consummated.

Jones was on a collision course with trouble.

Taking a phone call from a banker one day, Jones thought he was calling about an interest payment that was past due. The banker said they needed to talk but he never mentioned the interest. In the back of his mind, Jones had planned to secure a loan to pay the interest, but the banker had other things on his mind when Jones arrived at the bank with his daughter and an accountant.

"Charlie, can I see you by yourself?" the banker asked.

Jones said it was all right for them to stay but the banker insisted.

"No, Charlie. I'd like to talk to you."

Jones motioned for the others to leave. Then it was just he and the banker, an old friend with whom he had done business for years. Couching his words carefully, the bank officer said he knew Jones's company was going through tough times—and he assured him he was not alone. Now he got to the point of the meeting.

"Charlie, we can't lend you another dime," he said.

"What?" said Jones, who hadn't heard such harsh news in years.

"I can't lend anybody another dime," the banker explained.

Not since Poplar and Broadway had Jones been so close to the edge. Only now he was a somebody—or so people thought. In his heart, Jones felt he knew better, that he was an imposter. It didn't take much for him to revert back to the poor country boy who once had lusted after another boy's bicycle. The town was talking about this penthouse deal he had swung and here he was heading for the basement.

Back at his office, a brooding Jones looked at what he did have, not what he didn't. What he had in hand wasn't much—at least not in dollars and cents. What he had inside was a totally different matter. His confidence began to rebuild itself a brick at a time. The news at the bank sent him reeling, but, money or not, he developed a plan.

The cash value on his life insurance policy was $200,000. Getting an appointment with his GSA contact in Atlanta, Jones went to see him personally. He told the government official that the banks had cut him off and that all he had in hand was the cash value of his life insurance.

"I can't borrow money and I've already spent what I had. That means I can't finish the job. I'm willing to cash in my life insurance, but here is what I'm thinking. If you occupy part of the building, you'll start paying me. So what I need you to do is an 'aggressive occupy.' As soon as I get a section of the building finished, you occupy it. If you can't do that, I will have to stop where it is," Jones said, laying his future on the line.

The government official listened and said he would talk the unusual idea over with his superiors in Washington. He told Jones he would get back to him as soon as possible. Back in Macon, Jones waited on an answer, knowing what was at stake. When the call came, the GSA had agreed to Jones's plan. It would not be long before the government was ready to move into a 35,000 square foot section of the building, leaving more than half of it under construction.

That income, coupled with the shopping centers and the other properties Jones owned saved him. Because of his diversity and that arrangement with the GSA, he was able to pay the electrical contractors, the builders, the roofers and all the others involved with the renovation of the old BP site. Eventually, the GSA moved into the remaining parts of the building on Eisenhower Parkway. Nearly 30 years later, the government remains a dependable tenant in a building now totally surrounded by a busy shopping complex.

In a small town, there are few secrets and while Jones was enduring the financial and legal machinations, gossip was spreading that he and his company were about to go belly up. Jones was too busy to know what was being said around town. He found out when another local businessman showed up at his office and asked him point blank if he was going bankrupt.

Jones never has been sure what the fellow's motives were. But what he said was much too close to the truth. When the visitor was gone, Jones thought about what he had said. He was frightened. Such talk can be deadly for a freewheeling developer. It was as if he was again that new kid who had just moved to Thomaston from Molena. As a teenager, he bought bargain clothes on Pryor Street in Atlanta so he could keep up a good front at school. Thinking about what his visitor had just said, Jones felt he once more needed a way to keep up a good front, to show people he might be down but he was hardly out.

By then, it was late in the day, after what most folks considered normal business hours. Jones was still at the office and he took a chance that Jack Huckabee would be too. Picking up the phone, he called Huckabee, whose family had operated a Cadillac dealership in Macon since 1918. Jones had been buying cars from Huckabee's for a long time. And like Jones, his friend was still in his office.

"Jack, have you got a Cadillac, one of those long four-door models?"

Huckabee said he did, that he had ordered one of those models for a preacher who had changed his mind after the car was delivered. The sticker price on the window was $16,000.

Jones didn't let Huckabee see him flinch.

"I'll take it. I'd like to pick the car up tonight. But look likes I can't get out of here until about 7 o'clock. I know you'll want to be home by then."

He would wait, Huckabee said, and at 7 P.M. Jones walked into his office.

The Caddy was blue and loaded with all the extras. That $16,000 price tag was a hefty one for the 1970s, but the bottom line was not the major issue to Jones. The arrangements were more important than the price.

"I'll tell you what. I can't pay you cash tonight, but here's what I'll do. I will take the car and I will pay you a third in 30 days, a third in 60 days and the balance in 90 days," Jones said.

Huckabee said it was a deal. Only Jones had one more stipulation.

"I want you to do this one thing for me, Jack," Jones added. "If anybody asks you how I bought it, you tell them I came down here and paid you cash on the barrel-head."

For Charles Jones, that big blue Cadillac delivered a clear message whenever he was seen on the streets of Macon: How could a fellow be driving around town in a car like that if he is bankrupt?

This decision was not entirely based on ego. In the development business, it is sometimes more significant to appear successful than it is for you to be successful. A person in that field is selling himself and little else so packaging is important. You have to swagger and you have to sizzle. If the word spreads—and it usually does—that you are in financial trouble, your resources can dry up over night. Knowing these things, Jones was simply repackaging himself. If people heard the word bankruptcy in the same sentence with the name Charles Jones, they would picture him driving that big blue Cadillac and immediately discount the story.

"If you're driving a Ford or Chevrolet down the road and somebody passes you in a Cadillac, you figure it's because they're wealthy and they have the money to buy one and you don't. It doesn't matter if you owe millions of dollars, you must be all right if you can buy a Cadillac and pay cash for it," Jones says.

If he didn't know it before, he knew from that unexpected experience that some folks—even ones you think are friends—will gloat over a person's failures before they celebrate that person's successes. Charles Jones was in the process of completing the largest real estate deal that Bibb County had ever recorded. He had been a focal point in the volunteer group that went around the globe to secure new thousands of new jobs for Macon. Jones should have been on top of the world, but there were a few envious people around town who at some level would have liked to see him fall.

"And by the grace of God, I've never had to face that again."

17

Determination and Tenacity

They had no tent and they worked without a net. Come one. Come all. It's Brother Charles' Traveling Road Show, coming soon to a town near you.

Flying or driving all over the state of Georgia, they took their show on the road. They would feed you, give you something to drink and hand out a few brochures. Then they would spell out why it should be the mission of everyone in that room to help Mercer University get a school of medicine.

Preachers came, most of them of the Baptist persuasion with Mercer University diplomas on the wall of their study. Local pharmacists who had filled their first prescriptions at Mercer also came. There were plenty of attorneys, still practicing the law they had studied at Walter F. George. Other nearby Mercer alumni were usually scattered throughout the crowd. Local physicians were also invited. At the center of it all were the guests of honor: the Georgia legislators that soon were going to be asked to vote in favor of allocating state money to a private institution.

Using the local telephone book as his text, Brother Charles usually delivered the closing message, a rousing come-to-Jesus sermon on Georgia's dire need for family doctors.

There was pressure on Jones to deliver, but no one felt as much pressure as Kirby Godsey, still the new guy on campus at Mercer University. He was the university's new president, having succeeded the legendary Rufus Harris in 1979. Godsey was a rookie trying to prove himself to faculty, staff and alumni.

Not too many years before, Harris had been somewhat lukewarm to proposals of a medical school and in the beginning so was Godsey. His mind now changed by Jones and other supporters, Godsey joined the Mercer entourage on the road all over Georgia, telling the story of a long-shot project few people thought would ever see completion. At most stops, Godsey would lead off the program, making a few house-cleaning remarks, bringing Mercer folks up to date on the current events at the Macon campus.

Someone would share the stark statistics about health care needs in Georgia, telling those assembled about the shortage of family practice doctors in rural counties. Someone would explain the uphill political process and how the university needed their support in convincing Governor George Busbee and Georgia's General Assembly to help fund a medical school that would graduate family doctors to practice medicine in towns where the super highways didn't run.

Then along came Jones. Even before the group had boarded his company airplane or crowded into a car to travel to that night's meeting, he had been doing his homework about that particular community. As soon as they arrived at that night's stop, Jones would study the local telephone directory closely, searching the Yellow Pages for information.

"He would memorize the phone book and tell them what they had and what they didn't have. By the time he got up there, he would know more about that town than the people who lived there," retired Mercer administrator Johnny Mitchell says.

At every stop, Jones's approach was the same.

"You know how many veterinarians you have in this town? You've got five. Know how many druggists? You have three. Know how many lawyers there are? Seven. Know how many family doctors there are practicing medicine here? None. Who's more important, your family pet or your own little child? If I come to Georgia after I die, I want to come back as a dog 'cause we take better of them than we each other."

Jones would make them laugh, make them cry and make them think, telling them about the small towns and out-of-the-way counties in their state that had no medical doctor. He would tell them that the state of Georgia deserved a medical school that graduated Georgians who wanted to treat other Georgians—even ones that lived outside of Interstate 285. He would tell them how the Medical College of Georgia in Augusta and the Emory School of Medicine in Atlanta were just plain ignoring the plight of rural Georgians like them. He would tell them that if Mercer University was not successful in establishing this medical school that these needs might never be filled.

Godsey and friends were personally carrying the message to the people this proposed medical school would serve, tactfully and tactically employing them as unpaid local lobbyists. It was a lonely struggle, however. The Mercer faculty did not wholeheartedly support the proposal and the issue had never come to a vote of the university's trustees. The Macon medical community was skeptical as were its counterparts around the state and the country. Macon hospitals were opposed. The governor had said no as did many other statewide political leaders. The University of Georgia Board of Regents did not want to see a competitor for its medical college in Augusta—particularly not one that might drain state funds. The University Board of Regents was putting up political and academic roadblocks as was Emory University with its statewide influence in the medical community.

A handful of supporters thought otherwise—including Jones.

> If the right people were combined, I believed the medical school would receive the support of the people that would have to fund it. That would happen if we wouldn't

allow ourselves to be sidetracked. I wasn't going to let any studies, any stories in the newspaper or any politicians stop us—not even the governor. Come hell or high water, by God, it was the right thing to do. I wasn't going to sleep until dammit, that school was built, Jones says, still passionate after all these years.

Jones, according to Godsey, was somewhere between pre-occupied and obsessed—personal traits that were needed to get the medical school project off the ground.

"He believed in his heart that the well-being of this community was dependent upon our becoming a major health care center and that a medical college would become an important component," Godsey says.

Medicine had always played a prominent role in Macon's history. In 1849, seventy-five Georgia physicians met in a temperance hall in the city and adopted the first constitution of the Medical Society of the State of Georgia—now known as the Medical Association of Georgia. The state pharmaceutical association was formed in Macon in 1875 and the Mercer University School of Pharmacy opened there in 1903. Through the years, Macon's hospitals had treated patients from throughout Middle Georgia

Jones had first-hand knowledge of the Macon medical community. As chairman of the hospital board, he was involved in improvements of care and facilities at the Medical Center of Central Georgia in the late 1960s and early 1970s. Under the leadership of Damon King, that hospital had continued to prosper, adding many vital health programs. Other full service hospitals joined the Macon landscape along the way making health care a major player in the local economy as well.

Around those hospitals, there was a growing medical traffic jam. Restaurateurs don't enjoy isolation, believing that eating establishments feed off the success of one another. Physicians follow that same rule. Medical specialists usually cluster around major hospitals as do groups of doctors and support personnel.

Small towns did not have that advantage and young doctors coming out of medical school usually flocked to larger communities to start their practices. And with more and more students choosing to enter specialty fields, the number of family practitioners had been diminishing in every community.

That shortage was particularly acute in rural Georgia. "Need was never an issue," says Dr. Waddell Barnes, now a retired physician in Macon. "The state of Georgia desperately needed doctors in small communities. Cities all over South Georgia and Middle Georgia—the ones without physicians—were almost demanding this school."

Dr. Milford Hatcher of Macon chronicled that need in the 1960s when he was president of the Medical Association of Georgia. Visiting counties below the Fall Line, people were begging for help in attracting physicians and proper medical care. Some of these communities were served only by a pharmacist or even a veterinarian. Around that time, Hatcher and a colleague had talked to President Harris, measuring Mercer University's interest in opening a medical school. Harris listened to Hatcher, but at that time the Mercer leader thought such a project would be too expensive for a private institution such as Mercer to undertake or afford.

With more and more constituents complaining, state and national politicians began to explore the health issue. A study group known as "Goals for Georgia" was appointed by the Georgia Legislature to explore the issue. Its membership included Sam Nunn, a future United States Senator who was a member of the Georgia House, and Dr. Beverly Forester of Macon, the chairman of the State Board of Health. That commission also identified the compelling need for competent care in rural areas. However, as late as 1970, 25 percent of Georgia's 159 counties were without a licensed physician.

Jones was neither a politician nor a MD. But he did recognize there was an increasing need for another medical college in the state. It was an idea he had carried around in his head for sometime, one of the goals he had expressed when he was elected president of the Macon chamber. It was also on his mind when he traveled to Milledgeville for a meeting with legendary Congressman Carl Vinson in the early 1970s.

Bert Struby, the publisher of the *Macon Telegraph* & News, was chairman of Mercer's Board of Trustees and Harold Logan was the university's Director of Development. Joining Jones, they made an appointment with Vinson to ask the distinguished Mercer graduate if he would lead an ambitious fund drive for the university.

Meeting with Vinson at his office in the Baldwin County courthouse, they finished the university's business and posed for photographs. The group from Macon was ready to leave when Jones, out of the blue, changed the subject and asked the longtime chairman of the House Armed Service Committee a final question.

"Why doesn't Mercer have a medical school?" asked Jones.

"I don't know," Vinson said. "I've always wondered that myself."

That set Jones to thinking even more. Back in Macon, he thought of Rufus Harris. Jones had become acquainted with the Mercer president through a series of meetings Harris often held with local business leaders. Johnny Mitchell had made sure the two of them met. Those meetings grew into a lifelong friendship between Jones and Harris.

Jones approached Harris with the same question he had asked Vinson. Before coming back to Mercer—he had been dean of the law school in the 1920s—Harris had served as president of Tulane University. He was well aware of the value of its respected medical school. He also knew how costly such a venture would be. He did not want any single program to be a burden on the university's other schools of study. Weighing Jones's question, he finally agreed that Mercer University would be part of the planning for a local medical school.

Vinson was thinking too. In 1972—after President Richard Nixon had signed into law the National Health Care Bill—the longtime Georgia Congressman invited a number of Macon leaders to meet with him in Milledgeville. Vinson had examined the new federal health law. After studying the medical situation around the country, he said Congress had decided the federal government should finance twelve new medical schools located all over the country. One of them, according to the law, was to be built in Georgia.

"You get busy and form this school," Vinson told the group. "I want it at Mercer University in Macon."

Vinson made it sound simple, but it wasn't. Starting medical colleges took time, money and political capital—all in ample quantities. But this was a man who for decades had run the House Armed Services Committee. Generals, admirals and even presidents followed his lead. All the group from Macon could do was say "Yes, sir."

The congressman's conclusions were sound. Vinson recognized that Emory University would not support another medical school in Atlanta. In the past, it had kept Oglethorpe College from such a move. The state university system also would say no. Yet any medical college would require an affiliation with a four-year university that could grant accredited degrees. Mercer and Macon would be an ideal match.

Mercer did join the effort, but Harris was adamant that the university could not finance such a project alone. The chamber planned a campaign to raise $2 million in the community. In 1969, Hatcher had presented a resolution to the Bibb County Medical

Society asking that organization to endorse the establishment of a medical school and a health complex for Macon and Bibb County. Members were caught by surprise but the resolution passed unanimously. Reluctantly, the medical society pledged $200,000 as startup money. Research began on the mechanics of starting such a school although it would be thirteen years before it would open its doors.

Always the issue was financing. So when President Nixon came to Macon to speak at a Mercer Law Day program, local Republicans got an audience with him and secured a promise that federal funds would be set aside for the medical school—a promise Nixon mentioned in his speech that day.

Hopes were high, but that money would never come. Soon after Nixon's return to Washington, the Watergate scandal hit the news so the president had more on his mind than a Middle Georgia medical college. That was first among a series of setbacks that plagued the project. But no one wanted to quit—especially Jones, one of the project's most consistent supporters.

After Nixon left the White House, local supporters went to Washington seeking the federal support that the former President had promised to provide. They were told that before the government would allocate funds there would need to be $5 million in state or local dollars set aside. Governor Jimmy Carter agreed to put aside state money to be used when and if the Mercer medical school was opened.

With Mercer lobbyist Johnny Mitchell doing yeoman duty, the $5 million that Carter had pledged stayed in the budget for several cycles. But when George Busbee was elected governor he wanted to see bricks and mortar, not just promise and potential. Carter had made a commitment but he no longer had a voice in the state budget. Busbee did and money for the proposed medical school wasn't in it.

Dr. Douglas Skelton was serving as commissioner of Georgia's Department of Human Resources when, with little warning, Busbee sliced Mercer's $5 million from the state budget. The late Frank Pinkston, a Macon legislator, accosted Skelton in a capitol hallway.

"Where the hell is the Mercer money?" Pinkston asked.

Skelton tried to stay calm.

"Frank," he said. "The DHR budget is $300 million. I have some control over $295 million of that. The other $5 million is controlled down in the governor's office. Go see him."

Even though his sister, Jane Turton, was a member of the Mercer board of governors and very supportive of the medical school project, the governor had been hearing whispers from opponents of the proposed school. Busbee asked what qualifications graduates of the new school would have. Mercer officials assured him that each student would be required to pass the National Board of Medical Examiners test before he or she could graduate. Busbee still declined to restore the money to the 1981 state budget.

Busbee may have been seriously skeptical of the plan. He could have been testing the will of the Macon leaders, trying to determine if they were serious or if this was an outbreak of civic boosterism that would soon fade away. Then again, it could have been nothing but good old Georgia politics. Whatever Busbee's reasoning, Jones was not deterred.

Growing up in Molena, there had been one physician in the area. He was important to his family and to other folks who lived around Molena and Pike County. He remembered Dr. Grubbs, a country doctor who served folks from Concord to Woodbury. When someone in the Jones family was sick and had to see Doc Grubbs, he was always paid. Not always in money. Sometimes with a chicken or corn or tomatoes.

"And that never slowed him down," Jones says. "His commitment to that community was absolute. I'll never forget how much we appreciated that man."

Years had passed since those days and Jones could not understand why any Georgian should have to drive great distances to see a doctor. Everyone deserved a Doc Grubbs.

A meeting was arranged so that Mercer supporters could meet face-to-face with Busbee, a native of Albany. As the sixteen visitors filed into the governor's office that day, Jones noticed two prominent stacks of papers on the corner of the chief executive's desk. One was a report from the Medical College of Georgia. The other was a similar study conducted by Emory University. Neither supported a medical school for Mercer. Of that, he was certain.

Pleasantries were exchanged then Busbee said he knew why they came.

"I get a phone call and a letter every day from my sister Jane, telling me why I should support this project," Busbee said. He laughed, but the message he sent was serious.

Listening to the way the conversation progressed, Jones sensed that Busbee was not giving an inch. One by one, the visitors made their pitch but the governor still wasn't relenting. When it came Jones's turn to speak, true to form he was blunt.

"You've done a great job as governor without my help but I'm going to offer it anyway. See Governor, I was born in Molena, a town you've never heard of. We had a doctor in that little town that took care of us all. Nowadays, we've got towns in South Georgia where folks are dying for lack of medical care. The doctors we do have can't speak English. My grandmother was a Baptist missionary, Governor. She taught me that a man who forgets who he is and where he's from ain't worth his salt."

If the meeting wasn't over before, it was then.

Jones was growing impatient, but Godsey was moving more deliberately. He had been on campus two years before succeeding

Harris as president so he was well aware of what had been transpiring. Godsey was supportive, but he was not sure what direction was best for the university. As a Baptist-supported university, Mercer had $15 million in endowments at that time and Godsey had been told that it would require at least $100 million in endowments to start a medical school.

Seeking advice, he called Skelton, a Mercer alumnus who had served as DHR commissioner in Jimmy Carter's administration as governor. By that time, Skelton had left public service and was the vice chair of psychiatry and vice president for government relations at Emory University.

Skelton reported his findings to Godsey. "I looked it over and said from my perspective I wouldn't go forward with a medical school. It was a huge undertaking financially. I was not the only person to advise him that way. Several others did, too, for a host of reasons," says Skelton, now a senior vice president at Mercer.

Feeling the power and energy that was building throughout the community, Godsey bravely proceeded with the plans for a medical school—even without Busbee's support. While many so-called experts were saying no, the common people were saying yes.

In 1976, Mayor Buck Melton called for a referendum that asked voters to consider a $7 million bond issue to build and equip the school. Warren Berry, the president of C&S Bank in Macon, was charged with convincing voters at a time when local bond issues were failing all over the country. Macon was different. With Melton, Berry and others pushing, voters spoke loudly. An impressive 65 percent of the voters supported the plan. Melton ran the campaign like a political race, slapping bumper stickers on automobiles all over town.

A public campaign to raise money put more than $3 million in the bank. Those funds came from people all over the community, not just the bankers on Cherry Street. Everyone wanted to be a part of it. Included in the donations were very personal gifts—including the $25 pledged by an aging woman who had raised the money selling ice cream cones.

Now, here was Mercer, a private institution with hat in hand, in line asking for state tax dollars. The governor had turned them down, but they bypassed the leadership in Atlanta and took their request to the people. Busbee's sister Jane and her husband drove from Cordele to every one of those meetings to show folks that not everyone in the governor's family agreed with his decision to slice the medical school funds.

With their statewide tour of Georgia's small towns and rural counties, Godsey and friends inspired local folks to call their legislators and urge support for the Mercer project. Legislative leaders were getting calls at home from their druggist, their lawyer, their neighbor, and sometimes their preacher. All were underscoring the need for more family doctors.

From the onset, Senator Hugh Gillis of Soperton was among the strongest political supporter of the school. He attended many of the early planning sessions at Jones's home in Macon, usually strolling through the backyard garden and picking a few tomatoes to take home with him. A fixture in first the House then the Senate, Gillis put the medical college issue in simple, rural terms. "What this state needs," Gillis said, "are more doctors who speak English and more vets that will treat large animals."

At the same time Mercer was making its pitch for a medical school to legislators, so was Morehouse—a nationally known member of the Atlanta University complex. While Mercer was pledged to attract doctors for rural areas, the historically black college planned to graduate more African American physicians.

Georgia's legislative black caucus, led by Representative Calvin Smyre of Columbus, was supporting the Morehouse effort. The two-headed medical school proposal became a major issue in the 1981 General Assembly, spurred by an unlikely coalition of rural and black legislators. As Mercer's lobbyist, Mitchell was relentless, working the ins and outs of the state's budget-writing process to perfection.

Skelton was representing Emory University during that session of the General Assembly and he remembers the legislative hearings on whether there was a need for the two medical schools. Listening to the testimonies and watching the movement evolve, Skelton offered his superiors at Emory some private advice.

"Here's Mercer, a very respected statewide Baptist institution. Here's Morehouse, a widely respected black institution. I told Emory if the Baptists and the black leadership have become allies and have decided they are going to have two medical schools, they have the power to get that done. Back off, I said, you're just going to get hurt," Skelton recalls.

Going around the governor, both the Mercer and Morehouse medical schools gained their state funding by overwhelming votes in the House and Senate. The two schools still receive state dollars—thanks to that political coalition of rural whites and urban blacks. Whether one school would have been successful in securing state money that year without the other is debatable. But it would not have been easy.

After years of false starts, the Mercer University School of Medicine opened in 1982. Jones served as chairman of its first board of governors. When the second class convened in the summer of 1983, he spoke to the men and women who would be the Class of 1987. Jones was only supposed to welcome them, but in doing so, he shared the miraculous history of the school they were about to enter—an experience that would change their lives and touch the lives of rural Georgians.

"And that is what we are all about," Jones told the new class. "The mission of this school of medicine is to educate primary care physicians for service in rural and medically under-served areas of Georgia. We are not a medical school that will train physicians to cure all ills for all of mankind. We have a special charge from the citizens of this great state of Georgia to take care of the health needs of our own people."

Remembering the setbacks and failures, Jones told them that the medical school did not just miraculously appear on that site, that thousands of people willed it into existence against impossible odds.

Jones said in his remarks that day:

> It was the people of the city of Macon and Bibb County who provided us with this magnificent building and the pleasant furnishings we enjoy today. It was the people of small towns in Central Georgia who rallied to our cause and sent their free will contributions to help establish this school. We owe the people of rural Georgia not only a debt of gratitude, but we must now show them ways to stay well and avoid illness until the doctor arrives. And that means each of you.

More than two decades later, the Mercer University School of Medicine continues to fulfill its basic goal of graduating primary care physicians for the state of Georgia. It consistently ranks at the top of United States medical schools in percentage of graduates choosing that field of medicine.

"We have stuck to our guns," Godsey says. "We had a mission and we've been faithful to it. We have fulfilled the promises about the school of medicine that we made the people in Georgia when we traveled around the state back then. Promise made. Promise kept."

The success of the medical school also has helped Mercer increase in stature as a university. In the academic community, in the state and in the region, it is perceived as a major competitor in higher education. Godsey says Jones should share in that success.

He was the first non-alumnus and non-Baptist to join Mercer's Board of Trustees.

"I think Charlie, before his time, saw that the well-being as well as the economic and political strength of this community would be increased by a strong university. He not only thought that, he acted upon that concept. He adopted Mercer because he saw how intertwined the success of the community and the success of the university were," Godsey says.

The excitement created by the medical school opening in 1982 was shared by people all over Bibb County. Though few noted this at the time, it helped bridge gaps between the community and Mercer—wounds that had opened wide in 1963. It was that year that the university admitted its first black students. With little prodding, Mercer became the first private university in Georgia to accept minorities, a decision that led to the resignation of several angry board members. During the confrontational Vietnam era, Jane Fonda—a lightning rod of the anti-war movement still called "Hanoi Jane" by her detractors—spoke on campus in Macon. Her speaking engagement inspired hordes of sign-bearing protesters.

In a conservative town, Mercer University came to be perceived as a haven for liberal thinking. Though only minutes from the heart of Macon, the campus had become isolated from the community's day to day life.

That perception began to erode with the decisive referendum for the medical school bond issue. That vote could not have carried with only the support of Mercer people or the business community. That victory belonged to the voters all over town who had displayed pro-medical school bumper stickers on the backs of their cars and followed that up at the polls.

The medical school movement was spurred by a new president and a non-graduate who in some circles was still considered a new guy in town. Godsey says he was too naïve to know it could not be done and Jones was not about to tell him.

"I believed it could be done so we went out and sold it. It was a dream that people bought into and it is one that fortunately has been successful in its implementation," Godsey says.

Three years after Mercer's medical school opened its doors, Skelton came home to his alma mater as dean of the school. In its infancy, the school had struggled with constantly changing leadership and in 1985 Skelton became its sixth dean. With Jones chairing the school's initial board of governors they became an interesting team—Jones with his fire-from-the-hip style and Skelton with his methodical bedside manner.

> What you might call the academic tendency to ponder, Charlie has a problem with. He's quick to decide. We had a lot of debates during those first six months, discussing the mission and arriving at our own definition of primary care medicine. It was a learning experience for both of us. But I've always found Charles Jones to be totally committed to the goals of this school. You don't have to wonder. He tells you what he's thinking, what he likes and what he doesn't like. He respects you if you tell him you think differently and why you think that way. He is a tough guy with a big heart, Skelton says.

Mercer's medical school continues to grow and prosper and Jones continues to offer quiet personal support. In 1986, as its first group of physicians graduated, the room where the board of governors convened was officially named "The Charles H. Jones Board Room" in his honor.

Skelton says Jones's relentless spirit made a difference.

> He likes people who seek forgiveness rather than permission. If you think you need to do it, then do it. Frankly, they could have never built a medical school at

> Mercer without that kind of attitude. If they had waited on approval for their plans. If they had waited on total satisfaction from leaders at all levels. If they had waited for everyone to pull the lever that said yes, it never would have gotten off the ground. And thanks to them, men and women from all over this state are becoming doctors.

The medical school was also a way for Jones to honor an old friend. In 1984, he donated to Mercer Stone Creek Lodge and 350 acres of prime land worth $1.75 million. That bequest became part of the Marion S. Whitehead Memorial Scholarship Fund, named for the late dentist who was Jones's first business partner in Macon.

Other mentors weren't forgotten either.

In 1997, Jones wanted to endow a scholarship for deserving students at the medical college. Until then, most of his financial donations to Mercer—at his request—had been given anonymously. This one would be different. Thinking back on his education, he remembered that schoolhouse in backwoods Thunder and the teacher who first told him he could learn.

As a *Macon Telegraph* reporter wrote: "In a one-room wooden schoolhouse in a town called Thunder, the joy of learning struck Charles H. Jones like lightning. More than sixty years later, he paid tribute to the teacher who threw the lightning bolts."

Jones's tribute was a $100,000 scholarship to the Mercer University School of Medicine in the name of Doris Lawrence. A smiling Mrs. Lawrence was there at Macon's Woodruff House that afternoon in May of 1997.

"I'm so grateful that you are doing this in my honor and not in my memory," said Lawrence, who later retired as postmistress of Molena. She remembered Jones, too, showing off aging black and white photographs of him, his classmates and his sister Betty Jones Dawkins, another of her former students.

"She made every student feel important," Dawkins said after the ceremony. "There was no way any of her students wanted to play hooky. I doubt any were even tardy."

"She awakened in me the reward of learning," Jones added.

Dean Anne Hathaway of Mercer's School of Education, the speaker at the luncheon paying homage to Lawrence, talked about the influence of a teacher. "A teacher affects eternity; he or she can never tell where their influence stops."

Lawrence influenced Jones and because of his efforts, medical students are reaping similar rewards. Unlike other institutions that started with like goals, Mercer has continued to graduate primary care physicians—all of them Georgians pledged to serve Georgia's smaller communities—communities that continue to need qualified practitioners.

Jones is not one who just writes a check and forgets it. One of the stipulations of the Doris Lawrence Scholarship was that Jones would always know who its recipient is. Each year, he meets with the school's financial aid representative and goes over the names of the applicants. Jones does not involve himself in the selection process. He just wants to know the recipient's identity so he will be able to track the student's progress.

"This school truly will be serving this community and this state long after we're gone. Its mission is far greater than the sum total of us all," Jones says. "It truly is a life and death proposition."

Scores of people played important roles in the unlikely establishment of the medical school on the Mercer campus. All deserve credit. It took close to fifteen years to open those doors. Jones was part of the movement from the beginning. And those who were close to the struggle know how vital Charles Jones really was.

Years ago, Godsey wrote a letter to Jones spelling out what his friend had meant to the project. The letter was written in 1986, just after Jones—feeling his work done—resigned from the medical college's board of governors. Godsey thought it important to note Jones's steady leadership.

Godsey wrote:

> Your strong hold has kept all of us on track during a tumultuous ride toward accreditation and graduation. Even when we were ready to be disheartened, you would not hear of it in word or spirit. Your determination and tenacity proved the critical difference in assuring that we did not abandon our goal or our purpose…You will mistake reality and disregard the truth if you do not see and accept that you, Charles Jones, have been the most forceful voice and the most steady hand that has steered our course, enabling the school to move from dreams to reality and transforming what many believed to be fiction into fact.

18

Politics, Real Estate, and Family

His leg was lost. Now they were trying to save his life. Dave Thornton was strapped to a hospital bed and wired to machines. Doctors were fussing around him like South Georgia gnats. He could feel them even if he couldn't quite see them. Thinking he was unconscious, they talked openly. Graveyard talk, the kind of conversation that comes from too many days of treating trauma. There was no need or time for reassuring bedside manner. They all agreed that Thornton was not going to make it, that there was no way he could be saved. The bank was dry of his blood type and unless he received a transfusion very soon, he was going to die.

Time meant nothing to Thornton. Events were running together. The day had started off in the woods near Savannah and Chatham County. It was a lark, a getaway. Friends from Macon had invited him on a father-son hunt. They were bounding along on dirt roads when it happened. Thornton was sitting on the back gate of a pickup and he was crushed between the two trucks. The memory of what happened was fading but the pain wasn't.

The clock ticked in slow motion as friends and emergency people got him out of the woods. Medics had finally rushed him to Savannah, to the closest hospital. Doctors who examined him did all they could do. They filled Thornton with pain medicine as if they were doling out candy on Halloween Night. He deserved to be comfortable if nothing else. Without blood, they soon realized they could do nothing for him.

Hovering around him, the doctors and nurses discussed Thornton as if he wasn't there. Listening, Thornton realized they had surrendered. But he hadn't given up. He felt alone, more alone than he had ever felt before. In the real estate business, you're a loner. It's you and the deal. Little else matters. He was accustomed to dealing with big obstacles and high risks. That was what he did. This time, the obstacle was blood. The risk was bigger than some land deal, too. It was his life. He was strapped to a hospital bed but in his stupor he realized survival was in his own hands. He had to do something. He had to fight.

Blood could close the deal. Blood could save him. His mind was racing. If there was a shortage of his blood type in Savannah, then get some from another blood bank in another town, he thought. What about Macon? Who did he know who would have access to blood? Mentally, he moved through his Rolodex, name by name. He stopped at one name. He knew someone who could save him.

That person was Charles Jones.

The name was right there on the tip of his tongue, but what could he do about it? Thornton was somewhere between here and there. He couldn't move and he couldn't speak. He had a plan but to make it work he would have to communicate with someone. He had to move a finger or blink an eye. Anything to let them know he was there, that he could help if only they would listen. It took minutes and it took effort but somehow, finally, Thornton was able to make a finger quiver. It was will he didn't know he had. Again, he made it move. When was someone going to notice?

At last, someone did.

A woman he knew in Savannah was in the emergency room with him. She moved closer, bending down to hear. He whispered weakly, telling her what to do. Haltingly, he gave her names. Three men Thornton knew back home in Macon had airplanes: Kenneth Dunwoody Jr., Cubbage Snow, and George Peake. They could fly some blood to Savannah. Charles Jones, he was the person who could get the blood.

Jones was working at his office when the phone call came. It was nearly noon on a Saturday. The woman told him Thornton needed blood. If he didn't have a transfusion by 8 o'clock that night, he was going to die.

Jones didn't say so on the phone, but he really didn't know what he could do. He was chairman of the hospital authority, sure. But chairmen deal with budgets, roofs and linen—not with blood. Such things were in the medical domain, ruled by empirical MDs who act as if doctor is a regal title. Besides, it was a weekend. Who was he going to find at home on a Saturday and with such a short deadline?

Figuring he would line up the plane first, he called the three men Thornton had suggested. None of them were at home. Along the way, someone told him about an emergency plan the Georgia State Patrol sometimes used. It was a relay system that somebody called a Blood Run.

Calling the State Patrol office south of Macon in Perry, Jones explained the desperate situation. They told him such a plan was only used when it was authorized.

"I'm the chairman of the Macon hospital authority," he said without blinking. "I will make this an official request."

Satisfied, the officer said they would stand-by.

Time was getting shorter every time the clock ticked. Now Jones had to secure the blood. He ran down a list of officials on the medical staff and finally located the hospital pathologist who told him that like Savannah their blood bank also had a dire shortage of blood—particularly Thornton's type.

"But this man is going to die," Jones said, pleading.

Finally, to humor Jones if nothing else, the physician said he would go to the hospital and check the inventory on Thornton's blood type. Thirty minutes later, he called Jones. The news was not good.

"Mr. Jones, we do have two pints of blood here but I would hate to turn that loose. We need to have it here in case we need it for a local patient," the physician explained, following hospital procedure.

"Doctor, Dave Thornton is from Macon. He's a citizen, just like anybody else. We have to risk it. If he doesn't get that blood by 8 o'clock tonight, he's going to die."

"If you tell me to release it, I'll release it."

Overstepping his authority, Jones said to release it.

It was close to 6 P.M., by the time Jones called back the state patrol. The officer on duty said he would take it from there. Minutes later, a city police officer picked up the two pints of blood at the hospital in Macon and the race was on. At the Macon city limits sign, a Bibb County sheriff's deputy took the package, handing it off to a state patrol agent at the county line on Interstate 16. That scene would be repeated up and down I-16 as the precious cargo was passed from trooper to trooper.

Even after the blood was in the hands of the state troopers, Jones could not relax. More than six hours had passed. Six vital hours. He felt exhausted. Then he thought about Thornton, wondering how he must be feeling. He called Savannah and told them the cargo was on its way. No one has ever asked how fast those Georgia lawmen drove. But they made it, and so did Dave Thornton.

Thirty years later, sitting in a restaurant on Riverside Drive, Dave Thornton slowly re-tells the story of that day. The horror still gets to him. Several times tears interrupt his story. He is over 80, and he is still in the real estate business, still making deals.

"Twenty operations later, I'm still here," he says

The bond and the respect between Thornton and Jones is unusual. They are not close buddies. They still compete for land

and deals as they always have. They often see each other around town but nothing planned. Both of them remember this story. They just choose to keep it to themselves.

"Charlie bluffed his way through the whole thing, you know. He had no authority to get blood. Only a doctor could do that. He had no authority to set up that relay system with the state patrol. But he did. Well, I ended up losing a leg but I'm still here and doing well. I'm thankful too. I'm convinced if he hadn't sent that blood I wouldn't be here. I'm eternally indebted to him. I remind him of that, which pleases him very much. "

As Thornton leaves the restaurant, you notice the limp and the smile. There is shared respect between them. Jones remembers seeing Thornton working out in a Macon health club, noticing how hard he was working to rebuild his body. "And I have never heard him complain about his pain or suffering," Jones says.

Sharing such stories does not come easy for Charles Jones. Right in the middle of a poignant chapter of his life, he will crack a self-deprecating joke. This is part of his personal makeup and part of his generation's way of coping. For him, it is important to mask a feeling and to deflect the subject to something more comfortable.

Not that he doesn't feel. He feels deeply. But feelings are best kept private and personal. He's flamboyant and outrageous but that doesn't mean he doesn't hurt. He's competitive and combative but he is also caring and generous—to those he knows and to those he doesn't. He thrives on giving, but accepting doesn't come easy for him.

All of these things are Charles Jones.

Around Bibb County, he is a legend in some circles. Mention his name and folks usually have a story to tell. Most of the tales people tell about him involve business. Not everybody likes him but there's usually respect.

Old-timers remember the Ambassador. Others remember his successes with the chamber of commerce. More recently there is his involvement in downtown revitalization. There also are many stories told about his aggressive style and the unexpected things he says. Few people are allowed to see the other sides of him—and that's the way he likes it.

His devotion to his pioneer granny is heard when he repeats things she told him when he was a child. Affection he feels for his teachers has turned into generous donations. Feelings he has for his siblings has inspired quiet support. His friendship with Dr. Rufus Harris evolved into a lifelong commitment to Mercer—a school he never attended. In his adopted hometown, he has been a part of many of the good things that have happened for the past half-century. His connection to the Creeks continues with an annual pilgrimage to Chief Cox's Methodist Church in Oklahoma. His love of his grandchildren is shown in the tomatoes and cucumbers they grow together in back of his house.

More than any thing are the simple gestures.

A token of one hangs on the wall at his sister's home not far from the town square in Thomaston. More than twenty-five years have passed, but Betty Dawkins—Jones always calls her Betty Jean—still hurts. A mother never really heals from the loss of a son. This framed letter helped her cope with her son's illness and his death. It showed her the love of a brother and the genuine thoughtfulness of a fellow who used to live on Pennsylvania Avenue.

Jimmy Dawkins was a teenager when he was diagnosed with leukemia. He fought as hard as he could, but his parents were distressed. James Dawkins, his father, was a strapping ex-football star. He thought he could handle anything. But handling his son's illness wasn't easy for him either.

Uncle Charles knew what was going on. Jimmy Dawkins was on his mind when he packed for Washington DC. for a special visit with President Jimmy Carter. Jones had campaigned with the Peanut Brigade, a band of Georgia neighbors who went to cold, faraway states, knocked on doors and told folks about their friend, Jimmy Carter. Those Georgians were special to Carter, who invited them to the nation's capital for a celebration in 1977. The visit was culminated by a barbecue on the back lawn of the White House. There was food and fellowship, even performers from a Broadway production called "Your Arm's Too Short to Box with God."

Jones was walking the White House grounds that night when he saw Carter coming in his direction. At his side were the ever-present aides and Secret Service agents, but he was among friends so the president moved out ahead of them. Recognizing Jones, he smiled and stuck out his hand.

"How are things in Macon?" he asked.

"Just fine, Mr. President. And we're sure glad you're here."

The two Georgians chatted for a few minutes. But knowing there were scores of friends he needed to see, Carter excused himself. Before doing so, he said what people often say, telling Jones that if there was anything he could do for him, just call.

This time, Jones stopped him.

"Mr. President, there is something I'd like you to do for me and it's important. I have a nephew in Thomaston, Georgia. His name is Jimmy Dawkins. He's eighteen-years-old and he has leukemia. He's gonna graduate from high school in a few months. If you would have one of your aides or secretaries drop him a note from your office I'd sure appreciate it."

Jones had already written Jimmy's name and address on the back of a business card. He reached in his pocket and got the card, handing it to the President.

Carter said he would write the young man. The aide who usually took care of such matters was not close by so Carter stuck the business card in his pocket and walked away.

When Jones returned to Georgia in a few days, his sister Betty called. She was all excited. "Jimmy's elated," she said. "He got a letter in the mail today from President Carter."

Jones stopped her at mid-story.

"That's nice, Betty Jean. Now don't tell Jimmy this, I'm just telling you so you'll know. But presidents don't write letters. He probably has a staff of maybe fifteen assistants and secretaries that do nothing but type those kind of letters. He doesn't have time to do that."

Now it was she doing the interrupting. "You don't understand, Charles. It's a hand-written letter."

Both of them still marvel at the kindness of a man busy with world affairs who would take the time to personally write a sick young man he had never met. It was especially important to Jimmy Dawkins, who in a few months succumbed to the leukemia he had been struggling against for so long. That's why Jimmy Carter's letter still hangs in the Dawkins home.

There is more to this story but it is not a chapter Charles Jones tells. Betty Dawkins does. It explores that generous side that Jones ordinarily keeps to himself.

Jimmy Dawkins was in the hospital when his uncle came to Thomaston to visit. Jimmy talked about his future that day, how he wanted to graduate from high school at Robert E. Lee and how he dreamed of having a car of his own. Jones said nothing while he was there, he just listened. But in a few days James and Betty got a letter from him. A check for $3,000 was enclosed.

She still remembers the letter. "He told us to open a bank account with that money. He knew we were strapped, that everything was going to Jimmy's doctor bills. He was our only child, we had to do what we could. In the letter, Charles said he didn't want this money to go for hospitals, or doctors or medicine. Name this account 'Circle the Wagons,' because we are circling the wagons. We are going to get Jimmy that car."

The boy got his car as a graduation gift, Jones says, though he claims not to remember being involved. Betty and Jim do. It was an act they will never forget.

Jones hasn't escaped his own heartaches either. "Bumps," he prefers to call them. His business life has been charmed, but his personal life has had the usual setbacks. His 1973 divorce from Emily was a disappointment because people in his family had never gotten divorced. More importantly it distanced him from his four children. In later years, there also would be painful moments when he was emotionally estranged from his children. He has not been immune from hurt.

On a less human level, there was Christmas of 1974 when he received a frantic phone call telling him his house was on fire. He wasn't living there then, but his boys, Jeff and Dwight, were. The children, he was told, were safe but the beautiful house wasn't.

This charming house was special to him. It had been built in Monroe County in 1821, years before Bibb County was even created. It had been built in a part of Monroe County that later became part of Bibb County. He was proud of the house and of its past. When he bought it in 1964, it was a two-story symbol that his life was looking up. His family was ready to leave for Florida to see his parents when he looked at the house and the fifty-four and a half acres that went with it. He explained that he was in a hurry and the aging owner accepted a dollar bill as ernest money. For Jones, this place held chapters of happy memories.

When Jones arrived at the front gate, flames were grabbing the sky and eight-year-old Dwight was standing in the yard crying. The scared little boy was pointing to where a front window had been. Behind that window had been the family Christmas tree—the tree he and his Daddy had rescued from the woods the day before. Under the brightly decorated tree were the family's Christmas presents.

A *Macon Telegraph* photographer on the scene snapped a poignant photo of Dwight, Jones's youngest child. The picture was on the front page of the next morning's newspaper. Other newspapers picked up the photo. That scene put the season into perspective.

Closer to home, that fire symbolized a tragic political situation that went beyond Dwight's Christmas tree and the beautifully wrapped presents that had been lost. Folks outside the city limits looked at that scene and realized it could have been their eight-year-old in tears, their home ablaze.

Jones's house was in Bibb County, only blocks away from the city limits of Macon. Firefighters from the Macon Fire Department arrived that morning, sirens squalling. They wheeled into the circular driveway and readied their equipment. They were ready to fight a fire. But before they did that they asked if anyone was still in the burning house. Told that everyone was safe, one of the firemen radioed to the station.

Orders were given to pack up their gear and return to the station. This house was in the county, outside of their jurisdiction. The firefighters were ready to do their duty. Their hoses were unfolded and they were poised on the ground. As they pulled away from the burning house that morning, several of the firemen had tears in their eyes. Since the thousands of people who lived in Bibb County had no fire service, the house was lost, along with a family's memories.

As the house burned, friends had tried to intervene. A neighbor of Jones called Buck Melton, at the time an attorney for the Macon development authority. Melton called the fire chief who was a friend of his, but the official never would take his call.

"That's how much influence I had," Melton laughs.

In a few years, when Melton was elected mayor of Macon, fire service for the county became a major campaign issue. While he was in office, city service was extended to people like Jones. Fire plugs were to be installed in the county. One now sits across the road from Jones's restored white house.

"I had to pay $650 for that fire plug," Jones says. "Not everybody in the neighborhood wanted to participate so I paid the money myself. As far as I was concerned, I had already paid dearly for it."

More than three decades later, during another Christmas season, city and county officials were again discussing consolidation of services. Once more, there were few minds willing to meet. A creative reporter from the *Telegraph* called Jones and asked him to retell that story, probably hoping it would prod stubborn officials into working together.

The story of the fire is one that still makes Jones sad and still makes him mad. Later, he picked up the pieces and built another house on that property. It is a twin to the old one. Only the original chimney survives.

When he was making plans to rebuild, Jones fulfilled a promise he had made when he was pinching pennies to afford the house and the property a decade before. As he promised the former owner, beautiful white columns were finally added. After his divorce from Emily was final, he moved back into that comfortable house. Dwight grew up on these grounds. Jones has never moved again. This is home.

Through incidents such as the fire, Jones came in contact with politics and the people who played that game. Most of his life, he had been fascinated by that process. He remembered his father getting signatures on petitions that forced school officials to send buses to pick up his children out in the country. He remembered hanging around the General Assembly when he paged for Jimmy and Preston Bentley's father. He worked for the governor himself after he graduated from Georgia. He had seen up close the wheeling and dealing of recruiting new industry, remembering vividly the influence of a United States Senator's phone call.

So why not run for office, he asked himself. It seemed a natural thing to do. He had sold everything from Valentine's candy to Oldsmobiles in his store at Poplar and Broadway. He had closed million dollar land deals. He had sold the Japanese on Macon and he had sold the Indians on coming home. Running for office would be little more than an extension of those things. All he would have to do was sell himself.

Only voters had other ideas. Twice.

His first attempt at public office came in 1970 when he was a candidate for the Georgia State Senate. District 26 then included half of Bibb County and all of Jones County. Jones ran as a Republican, opposed by Democrat Bert Hamilton. Jones narrowly carried Bibb but lost in Jones County by a 2-to-1 margin. The district gave it to Hamilton 8,129 votes to 7,340 for Jones.

Twelve years later, with newly drawn senate districts, Jones tried again. Veteran Lee Robinson—later the mayor of Macon—was giving up the senate seat so there would be no incumbent in the race.

In the summer of 1982, Jones announced he would be a candidate for Senate District 27, and it seemed tailor-made. The district's new boundaries included Lamar, Monroe, Crawford and Upson counties along with a section of Bibb County. To Jones, the voters would be home folks, for he had lived in that part of Georgia all of his life. This time he ran as a Democrat, explaining that in 1970 "the population was of that nature." Now he was returning to his Democratic heritage.

"I thought running again would be an interesting thing to do," Jones says. "Being a senator wasn't an all year thing. It wouldn't be like holding office for twelve months a year. I thought that would be a way for me to serve the people in a more significant way than I had been serving them. I thought it was the thing to do."

So did his friends. Encouragement came from every direction—from Macon and from the other counties. A delegation from Thomaston came down to a planning session at Johnny Mitchell's house in Macon to urge Jones to run.

When he announced he was a candidate, Jones did it first at the State Farmer's Market in Macon then again in front of the courthouse in Thomaston—the same building in which he found out he wasn't named for Charles Lindbergh.

"My roots are in this part of Georgia," Jones proclaimed.

Without an incumbent in the race, the campaign was a free-for-all. Jones was opposed by Billy Harris, a former chairman of the Monroe County Commission, and Jimmy Matthews, the mayor of Barnesville. With three candidates in the race, it was a busy summer—speaking to civic groups, sticking signs in the ground and smiling at everyone you met.

Though he appears confident at what he does for a living, being out front as a political candidate did not come so naturally for Jones. Still, in the August 10 primary, Jones led the field of three, out polling Harris by 440 votes. Matthews trailed the other two but his votes would prove important in the runoff. So would the votes in Bibb County where both Harris and Jones deduced the runoff would be won.

Along the way Macon newspaper columnist Bill Boyd wrote a piece about Harris. After it appeared in the *Telegraph*, he got a call from Johnny Mitchell who asked Boyd to come by and visit Jones at his home.

Boyd did just that, joining Jones in chairs next to his swimming pool. Boyd sat between Jones and the pool. Jones soon mentioned the effusive column Boyd had written about his opponent.

"When you gonna write something nice about me?" asked Jones.

Boyd said he didn't usually write columns about politics so he didn't think he would be writing anything about Jones. Boyd, however, did later write a very negative column about Jones.

Matthews was not personally involved in the runoff election that followed but that did not keep the Barnesville mayor from chiming in his opinions when reporters were around. In endorsing Harris, he said the Culloden farmer was "one of the finest people I have met in my life." Jones, he labeled "flamboyant" and a "big shot."

Though Harris and Jones were debating many pertinent issues in the campaign, one matter overshadowed the others. Instead of talking only about city-county consolidation for Bibb, roads, sewage problems, taxes or proper medical care, they spent a lot of time discussing how much money Charles Jones had spent on the senate campaign, how much land he owned and how many dollars he had in the bank.

There was little doubt that the Macon developer spent more money than either Harris or Matthews in the primary. Jones shelled out nearly $30,000 while the other two spent a combined $13,000.

Harris started talking about Jones trying to buy the post and lamented that it was getting hard for an "average person" to run for office. Matthews joined the discussion by saying election day was becoming auction day. A week before the final vote, state expenditure reports showed that Jones had spent five times more than his opponent on the race.

"I should have spent more," Jones now laughs.

In the primary, Jones had attracted 3,626 votes in Bibb County compared to Harris's 2,389 and Matthews's 1,464. Harris was confident that in the general election he would do well in Bibb, figuring the Matthews' voters had already had a chance to vote for Jones and didn't.

Jones was also confident. His campaign hinted that Harris wouldn't be good for Bibb County, that he represented the rural cause. "People have realized their self-interest is at stake," Jones said in a newspaper interview the week before the election.

Looking back, Jones believes the race was effectively won by a newspaper ad Harris ran in the final days of the campaign. In that advertisement in the Telegraph & News, Harris said Jones was personally worth $4 million. That statement planted a seed in the minds of voters in the district that Jones was rich and they weren't. Jones says it was a master strategy on Harris' part.

"Except he understated that figure by several million dollars and my creditors started calling me," Jones says, cracking a joke at the memory. More seriously, he says the tactic was smart.

"In Georgia, having money was not a recommendation in those days. I don't know what it is today. It killed the deal for me. If you're in Massachusetts, you can have a billion dollars and still be a candidate. That's not the case down here. You get no credit for employing several hundred people or paying X-number of dollars in taxes," says Jones.

On the eve of the August 30 election, Jones received the editorial endorsement of the *Telegraph & News*. Four years before, a newspaper survey had ranked Jones as the sixth most powerful person in the city. The editorial writer cited those involvements, noting that Jones had been in the forefront of progress in Bibb County. The newspaper said it was supporting his senate campaign for several reasons:

"One is that he has ties with Crawford, Lamar, Upson and Monroe counties which should stand him in good stead representing them all along with the portion of Bibb in the district. More important, he has a record of proven performance as a businessman and civic leader which attests to his energy and his ability to get things done. He has paid his dues."

Voters did not agree. Harris won the seat with 11,947 votes. Jones trailed with 9,850. A dejected Jones was hurt that he won his home county of Bibb by only 250 votes. He carried his native Upson County 3,403 to 2,263. Harris prevailed in Crawford, Lamar and Monroe by substantial margins.

Harris took a final jab. "It proves hard work and friendship can mean more than all the money in the world can buy. This proves it beyond a shadow of a doubt," Harris said on election night.

With his arms around his tearful twin daughters, Jones conceded after results from Monroe County were posted at his campaign headquarters on Riverside Drive.

"I personally had my wings clipped by the voters of the 27th District tonight," he said. "I want to send them this message: clipped wings can grow again, and mine will. Now, let's have a party."

His wings grew back, but his interest in running for office did not. Several years later, Matthews looked back on Jones as a political candidate. He said the Macon man was a fierce competitor who was driven and tenacious. "He likes a good scrap," Matthews said.

But that competitive nature didn't play well in politics. "He came across too strong. People didn't perceive him as being sincere. What he was saying came across as political (bull) instead of sincerity. I believe he overdid his campaign and spent too much money. People read into it that he was trying to buy the seat," Matthews said.

Jones does not dispute what his one-time opponent said. Analyzing himself, Jones said politicians need a temperament and patience that he does not possess. Voters did him a favor, he believes, because through that political defeat he matured in ways he had not before. When he said he would run, he was doing what others wanted him to do instead of following his own lead. Though he wanted to serve, he never seriously considered what he might do if he was elected.

"I am grateful for the people who voted for me and I am equally grateful for those who did not," he says. "We do learn from our mistakes and that defeat certainly taught me lessons I couldn't have gotten in any other way. More than anything I learned, to my own satisfaction, that you really can do just as much as a volunteer as you can if you hold some kind of office. I think Granny would agree with that too."

A defeated Jones was still a winner in real estate. His business was expanding by the day and so were his holdings. His touch was magic, though he confesses that wasn't always the case, pointing to plots of undeveloped land that bring in nothing but a tax bill. In 1985, his company owned five motels in Bibb County alone, along with properties in Forsyth, Perry, Fernandina Beach, Florida and New Smyrna Beach, Florida. The company soon moved into the food supply business to service their motels and in 1985 alone had three strip malls under construction in Macon. It was a busy time.

His son Jeff, just out of the Navy, joined the company in 1981 followed in the coming years by daughters' Jan and Judy's husbands—Steve Hay and Paul Ward. By 1988, Dwight, his youngest son, would need a job. Charles Jones Enterprises had evolved into a true family business.

"I had to grow it," Jones says. "We needed the jobs."

As a matter of business tactics, Jones decided his name should not be on the marquee. It was an advertisement he didn't need, often giving clues on his future plans. Changing the company name to Riverside Development Inc., he sought to move into the background. The company name was changed a final time in 1982—the same year he ran for office. Latching on to a personal passion and to local lore, the company became Ocmulgee Fields, Inc.

To Jones, it was an obvious decision. "When the Creeks were here, a fifteen mile stretch of land alongside the Ocmulgee River was called Old Ocmulgee Fields. We just dropped the word old. The name was very appropriate. I was dealing in land Indians used to own. It was a very legitimate name," he says.

The company weathered uneven economic times during the late 1980s. During one down period, when they concluded they could not afford another high-priced executive, Jones personally moved into the Holiday Inn on Riverside Drive and served as general manager for four years—running the whole company from that little office in the hotel. "Know what? We made the same profits during that four years of recession that we had the four years before," he proudly notes.

His patience paying off, the land along Riverside Drive and Tom Hill Sr. Boulevard began to flourish. Jones was soon landlord to a national bookstore, a multi-screen theater, and a major supermarket. Other developments were also paying off. Call it luck or call it foresight, but in a short amount of time several roadways in front of Ocmulgee Fields shopping centers were widened, opening up needed access to the stores and his tenants.

Just out of college in 1988, Jones' son Dwight moved into the office next to his father. Watching Dwight maneuvering in this new territory, Charles Jones felt proud. Dwight had lived with his father after the divorce and now Jones was seeing him in action as a grownup. He liked what he saw. By 2000, Charles's son Jeff Jones had left the company a second time to start his own development firm.

But in 1992, near the end of May, Jones's world was changed. His effervescent daughter Judy—one of the twins—died from positional asphyxia. She was just 41 years old.

Jones tried to weather it but people around him knew he was distressed and in pain. "Death is a circumstance that comes to us all," Jones says. "I tried not to spend a lot of time in that valley of despair and despondency because the more time you spend there the deeper the hole becomes. I tried to look at the blessings I've had because they are just as much a part of life as the disappointments."

Local banker Bob Hatcher was one who sensed the upheaval in Jones's life. They were friends, having worked together on civic projects for many years. After Judy's death, Hatcher noticed the changes in Jones, not knowing that in a few short years he would endure a similar loss. His son Joel was later killed in an auto accident at the age of 20. One of the first people to call Hatcher on the telephone was Charles Jones.

"When he said he understood what I was going through, I knew he did. He and Dwight ended up giving a lot of money to Stratford Academy in Joel's name. That, I thought, was awfully generous and thoughtful," says Hatcher, the president of BB&T Bank in Macon. "There is a very deep, warm side to the man that people don't know. Having lost children, we have another level of friendship and a bond that is important to me and important to Charlie. I think that says an awful lot about the human spirit within the individual."

Jones still finds it difficult to talk about Judy's death. "I'd rather dwell on the blessings instead of the bumps," he says.

But beyond those rough edges, Hatcher says, there is a core of generosity, softness and sentimentality. "You have to look hard for them," he says. "But they're there. Charlie is a great human being. He really is."

19

Ves

Theirs is a union that was truly blessed—by a Baptist minister, the distinguished president of a Southern Baptist university and, if those two don't impress, by the King of Rock 'n' Roll.

"The worst Elvis impersonator I've ever seen," Charles Jones says. The two preachers and Elvis did not officiate in the same sanctuary. The formal marriage of Charles and Ves Jones was held in the campus chapel at Mercer University. The King offered his "hunka, hunka burning love" later, in Las Vegas, when the newlyweds were vacationing there.

Ves Jones remembers one of the vows the pseudo Elvis asked the groom. "He wanted to make sure Charles wasn't going to be a mean, mistreating hound dog or something like that."

Their true ceremony on November 21, 1998 was much more traditional. The Reverend Steve Johnson, a Baptist minister, presided along with Jones's longtime friend, Kirby Godsey, an ordained Baptist preacher as well as the president of Mercer University.

The ceremony was small and quiet. Only a few close friends and family members were invited—people they dearly loved. The ministers also were special. Johnson was Jones's late daughter's pastor. After Judy's death in 1992, the two men frequently joined each other for lunch. Godsey and Jones's friendship had grown over the years and the Mercer president was delighted when the couple asked him to participate in their wedding.

"They did a good job," Jones says, his eyes twinkling. "They got me saying 'I do' to things I thought they should have left out. They let Ves off pretty easy, I thought."

Though he makes jokes now, this was not a decision the two of them rushed into making. They had known each other since 1986. A native of Gray, Georgia, Ves had moved to South Florida. Jones began visiting Ves in Florida in 1993, and as the relationship blossomed, Charles visited her often, eventually leaving an automobile at the Boca Raton airport so he would have his own transportation there.

It was a loving relationship he found joyful and playful and so did she. The two of them rode bikes together, read books together, traveled together, exercised together and enjoyed themselves together. Even with those attributes, marriage was not something they wanted to hurry into.

Age was an issue, but not to them. "I tell people that there is an age difference between us—and that because of it I have trouble keeping up with him," says Ves, an accomplished artist in her own right.

Their relationship helped Jones rewrite his life. Ves was able to smooth out the rough edges and turn down the volume. She helped him expand his interests, calm down his unpredictable personality, and refocus where he was going with the rest of his life. Jones had all but disappeared from public life and it was more than a coincidence that once Ves was in the picture he began to reemerge—getting very involved in downtown revitalization and in higher education.

Most of his life, Jones saw work as his only outlet. As a young person, he cared little for the games of football and baseball his friends enjoyed playing after school. Instead of play, he went to work at the theater or delivering newspapers. Later in life, he couldn't see the attraction of playing golf either. He would enjoy an occasional tennis match, since it was an activity you could play in an hour or so under the lights—after work, of course. Jones was competitive, anyone who knows him would verify that. But his competition was in the game of business. But that was about to change.

Friends of Ves in South Florida did not know what to make of her frequent visitor from Georgia. She was an avid bike rider, competing in races all over Florida. Ves rode an expensive bike with gears, shocks, and all the other bells and whistles a competitive rider expects. On one of his visits, she asked Jones what he wanted to do that afternoon. Knowing of her passion for riding, he suggested a bike ride.

She had her own bike, but she didn't know what Jones was going to ride. Her nine-year-old nephew often visited and Ves had bought him a trick bike, one of those small models that young people use when they're showing off by doing wheelies and spinners.

"I wish I had a bike for you," she said, suddenly remembering the one in her garage. "Oh, I do have one you can ride."

Pretty soon, they were starting down a nearby bike trail. Ves was on her fancy bike. Jones was on that trick bike, his knees hitting the handlebars as he pedaled. Their ride wasn't a short one either.

"You know Charles. He wasn't content to just ride a mile or so. Pretty soon we're having lunch in Delray—25 miles away," she says. After eating they started the demanding ride back to Boca Raton.

"Keep in mind, I have eighteen gears and Charles is on this little bike just a pedaling. We were on the beach side and it was just beautiful. I started noticing that if my wheel was the least bit ahead of his that it would drive him nuts. He had to be in front."

She didn't say so, but Ves wanted to be in front, too. When they got to the long bridge leading in Boca Raton, she made her move, figuring Jones wasn't paying close attention.

"I dropped the bike into gear and just flew by him. I even waved as I went past. Before he knew it, I'm flying down the other side of the bridge leaving him behind," she relates.

As it was on that bike ride, Jones wanted to be heard. "A few minutes later," he says, "she had forgotten I was even in the state of Florida. She was feeling pretty comfortable by then. And all of a sudden—whoooooom, here comes that old man on the trick bike."

"It was the kind of thing you had to see," Ves says. "It didn't matter to him that he might have a wreck. But by George, there was no way I was going to end up first."

On another Florida trip, they went riding in the Everglades. This time they rented bicycles. "She got me an old raggedy one, too," jokes Jones. They had finished their ride and were turning in their rentals when some bike-riding friends of Ves showed up on their rough-tough mountain bikes. They told her about a trail they had cut out through the swamp using machetes to slice the bamboo. The new trail was an endless string of peaks and valleys with razor-sharp bamboo slivers below you when you jumped over the valleys.

"You gonna ride the course?" one of the riders asked Ves.

No, she explained. She and Charles were about to leave. "I knew what they were thinking," Jones says. "You've got this old man with you and you're not going to ride."

Jones encouraged Ves to ride the course but once more there was no bike for him. However, one of her friends was hauling an extra one—a really sleek mountain bike with super-duper gears—equipment Jones had never seen or used before.

Off they went, with Jones trailing behind the group. They stayed that way through the first section of the course and by then Jones decided that he had figured out that fancy bike. The experienced riders were moving along at a pretty good clip when Jones suddenly passed them, making the hazardous jumps like an old pro.

Until he flipped. Ves describes the scene: "There was a bamboo sliver shooting up in the air. It flipped his bike over and over. His arm came down on that bamboo root and the cut was awful. Blood was everywhere. Charles was turning white. But you know what? He got back on his bike. He was not going to let that other fellow beat him. Meanwhile, he was bleeding to death. I finally got him to stop and rest. I took off my shirt and used it to wrap his arm."

Jones remembers more: "This guy, he was about 25 or so, he says, 'Well, I guess you all are going to pack it in now.' My skin was hanging off my arm and he has no sympathy for this Great American who has been out there riding with him. All he can say is 'Are you going to pack it in?"

Pack it in, they did. At a nearby emergency room, they waited for medical help. Jones's name was finally called. Once the doctor took Ves's shirt off the arm and looked at the wound, he was full of questions, wanting to know what had happened and why they had waited so long to get to the ER. Not that the doctor would have understood why it was so important to Jones to be in front of the bike pack.

To Jones, it's energy. He has had an extra dose of it for as long he's been on this earth. It is something for which he's grateful. It helped him earn the money for his parents' dining room set. It helped him raise those chickens and pay his college tuition. It helped him squeeze out a living for his young family at that old drug store at Poplar and Broadway. It has helped him be the success that he is. It can also be a curse.

With Ves in his life, he channels that energy in different ways. They bounce here and there, traveling when they want to and staying home when they need to. When Jones wants to plant a garden with his grandson, he does. When he wants to pull a stint with the grounds crew at Ocmulgee Fields, he does—outworking the surprised younger guys in the process.

20

Shakin' and Movin'

Over the years, when he wasn't working for himself, Jones was working for the community. He had been out of that loop for several years but before long, he began to discover new ways to get involved in Macon and the state at-large. Two opportunities came in 1994—nearly a quarter century after he first jumped into industrial development and the efforts to secure a medical school at Mercer.

It had been a long time since Macon had been represented on the University System Board of Regents. Governor Zell Miller was considering Jones but some people were concerned that even though he had graduated from two state schools—Gordon College and the University of Georgia—he was too personally connected to Mercer University, a private institution.

Miller wasn't concerned in the least. The two of them had become friends through their common interest in the Mercer medical school. The governor wanted someone with a strong background in business and construction on the prestigious board that oversees the state's thirty-four colleges and universities. He also wanted someone who would think for himself. Jones was a good fit on all three of the governor's needs.

Jones joined the sixteen-member board in the fall of 1994, taking the oath of office on a six-year term. Miller did not want Jones to represent the Macon congressional district. He wanted him to serve in an at-large role. Jones assured him he would be as interested in Abraham Baldwin in Tifton as he was East Georgia College in Swainsboro.

Though he did not know it at the time, the governor was trying to force a left shoe onto a right foot. The Board of Regents is traditionally a staid, proper panel of prominent and successful men and women who are interested in higher education. The regents might be compared to the Rotary Club. Other civic clubs sell Christmas trees, push raffle tickets or cook barbecue—all in the name of raising money for whatever worthy cause their club adopts. Rotarians, on the other hand, want to do good deeds, but they prefer to merely write a check and make a donation. Let the Lions sell tickets.

Through most of his life, Jones has never been a joiner. He has always been the fellow with mud on his boots instead of the executive in the fancy office with the freshly polished Italian loafers.

"I see too many times people who think being a member of something is a reward sufficient into itself. That nauseates me. I don't understand people who join organizations or committees just so they put them on their resume. When I go to a meeting, I sit there and wonder 'When do we do something?' "

Joining the regents, he didn't wait to wonder that. He started to work even before the governor gave him the oath of office. Jones realized immediately that he knew very little about the schools he was about to help govern. Most of them he had never seen. To him, this was a simple and obvious thing to do: he intended to visit every school and every campus in the state system.

This was just the way he operated. When he joined the local hospital board, the loss of bed sheets was an ongoing issue. Sheets were disappearing daily. Using his experience in the motel industry, Jones visited the hospital laundry. After that one visit, he established a new policy. "Don't give anybody a clean sheet until they turn in a dirty one," he decreed. Without that hands-on experience, he would have been as puzzled as the others were.

Methodically, he began his tour of campuses, spending about two days at every school. He proposed to visit every one within a year. The unexpected bonus was a renewed interest in his state. As he drove along the highways, he would look at the crops on the side of the road, stopping to ask questions of the surprised workers, remembering the advice of his mentors at Poplar and Broad who told him to go to the source for knowledge. At the schools, Jones was surprised at the reaction he received. The college presidents were at first suspicious of him and his motives. Some told him there had never been a regent on their campus before.

"I was shocked that they were shocked," he says.

As he continued to travel, Jones was criticized by a few of his fellow regents who complained that he was invading their district by going on the campuses in their home territory.

"I didn't care. I knew that if every one of them got in there or did it as a group that they would come back to the meetings in Atlanta with their own opinions. They would not be depending on the chancellor's staff or on written reports."

The free-thinking Jones wasn't shy about sharing his findings either.

"If you're devoted to the whole system, then you have got to leave Atlanta and see the system. That was not a sacrifice to me," he says. "It was a joy. The reward was in seeing every school and every president."

His experience was joyful but what he observed on some of those campuses made him angry. While funds were pouring into the major institutions such as the University of Georgia, Georgia Tech and Georgia State, the smaller campuses were being overlooked. He remembers particularly his visit to Bainbridge College, one of the system's newer community colleges. It was located in a corner of the state on the road to nowhere.

"It would make you cry," Jones says. "We were walking the campus and we came to this structure where they had art. I had already been to other schools where we had just finished multi-million dollar fine arts auditoriums. There they were in Bainbridge, going to class in a trailer. God will have to forgive me because I won't change down here. But they still were using that trailer when I left the board. Their voice down there is inaudible. I mean, how is anyone going to hear their voice way up in Atlanta?"

Seeing the need for improved facilities first hand, Jones was asked to be assigned to the board's building and grounds committee. In the coming years, he reorganized that committee from top to bottom, replacing its director in the process. "That department was pitiful," he says.

Doing his math, he figured out that if the student enrollments of the other thirty-one institutions were considered together, they were serving more students than Georgia and Georgia Tech. Yet, they were only getting $8 million a year from the state to maintain their buildings. Jones soon became the voice of the state's smaller schools, concluding they needed someone at the table in Atlanta representing their interests. He equated what he saw with his own experience operating motels.

"If you have a budget motel and you don't renovate it, people don't stay there and you lose occupancy and you lose money. At the same time, you're spending money to keep up your franchise locations and you do more business. You have to have a level playing field and keep up all of your properties. It was the same way with the university system. You ought to have a level playing field. But out of sight, out of mine. If you don't see those campuses, it's easier to ignore their needs. I decided I would see them."

While often distressed at the conditions of the facilities, he was impressed with the leadership and the educational process that he saw. At Abraham Baldwin, he learned that students are allowed to bring their horses with them, that the animals are in barns near the dormitories. He discovered that more pre-dental students came out of ABAC than any other in the system. At Valdosta State, he saw the passion for his school of in Hugh Bailey, the president, a man who had survived a childhood bout with polio. He walked the grounds at Georgia College and State University in Milledgeville and saw the dangers caused by massive columns attached only by cables that tied them to the roof.

"If the fire inspector had inspected that school, he would have closed it down," Jones says. "If it was a private business, we would love to close them up. I asked the president about it and he said, 'Well, we've talked to them up yonder and I can't get anybody to finance this kind of stuff.'"

Jones pushed hard for the installation of an ongoing fund for future construction and maintenance needs that the board of regents still uses today. When he checked last, more than $20 million was in that account. For him, none of these things seemed that extraordinary. He was just doing the job the way a hard-nosed businessman would.

His labors eventually paid off. "Later on, we were able to fix those buildings at Georgia College. We installed air conditioning in their dormitories. We also air-conditioned an auditorium there that hadn't been used in years because of the heat. Visit it today. It's a beautiful campus. So are most of the institutions in the system," he says, showing a pride of ownership that goes beyond a seat on the board.

Eventually that pride got in the way of his service. He had grown impatient with Chancellor Steven Portsch and his staff. He decided to resign, knowing that he wasn't willing to give in and concluding that Portsch wouldn't either. He left with a year remaining on his term. He was also living up to an adage he often followed.

"My attitude has always been that when you are asked to participate in a position, you serve and you have goals in mind. Once you reach those goals, you get out of the way and let somebody else have a run," he says.

While he was disappointed with some things left undone, he was proud of the work done at Macon State College. Founded in 1968, it had been a two-year school forgotten by the community and ignored by the state. By the time Jones joined the regents, MSC was in shambles. Enrollment was steadily evaporating and so were its finances. Cutbacks had been drastic. Twenty-five faculty members had been laid off. The athletic program had been eliminated. New academic programs had been authorized by the state but no money was available to staff them. The school also was between presidents.

David Bell took over at Macon State in 1997 as the school's interim president. He came aboard when his wife, Nora Bell, was named president of Wesleyan College, a private women's college in Macon. Usually interim leaders are temporary appointments and are not considered for the permanent position. Bell was an exception, and it was Regent Jones who made the motion to hire him permanently. A framed copy of the minutes of that board meeting now hangs in Bell's office.

Bell was introduced to Jones on his first visit to the Macon campus, the day he was introduced to the students and faculty. In the years that followed they met regularly, sharing a monthly lunch in the college president's office. Their discussions were blunt. Bell soon discovered that Jones did not want him to put a spin on the news. He wanted facts. He expected the college president to tell him what the college needed and why. Bell soon found that Jones would be an important ally.

What we did was like repairing a ship at sea," says Bell. "We could not go in for dry dock. We had to repair

> things as we went. There was no time to worry about political matters. Charlie gave us the freedom to act. He was right there by my side. He is so creative, always a wealth of ideas. He could put us in touch with people that a new person in the community could not meet so quickly. He took this college under his wing. He became our champion It was time for someone to ride in on a white horse and do that for us.

Ves Jones remembers a holiday party several years ago when her husband went from person to person drafting key people to join the board of the new MSC Foundation. He tabbed the usual suspects, local leaders that had worked with him on projects over the years—from Buck Melton to Waddell Barnes to Bob Hatcher. Jones took them one by one to the campus and sold them on what the school could be and what a thriving Macon State could mean to the area. That board would provide a spark and a community spirit that had been lacking on the campus.

With the help of Jones and that board, financial support has grown and so has the school. When Jones and Bell went to work, the school's foundation had $350,000—an amount that is now more than $4 million. That comes out to a 1,100 percent growth. Three chairs for eminent scholars have been created through $1.5 million raised locally with a matching amount from the board of regents.

"Charlie shined the light on us. He saw our potential," says Bell. Remembering his own background as a student, Jones also focused on the needs of the students. He needed someone to encourage him and he needed financial help to pay his way. Bell says Jones seems genuinely interested in the care and feeling of young people.

"That emanates from him. He is interested in them as students and he wants them to have a better life. He cares. He knows that a lot of them don't have much money and that this public college hold tremendous promise for them. He came up the hard way so he understands their needs," Bell says.

Over the past five years, Macon State has become the fastest growing institution in the state system. Its enrollment has spiraled at a time many of its sister institutions have been experiencing a drop. Between 1998 and 2001, student enrollment increased 30 percent, growing around 12 percent a year. Contracts for more than $38 million in new campus construction have been let and the base budget is up more than $6 million. A $5 million satellite campus will open in Warner Robins in 2003, filling a long-standing need for educational facilities for Houston County and Robins Air Force Base. Heretofore, Warner Robins had been the largest city in the state without a higher education presence.

"Charlie knew a good investment, didn't he?" Bell laughs. At a time the college was looking to the future, downtown Macon was stuck in the past. It was a malady shared by communities around the country, spurred by the evacuation of merchants and customers after the construction of shopping malls in the 1960s and 1970s.

Macon was no different. Its infrastructure was crumbling. The city had lost its locally-managed banks, textile mills and utility companies. Retail outlets had long ago moved to suburban malls. There had not been a major downtown office building erected in more than twenty-five years. There had been well-intended attempts at inner city revitalization but little progress had been made. Only the historic churches, city hall and the federal building survived along Mulberry and Cherry streets. Downtown had turned into a 5 o'clock ghost town.

As a real estate developer, Jones had never seriously focused his interests on downtown Macon. As a newcomer in town, he had served his time there running that drugstore decades before. After that, he built the city's first motel and its second shopping center—neither in the downtown area. He had left downtown and never looked back. Years ago, an offer had been made for him to take over the Hilton Hotel, which now operates as the Crown Plaza, but he refused. He also turned down overtures that he build a Holiday Inn somewhere downtown. He appreciated the value of a vibrant downtown, but his successes had come elsewhere.

Juanita Jordan, the director of the Peyton Anderson Foundation—a philanthropic trust—was among a group of Macon leaders that in 1994 desperately wanted to breath new life into the city core. She knew Jones and she knew he was seldom short of opinions. The Georgia Music Hall of Fame was under construction near the old rail terminal and her group thought its opening might lead to renewed interest in the downtown area.

"I went to see Charlie to pick his brain," Jordan says.

Jones had a single piece of advice.

"I need to take you to Columbus," he told her.

Serving on the Georgia Board of Regents, Jones had become friends with William B. Turner, a Columbus businessman and civic leader. Turner's grandfather, W. C. Bradley, had been the Coca-Cola Company's first chairman of the board. A member of his family served on that powerful board of directors for most of the next seventy-five years. Turner himself was a major investor in Synovus Financial Corporation in Columbus, the state's largest bank-holding company outside of Atlanta. An unpretentious person, he seems to be most proud of the Sunday School class for teenagers that he has taught for more than forty years.

More than anything, Turner is generous. Through the Bradley-Turner Foundation, he and his family have been the impetus behind a re-energized Columbus. Their gifts often came in the form of challenges. Before a group can receive their funding, it must raise matching dollars. Turner's vision can be found on projects throughout Muscogee County—particularly in the RiverCenter for the Performing Arts, an impressive facility that was built with a melding of city, state and local dollars. Its stakeholders include the University System Board of Regents and Georgia Department of Natural Resources.

Turner's office at the W. C. Bradley Company is between Broadway and the Chattahoochee River. Because of its historic location and because of the properties it owns in the area, his company has always taken a keen interest in the fortunes of downtown Columbus. Like Macon, the Columbus downtown fell on hard times, turning into a string of wig shops and vacant store fronts. Those problems ultimately led to the formation of Uptown Columbus Inc.—a non-profit group whose goal was a more viable downtown.

These days, downtown Columbus is blessed. It features the sprawling TSYS headquarters, nightlife that includes restaurants, clubs and community theaters, a growing downtown campus for Columbus State University and the Coca-Cola Space Science Center. On the drawing boards is a new riverfront office for Synovus Financial Corporation, a new YMCA, a pedestrian bridge to Phenix City and a series of city-owned parking garages.

Jones wanted Jordan and the other Macon leaders to study first-hand what Columbus had accomplished. For years, he had heard Turner sing his city's praises, always inviting him to come and see for himself. Now Jones was going to accept that invitation. An ironic twist was that in the early 1970s a group of Columbus business leaders—starved for an alternative to its dying textile industry—came to Macon to learn from Jones's success in attracting new industries.

Making the arrangements with Turner, Jones asked the Macon contingency to fly with him to Columbus and see what was happening in that West Georgia community less than 100 miles away.

At the Columbus airport, Turner met them in his yardman's van. He drove the visitors downtown where they met with Uptown Columbus personnel and other city officials. That was the first of several visits the Macon group made to Columbus, learning something new on every trip.

"We were excited," Jordan says. "We figured if Columbus could do it, we could do it."

Columbus had a new 10,000 seat arena. There was the RiverCenter for the Performing Arts, a new public safety building and a forty-six mile Columbus Riverwalk meandering alongside the Chattahoochee River. Its downtown medians were being recreated. Sidewalks were being built and recreation centers were springing up all over town. Most of these projects were financed by a unique blending of public and private funds. Public-Private Parnerships had become an overused phrase in the Columbus vocabulary.

At last it came time for the Macon group to apply what they had learned. After three visits to Muscgoee County, interested people got together for lunch at a meeting room in downtown Macon. Energized by what they had seen, they all wanted to create an organization similar to Uptown Columbus. Everyone around the table agreed to put up $10,000 as seed money for their organization. Kirby Godsey was elected chairman. It had been a long afternoon but before they adjourned they wanted to settle on a name for their fledgling organization. Someone suggested Uptown Macon, taking a cue from Columbus.

That name didn't set well with Jones, who proceeded to give the group a quick lesson in Macon history. He told them that Fort Hawkins was built in 1807 and lasted until 1827, built to trade with the Muskogee Indians. Traders began to live outside the walls of the fort, all the way down to the Ocmulgee River. The village they spawned came to be known as Newtown, Georgia, and in 1821 the state legislature recognized it as an incorporated city. Macon was unincorporated in 1823 and seven years later the two were merged.

"There was a Newtown before there was a Macon," Jones said.

Godsey had heard enough. The group adopted NewTown Macon as their name. Two years later, again following the lead of Columbus, NewTown contracted with LDR International, nationally-recognized that consult with cities and organizations that are dealing with urban problems. LDR visited Macon, interviewed public and private leaders, studied the downtown area then issued a report on their findings.

Among LDR's findings were that the Ocmulgee River was an untapped resource, that the Medical Center of Georgia will play a role in the city's future and that downtown should build on the strengths of its downtown buildings, streets and parks.

Jones has played a part in each item on their survey. He had long discussed the value of the river, had been an instigator behind the expanded hospital and in the future he would play a role in the development of the first of many downtown parks.

"He's our lightning rod," Jordan says. "I call him our guru. I identify with him in every way. We are both goal-oriented. We're not into the process, just the results"

To Godsey, the results of the NewTown movement are many—some tangible, some not. One of the intangibles, he thinks, is the diverse group of local people that have been brought together under this single umbrella. In a community divided along city and county lines as well as racial lines, that is important.

> I love this community. Of course, I've been here quite a while now. I think Macon has what I call the gift of geography. We have so much going for us and we are in such a wonderful location. We have only needed to ask more of ourselves, to use our imagination and see what we can become as a community. Charlie is one of those people who is capable of seeing what others cannot see. I think that's why he is such a leader. He shared those traits through NewTown, Godsey says.

Jones agrees that the strength of Macon depends on the strength of its core. That strength depends on the involvement of the private sector, not just public officials.

Says Jones:

> For all of us to swim rather than sink, we have to give our attention to downtown Macon. My company is going to. Neither I nor Ocmulgee Fields own anything downtown. Our interests are elsewhere. We are just not into the kind of businesses that would succeed in downtown Macon. But the restaurants and clubs, the Tubman Museum, the Sports Hall of Fame and the Music Hall of Fame and the Mercer Law School. That's New Macon, and it has to be encouraged.

Jones has encouraged through personal investments and through funding from the Charles H. Jones Family Foundation. He has made significant bequests to the Tubman African American Museum and for the construction of Gateway Park. Located up the hill from the Ocmulgee River, it is a new greenspace designed to serve as a gate for a $7 million river walk proposed by NewTown Macon. Eventually, it will become part of a planned Ocmulgee Heritage Greenway.

"I've always been in the giving business," he explains. In June of 2001, that downtown park officially became the Charles H. Jones Gateway Park. A dedication ceremony was held at the park that sits on the corner of Riverside Drive and Martin Luther King Boulevard, up the hill from the river. The park is the first visible accomplishment of NewTown since its inception in 1996. Mayor Jack Ellis of Macon was there along with a lineup of political and business leaders. Georgia Governor Roy Barnes served as the guest speaker for the event. Barnes paid special attention to Jones, the guest of honor whose $500,000 donation helped make the park a reality.

"He dedicated time, talent and money and I thank him on behalf of all Georgians for his great commitment. The heart of a great community is not found in its buildings, but its people. It is clear that Macon is fortunate to have so many dynamic, caring citizens who want to continue to protect the city's heritage and sustain its success," Barnes said.

For Jones, it was an opportunity to comment on Macon's proud history. Remembering an early goal that Macon would become a successful inland port, he connected its past with the challenges of its future.

"We need to catch the spirit of our founders," he said. "We've got to run fast to catch up with our ancestors and other Georgia cities. It is now our time to plant some seeds for the harvest of the future. Macon can lead again."

Falling back on his own history, Jones grabbed a page from a speech he made two decades ago to visitors on the Red Carpet Tour and the governor of Georgia, Jimmy Carter. Some of the folks standing the sun that afternoon recognized the words. Only this time, he directed the punch line at Barnes, the sitting governor.

"Governor Barnes, we have a special request we want to make to you. We know you are a spiritual person. So when you are doing your daily prayers, we ask you to begin it with these words: 'Oh, God, what can I do today to again make the great city of Macon a world-class inland port city?'"

21

Blessed

Clustered on the roof of the Broadway Lofts were friends of the Tubman Museum and friends of Charles Jones. Enjoying their drinks and the skyline of downtown Macon, few of them understood the haunting significance of the view below.

Fifty years ago, folks standing on that roof would be looking down on Dr. Glass's old drug store at the corner of Poplar and Broadway. It had been around. People say city council met there in the old days. By 1951, it was called Charles Jones & Co. The guy who ran it answered to Doc. He was a whirlwind in a white jacket, whizzing all over that store selling liver and kidney pills and 'git up and go' potions. Made pretty good coffee too.

No one on that rooftop in the fall of 2001 had ever heard of Doc Jones. The buildings they were peering down on now house the beautifully restored offices of the Mercer University Development Department and the box office of the Grand Opera House. Along the way, Broadway became MLK Boulevard. And those people would not understand the depth of the ocean that separated Poplar from Cherry or how rare a $10 bill would have been in Doc's cash register.

People came to the penthouse of the upscale lofts that night to honor Charles H. Jones, the man folks in this neighborhood used to call Doc. In that other life, he was a frightened country boy posing as a grownup. He came to town with an old car and a new diploma. He could have been swallowed up on Poplar and Broadway but he wouldn't let that happen. He has returned to the old block this night in 2001 so supporters of the Tubman African American Museum can say thank you for the generous gifts he has bestowed on them.

As his friends gathered for dinner in the penthouse suite. Charles Jones was seated by a window. Through it you could see clearly the corner where he first set up shop. Ben Fitzpatrick and J. A. Smith are long since gone and so are the Saturday regulars who shopped with their money tied up in dingy handkerchiefs. That corner has changed and so has Jones, a millionaire developer who used to push German screwdrivers to customers with grease under their nails and now signs high dollar leases.

"I've had my bumps, but the blessings have always outweighed the bumps," he says, giving a philosophical spin to a career that only he could have ever imagined.

By the following year, 2002, he had taken down the Ambassador, the motel he built by the grace of God and Macon Federal. On a hill looking down on Riverside Drive, that quaint motel was the last surviving reminder of those years when he, his wife and three babies crammed into an apartment created from rooms over the motel office. Now he lives comfortably in a two-story house with white columns on the porch, distinguished trees in the front and tomato vines in the back.

Only a few people who come in contact with Jones grasp the enduring influence he has had on his community. He is Macon's most important unknown. Little notice is made of the thousands of jobs he attracted, the modern hospital he helped build, the medical school he helped secure or the college campus he helped rebuild. The *Macon Telegraph* listed him as one of the city's most influential men of the century. Yet few know his name.

Those who do know him and his story marvel at all he has accomplished for his adopted community in a fast-moving fifty years. But not even his friends fully understand the man and his complexities.

He quotes the Bible flawlessly and can recite verses he learned as a college freshman. He knows local history better than a professor. He follows politics as if it was a contact sport and still cries when he remembers a sermon a visiting fellow preached at his church back in Thomaston.

This is the same man who has survived in a cut-throat business by being more energetic, more aggressive and more willing to work than the next fellow. He offers his employees a share of the profits but expects them to work as hard as he does. If they don't, they can share another man's profits.

Health care executive Ben Porter says Jones has an evangelical calling to make things happen. "If you look for the epitome of a self-made individual, Charlie fits the bill. He's an original. You could categorize him a loner who has his own agenda and the determination to get it done. He has the qualities to make wheels turn."

Porter believes people who start life with nothing conduct their business with an entirely different flair than ones who were born with a silver MBA in their mouth.

"The risk-reward feeling is totally different. If you start with nothing, what do you have to lose? You're willing to take more risks. That's Charlie. He's always been willing to take risks."

Jones has always been a man who enjoyed the game as much as the victory. He thrives on competition. He can be combative, even willing to force his wife's bicycle off the path so he can win a race they weren't even running.

Kirby Godsey has seen that side of Jones. They have worked together on a variety of levels and a number of assignments. They were part of the relentless team that made the Mercer Medical School a reality and now they are partners on NewTown Macon.

He even officiated at Jones's wedding. But Godsey does not profess to know him well.

"I don't know that anyone knows Charlie completely," Godsey says. "I certainly can't say I do. He is so very unique. Some people who are leaders don't have substance. Charlie is a leader with substance. He is also verbal, verbally persuasive. Even now, he is looking for his next challenge."

Jones has been successful but not always popular. As one person said of him, "You can argue at the way he does things, but you can't argue with his results." Such an opinion would explain his two unsuccessful attempts at running for public office—campaigns in which he barely carried his home county. With time off to regroup, he was back in the game with a double dose of energy—"Inner energy that propels him forward," as banker Bob Hatcher describes it.

Over the years that energy has been channeled into making money and carrying out civic assignments. The holdings of Ocmulgee Fields Inc., his family-owned company, speak for themselves. So do the community projects on which he worked.

Even now, YKK, Brown & Williamson, GEICO, and the Medical Center are four of the community's largest employers. Each bears Jones's fingerprints. The Mercer Medical School has graduated 600 physicians and 400 of these men and women have completed their residencies. Every month, 100,000 people—mostly Georgians—are treated by a doctor trained at Mercer. Jones was the push behind that project, too.

Every month during the nearly five years he served on the University System Board of Regents, Jones would bring up the subject of Macon State College. When, he always wondered, would MSC be granted four-year status. At last, it was, and it is now the fastest-growing institution in the state system—poised to expand into Houston County.

David Bell, the president of Macon State, is grateful for Jones's efforts. He says Jones is absolutely unique, the kind of multi-faceted person he enjoys working with and for.

"There are enough of us academics around," Bell says. "We need more men like Charlie Jones, men who bring something very important to the table. He is not a carbon copy of anyone and is original to the core. I like that. An artist would use a lot of paint and a lot of colors in the painting of his portrait."

If the issue is business or land, the public Jones can strut like an Upson County peacock. Yet, he will tell you that he has always been able to get his ego out of the way so it doesn't interfere with his next move. The private Jones is cautious, even shy, reverting back to the country kid who overnight became a city boy. Mixed together, he could be portrayed as an egomaniac with an inferiority complex. But as his son Dwight notes, "his heart is always in the right place."

With his heart, Jones has supported most of the worthy causes that come along, in Thomaston as well as Macon. Ves says he will even offer quiet help to needy strangers he reads about in articles he clips from the morning newspaper. Giving was a trait he learned from his Granny and one he practiced before he graduated from high school, saving money he had earned to buy his parents a dining room table. Jones enjoys giving but finds it difficult to accept gifts in return..

"He's a little man with a big heart," says childhood friend Preston Bentley. Giving is easy to him because he doesn't believe in ownership.

"We have the use of certain properties that we've developed. The land we own was here before we got here and we won't take it with us when we go to heaven. I don't own one thing. I only have the responsibility to be a good steward over what I have. This house I live in was built in 1821. We are the eleventh family to live in it. Who owns this house? Out of 11 families, who owns it? I know I don't. I don't have the burden of ownership. I have the burden of responsibility and stewardship. I have always known who owned my company and it wasn't me."

Today, Jones is simplifying his life. The Ambassador was torn down and other motels have been sold. He is scaling back and slowing down, living within the speed limit for perhaps the first time in his life. He goes into the office when he wants to and wishes he didn't have to go at all. With the caring influence of Ves, he has mellowed.

"Reginald Trice wrote me a letter before he died and said of all the things I have accomplished that marrying Ves was my greatest accomplishment. He was right, too."

Not that he has shut down. "I have a diversity and width of interest that I think is a gift of God. It is a blessing on one hand and a curse on the other. It would be a lot easier to be sitting on the front porch somewhere, spitting, chewing tobacco, reading the *Atlanta Constitution* and taking a nap every morning by eleven. But that's not me. I want to learn. I want new experiences. I want to read. I want to travel and show Ves the places I have been, the things I have seen, some of them places not far away."

After many years of saying yes, he has begun to say no. He even claims not to know what's going on in his company—leaving such matters to his son Dwight. Not that he regrets the involvements he has had. There are three kinds of people in the world, Jones says. One who makes things happen. One who lets things happen. One who doesn't know what in the hell happened.

"For years, I was one of those people making it happen. But there's no question about it, I'm in that third category right now, the ones who don't know what's happening."

He exaggerates, of course. Go into his cluttered study at home you can tell he is an avid reader with plenty of books read, and plenty yet to be read. His passion for politics still burns. And, he still keeps a small notebook in his pocket on which he writes updated phone numbers and keeps up with more appointments than he will admit.

More than all of those things, he is enjoying watching his son Dwight learn to 'swim on his own.' After his parents divorced, Dwight continued to live with his father, turning the rambling acres around their house into a family zoo. Theirs is a bond that goes beyond father and son. Now Jones is having the pleasure of watching his youngest son manage the family business, and he likes what he sees. Dwight and his family built their home in the back of Charles and Ves. Between the two houses is a well-used path on which they speed back and forth on a golf cart.

But when the juices get flowing, Jones can still get excited about the city's need to commemorate the first Christian baptism in North America—a rite carried out on the banks of the Ocmulgee not far from town. He still wants to see an Indian museum in Macon, a living memorial to his friend Chief Cox. Remembering the unnecessary burning of his own home, he wants to see the city and county consolidate, something he has supported vainly for decades.

"But I don't want to build another motel or develop another shopping center," he says.

Life is good, even if he wasn't born with the luck of Lindy.

"My life's been more fortunate than successful. I am truly blessed."